Gilchrist, Oregon:
The Model Company Town

by
John C. Driscoll

This other Eden, demi-paradise,...
This happy breed of men, this little world,...
This blessed plot, this earth, this realm, this England

—William Shakespeare
King Richard II. Act ii. Sc. 1.

Copyright © 2012
by John C. Driscoll

All rights reserved. No part of the material protected by this copyright notice may be reproduced or utilized in any form or by any means, electronic or mechanical, including photocopying, recording or by any informational storage and retrieval system without written permission from the copyright owner.

ISBN: 978-0-9840784-1-7

Printed and bound in the United States of America by
Maverick Publications • Bend, Oregon

Dedication, Thanks and Acknowledgements

This book is dedicated to William F. Steers. I never forgot what you said, what you predicted. You were right; time has borne out your predictions.

Thank you to Mrs. Mary G. Ernst, Gil Ernst, Stewart J. Gilchrist, Jim Childre, Mr. & Mrs. Louis Jordan, Mr. F. A. Hendry, Mr. B. E. Hill, Milton Hill, Kathy Stice, Charlie Shotts Jr., Fred Southwick, Tom and Karen Steers, Todd Kepple and The Klamath County Museum's Staff, Donna Smith and the staff of the Lauren Rogers Museum, Laurel, Mississippi.

William Faulkner: Your writing inspired this book by showing me why Gilchrist matters, why each town such as Gilchrist matter more than all the worlds cities combined.

MJC: You, (I am not unmindful of the irony), were this book's muse at its inception.

Gilchrist Mill – Circa 1939-1940
Collection of F.A. Hendry

Table of Contents

Chapter I	Company Owned Camps and Towns	1
Chapter II	The Gilchrist Timber Company: Laurel, Mississippi and Before	13
Chapter III	1938-1941: The Move West and Building the Town	31
Chapter IV	1941-1946: World War II and the Strike	85
Chapter V	1946-1982: Gilchrist in its Heyday	115
Chapter VI	1982 to 2012: The Wake of the Flood	151
Endnotes		165
Bibliography		177
Index		181

Frank's Corner
Collection of F.A. Hendry

Joseph W. Fordney
Collection of Mrs. Mary G. Ernst

Frank W. Gilchrist
Gilchrist Timber Company Papers,
Klamath County Museum.

CHAPTER I

Company Owned Camps and Towns

"The brother worked in the mill. All the men in the village worked in the mill or for it. It was cutting pine."

— Light In August *by William Faulkner*

Company towns and company camps have existed in North America since the reign of Henry VII, when fishermen established camps on Newfoundland to provide a base of operation for crews working the Grand Banks. By 1900, at a time when less than half the population of the United States lived in cities or towns, 6 percent of the country's population lived in company towns. Approximately 2,500 company towns and an unknown number of company camps existed in 1900.[1] These towns and camps varied by region and era as well as the inclination of the owners and managers of the firms which established these towns. The diversity of company towns is a consequence of the size of the United States and a well-established tradition of social experimentation on the part of leaders in the productive sector. In consequence thereof, company towns as varied as Lowell, Massachusetts; Pullman, Illinois; Morris Run, Pennsylvania; Gary, Indiana; Scotia, California; Port Gamble, Washington; and Kannapolis, North Carolina, were established over a period of approximately 150 years.

What both company camps and company towns had in common was a single industry that employed virtually all the community's occupants. The other characteristic shared by company camps and towns was that they were constructed by an employer to provide housing for its employees.[2] Tentative longevity was what distinguished a camp from a town. Camps were impermanent; towns were permanent. Towns were provided with more amenities than were camps. This generalization is useful for the purposes of this book, though there are numerous exceptions to it.

The size of a company town could vary from a few hundred to as many as several thousand people.[3] What determined the population of a company town was the size of its labor force. Some company towns were administered so that all aspects of the town, including the personal lives of its employees, were regulated. Other company towns, such as Gilchrist, only controlled those aspects of town life that pertained to the preservation of order and company property.[4] The relationship between the management of a company town and its employees depended on the company's policies as well as the character and extent of its paternalism. If the management of a company town dominated the lives of its employees, compelled them to live in houses which it rented to them at exorbitant rates, and paid them low wages as well, it usually had antagonistic relations with its personnel. Good relations prevailed between labor and management in those company towns where community services were provided and adequate housing was available at low rates. Gilchrist was a successful company town because an amiable relationship existed between the people who lived in it and the company that owned it.[5] The success of Gilchrist can be attributed to the circumstances of its history to include its leadership and management.

Most employers established company towns

as a means of assuring a stable, loyal work force. A few employers established company towns to generate additional income for their firms. Some employers established towns for idealistic reasons. More often than not, employers were motivated by more than one of these purposes when deciding to establish and operate their towns.

Policies regarding residence in company towns varied and changed, too. Pullman required its employees to live in its town. Other companies, including those located in New England that built model towns, limited opportunities to buy or rent houses to skilled employees and management. Some companies limited residence in their towns to current employees, then later modified the policy to allow retired employees to continue to occupy their houses. Occasionally companies allowed employees to continue residing in their houses when laid-off or on strike.

Company towns were characterized by variation. Some companies built towns with the intention of selling the houses to their employees. Others rented the houses to their employees. Still other firms sold some of the houses to employees while renting others. Some companies performed all functions one associates with municipal government, some none at all, while others provided a fluctuating number of municipal services. At least one company ceded municipal functions to its employees and then reassumed them when the employees proved unable and unwilling to furnish them.

How a town's housing, services, and businesses were provided and administered, whether the company that owned and operated the town did so to make money as well as provide for the needs of its workers, depended upon the intentions of its owners. A very few companies built towns to make money as well as attract a labor force. In such towns as these, the rents exceeded market rates. The former objective tended to work at cross-purposes with the latter one. Employees living in such towns were expected to live in company-owned housing and patronize the company store. There were rare instances of companies that derived income from providing town residents with municipal services. Towns operated in this manner engendered hostility, and then failed. Pullman is the best-known and perhaps most spectacular failure resulting from operating a company town as a source of revenue from employees who were compelled to live in it as a condition of employment.

Employers' motivations for establishing company towns included idealistic ones. Such towns were not unique to New England. Some employers constructed, organized and operated their towns in manners which suggest the influence of the Transcendentalist, then later Progressive movements. Company towns established by employers whose objectives included improving their employees while bettering their lot tended towards paternalistic management practices. Examples of such company towns include Pullman, Illinois; Lowell, Massachusetts; and Indian Hill, Massachusetts.

Beyond a single industry and construction by an employer to provide housing for his employees, there was a great diversity of patterns for the organization of company towns. Not all company towns were rural and many were located adjacent to cities. Pullman, Illinois, and Gary, Indiana, are two of the better-known company towns which were established near major urban centers. Fairfield, Alabama, was a suburb of Birmingham, Alabama. Its streets followed the topography and were not laid out on a grid.[6] There were company towns associated with most every imaginable industry to include automobiles, shipbuilding, electronics, consumer appliances, textiles, plumbing fixtures, and candy. The productive sector built the United States into the world's preeminent economy which was supported by their own towns.[7]

There has never been a general pattern for the organization and operation of a company town. Some companies built towns then rented the houses to their employees; others sold the houses to their employees. Indian Hill, Massachusetts, a suburb of Worcester, Massachusetts, was built to resemble a New England village. Its houses were sold to its residents, employees of the firm which built the town, on favorable terms through company-financed mortgages. The opportunity to buy a house in the town was a benefit the company used to attract and retain employees.[8] The Calumet and Hecla Copper Company of Michigan built houses which it rented to its employees for nominal sums and also leased land to its employees on which they could build their own houses.[9] The semi-detached houses built by the Norton Company for its town,

Indian Hill, proved tremendously unpopular with its employees, who preferred single-family houses with yards and clearly defined boundaries to each house's lot.[10] United States Steel built craftsman-style houses, inspired by the garden city movement, when it constructed Corey, Alabama.[11] Between 1900 and 1920, forty industrial towns were built. All were composed of single-family houses. Their appearances varied from town to town. None was laid out on a grid; all were park-like.[12] Company town rents, contrary to a common erroneous belief, rarely exceeded the prevailing market rate for similar houses.[13] Attempts to compel employees to rent company houses, much less rent them at above-market rates, invariably failed, as is what happened in Pullman, Illinois.

The availability and operation of services and amenities available in company towns also varied. Stores in company towns were sometimes operated by the company, though more often than not they were operated by concessionaires who leased the space their businesses occupied from the firms which built the town. The company store located in Potlatch, Idaho, operated out of a three-story building. It sold goods whose prices and selection was sufficiently competitive that it drew customers from throughout the region in which it was located. The store continued to operate after the town ceased to exist as a company town. It appears that most company stores were operated by concessionaires, not by the companies. The abusive company store was not merely an exception; it was an anomaly.[14]

There were firms which issued their employees script; most did not. Even among the firms which did issue script, there was significant variation in the reasons for its issuance and the manner in which it was managed. Script, as often as not, was issued by companies when adequate supplies of cash were not readily available. Most companies provided subsidies for recreational activities for their employees who lived in their towns. All company towns were, ultimately, the product of the leadership and management practices of the companies which established them. Pullman, Illinois was a company town which was defined by its restrictions and George Pullman's utopian philosophies. Hershey, Pennsylvania, and Scotia, California, were extraordinarily long-lived company towns characterized by benevolent leadership and mildly paternalistic management practices.[15] There were a handful of company towns which were intended as utopian exercises and even fewer which were purposefully exploitative, which by design tended to either extreme of the spectrum. Both utopian and exploitative towns tended to quickly fail.[16] The majority of company towns, particularly the ones which long endured and are fondly remembered, fall towards the utopian end of the spectrum. They did not engage in the meddling paternalism which characterized the utopian company towns operated by progressive members of the productive sector during the nineteenth and twentieth centuries.

In 1645, Brain Tree Iron Works established near Boston a company town which was one of the earliest in the United States.[17] Privately owned and operated towns connected with the industrialization of the United States began to appear in the early 1790s when Paterson, New Jersey, and Humphreysville, Connecticut, were established.[18] Companies establishing these towns carried on a practice from Great Britain to provide employees with housing.[19] Often, but not always, companies built then operated the towns due to their isolated location and the employees lack in resources to build their own houses. Towns were needed to retain work forces. By 1815, more than 170 small mills had been established, each of which had a village to provide housing for the firms' employees.[20] Absent from these early nineteenth century company towns was the comprehensive planning which was typical of company towns built during the last third of the nineteenth century.

Lowell, Massachusetts, established in 1821, was one of the first markedly utopian and paternalistic company towns established in the United States. Its leadership decided on these management policies as a way of attracting and retaining a work force which was largely drawn from single women who lived on farms before relocating to Lowell for a few seasons before returning to their fathers' farms then, as often as not, marrying. The mill functioned in loco parentis for these young women to pacify the concerns of parents who allowed their daughters to work in the Lowell textile mills. The mills provided chaperones and extensive programs of improving activities for their employees when not at work. It was one of the first large-scale planned industrial communities as well as the first of a succession of progressive and utopian company towns which attempted to exercise extensive control over the activities of its employees.[21] Charles Dickens, who visited Lowell during the 1840s, favorably contrasted the town with the mill towns of Great Britain.[22] Lowell, as has been the outcome with other progressive schemes, whether by members of the productive sector or the government sector, was not ultimately successful. Its residents chafed under the restrictions imposed on them.

During the 1830s, Phelps-Dodge, established the first of its company towns. The first was established by the members of a pair of Calvinist families from New York. The firm, which operated company towns in various locations until the 1950s, used the Golden Rule as the basis for the operation of its towns.[23] Phelps-Dodge combined benevolence with mild paternalism. Company towns which were managed using variations of the Phelps-Dodge policies were generally pleasant places to live, whose residents recalled with regret the passing of these towns. Few company towns employed the dramatic forms of control which characterized Lowell. Industries, particularly those that needed to attract skilled workers, did so by building attractive towns where the company's authority was subtle if at all evident.[24]

By 1861 Lowell, Massachusetts, had ceased to exist as a progressive and utopian company town. Lack of interest in the scheme on the part of management and changes in its work force from single farm girls to immigrants were significant factors for some company towns to change ideologies.[25] The benevolent and mildly paternalistic type established by firms such as Phelps-Dodge continued to quietly endure. The meddling and progressive company town retained an inexplicable attraction to some members of the productive sector, which resulted in the return of variations of this type of company town in another generation.

The accounts of abusive company towns say more regarding the prejudices of the individuals who have popularized the aforementioned perception of company towns than they do about the actual existence of such towns. They were very rare and, where they actually existed, were limited to a thirty-year period beginning in the 1870s, and were concentrated in coal country, particularly in Tioga County, Pennsylvania. As often as not these firms, as were their towns, were short-lived and undercapitalized.[26] Debt peonage then, as now, was illegal. Owing one's soul to the company store only worked when employees chose to stay in place rather than leaving. Mismanagement of consumer credit, whether to the company store or a bank offering a credit card, also occurred among employees who found themselves mired in debt.

The song "Sixteen Tons" which has done much to popularize an erroneous stereotype of company towns, was written in 1946 by Merle Travis. He was living in Hollywood at the time he wrote the song. Merle Travis, born in 1917, was the son of a coal miner. At the same time he wrote "Sixteen Tons," he also wrote "Dark As A Dungeon" which attempted to explain the coal miner's attraction to work underground. Tennessee Ernie Ford's cover of the song, which received extensive airplay during the 1950s, coupled with the his televised performances of the song, did much to cement a negative image of company towns in the minds of numerous individuals who never had any contact with the residents of company-owned towns.[27]

Companies which paid in script did so for no single reason or combination of reasons. Some did so as a matter of convenience for both the company and its employees. In companies which were isolated, where there were no readily available competing businesses, payment in script or a combination of script and cash was a logical practice. The availability of cash sometimes proved a factor when companies decided to issue script. When abusive company store arrangements, such as the one sung about by Tennessee Ernie Ford in "Sixteen Tons," did exist, they weren't sustainable. Inevitably they engendered labor discord which ultimately proved the arrangement's undoing.

The doctrine of mutual advantage began to significantly influence the construction and management of company towns. A variation of the Golden Rule employed by Phelps-Dodge, improved working and living conditions for their employees, affording economic advantage that would benefit both workers and employers.[28]

During the early 1880s, George Pullman decided to build a town for his employees. He was a

Progressive and his town succeeded in combining all the usually meddling, sanctimony and experimentation typical of the Progressive movement with most of the other least successful company town management practices.[29] George Pullman attempted to operate Pullman, Illinois, as a profit-making venture while managing the lives of his employees. The town was owned and operated by the Pullman Palace Car Company. Its employees were required to live in company-owned houses, rented to them at rates in excess of those charged by landlords in neighboring communities. Even when the Pullman Company reduced the wages of its employees, it did not lower the rent for its housing. The combination of Progressive paternalism and profit-oriented policies which the Pullman Palace Car Company used to determine the administration of its town made the community an unsuccessful enterprise, and contributed to the Pullman Strike of 1894.[30] Pullman, ironically considering the scope of its failure, influenced an entire generation of individuals who went on to build company towns based on the Progressive movement's concepts of management and labor.[31] Providing better living and working conditions were ideas which were more in harmony with the Golden Rule practices of Phelps-Dodge than the meddling by Progressives which characterized Pullman.

During the 1880s, companies began constructing towns which were the antithesis of towns such as Pullman. Scotia, California, one of the longest lived of all company towns, was founded in 1882 as Forestville. The Murphy family acquired it during the early 1890s and built a pleasant, well-maintained town. Extensive provisions, including a theater, parks, and playing fields, were provided for their employees' leisure time. The Murphys' lumber company was one of the first on the West Coast to practice sustained-yield forest management. The benefits its employees received included full medical, pensions, and scholarships for their children. The town still exists though it ended as the Murphy family's company town in 1985.[32] Hershey, Pennsylvania, founded in 1900, is yet another example of a model company town which still exists. The town's houses at the time of its construction were equipped with electricity and central heating. Amenities and benefits included a zoo,[33] medical insurance, life insurance, garbage removal, and a junior college, was constructed for the residents of Hershey. The town became of sort of a Disneyland precursor, attracting tourists coming to see the chocolate works.[34] Residence in Kannapolis, North Carolina, which existed as a company town from the early 1890s until the 1970s, grew to a population of 36,000. It was built and managed with an eye toward attracting, then retaining for the long term, employees who might otherwise not choose to take employment in the firm's remote location.[35] Company town owners provided their employees with extensive athletic and recreational programs and facilities as an alternative to frequenting saloons. Sports and improving leisure, it was expected, would improve the health and morale of employees and their families which would increase efficiency.[36] By 1900, 92 percent of all southern textile workers lived in company-owned towns. Mill housing had obvious economic advantages for owners and employees.[37]

After 1900, in spite of the Pullman fiasco, over 70 planned industrial settlements were constructed.[38] Planning and constructing company towns provided commissions for many of the preeminent architects of the early twentieth century. George Gibson McMurtry commissioned Frederick Law Olmsted to design Apollo, Pennsylvania.[39] Employers accepted the claims by design professionals that they had unique knowledge that gave them mastery of the industrial environment. Mill owners who entirely relinquished the design of their towns to these nascent technocrats were often left with expensive and unsatisfactory results.[40] The company housing constructed during the 1920s in Torrance, California, failed because the individuals for whom they were built found their design suggestive of poverty and austerity rather than the emancipation which was the architect's intent. The employees for whom they had been designed preferred bungalows to the spare and spartan boxes the architect had designed.[41] The professional designers of company towns failed when their concern was for an abstraction called "the people" rather than taking into account the aspirations of the individuals who lived in the towns they designed then built.[42] This failure was writ much larger when these planners moved on to designing, then constructing urban renewal schemes and public housing projects. Here they were more or less exempted from the consequences of successive failed designs, providing they were politically connected. Planning and designing company towns attracted numerous architects who subsequently drifted into urban and suburban planning for government entities. For these architects, city planning for governmental entities proved more attractive than planning for companies, since they had the force of law to implement their schemes as well as budgets. These budgets were the product of politics as opposed to the tempering effects of profit and loss, which was the case when planning, then building towns when employed by members of the productive sector.

Leadership and its attendant management practices more often asthan not was what determined if a company town was pleasant and serene or discordant and acrimonious. Hormel saw forty years elapse without a serious labor dispute. It coupled generous benefits with support for local charities and policies which allowed employees great latitude with regard to hours worked, so long as production objectives were met.[43] Some owners and superintendents combined varying degrees of control over their employees' lives with direct interest in their welfare to include devoting considerable attention to building personal relationships. This included not only Christmas presents and listening to workplace complaints but also extended to assisting with financial and family problems. Progressive firms attempted to compel temperance, using more intrusive practices. The owner of Bynum Mills, North Carolina, made the rounds of his town at nine o'clock on work nights to enforce lights out.[44] In spite of such eccentric practices, by 1920, Bynum Mills had developed into a cohesive and homogenous community that constituted a sort of extended family.[45] The mill owner or his superintendent lived in the company's town. They were members of the community. The management of southern company towns was influenced by the ideals of the antebellum south. Here, company towns were operated by owners or superintendents who had been brought up on Walter Scott and the tales of English squires and cavaliers who saw their relationships with their employees, with the residents of their towns, in terms of the reciprocal obligations of lords and vassals. Resident owners in the West and the South, because of the isolation they shared with their employees, developed intense and personal bonds which made for mutual respect, loyalty, and shared obligations. Company towns contributed significantly to the beginning of the South's recovery from the damage done to it by federal armies which had invaded it during the War Between The States.[46]

The company towns constructed from 1910 to 1925 were usually designed with the intent to sell the houses to the company's employees. These towns continued the practice of attracting and retaining employees by raising the standard of living for those employees who decided to reside in the company's town.[47] Kohler, Wisconsin, was one of the towns constructed during this period. Kohler Improvement Company, which was a part of the Kohler Company, built the town's houses then sold them to its employees. All the town's amenities were provided by the Kohler Company. The town still exists with a population reaching 1,926 in 2000. The Kohler Company remains the town's principal employer and benefactor.[48]

The national decline of company towns began during the 1920s with the advent of the automobile. In 1930, even after ten years of contraction, 2 million residents of the United States continued to live in company towns.[49] The towns were expensive to operate. Automobiles provided employees with a degree of mobility which made most company towns less isolated.[50] It was no longer necessary for employees to reside within walking distance of their places of employment. The emergence of the automobile as an item affordable by most consumers rendered company towns less necessary in many regions of the country, while spurring the development of company-operated camps in other regions. Oil companies, beginning in the 1920s and continuing until the 1950s, began building camps to provide housing for men who were working the oil fields. These temporary settlements were established in remote locations. Little was offered in terms of amenities. They weren't designed as places where men would bring their families. Rent was often as little as three dollars a month.[51] Another camp, the one established to house the employees of the consortium of six companies which built the Hoover Dam, sparked the development of Las Vegas as a center for gambling and other associated activities. The camp the firms built was dry and largely devoid of women. Las Vegas began its transformation by catering to the desires of the builders of the Hoover Dam.[52]

During the 1940s, the resurgence of company camps continued. Some camps, such as Hanford, Washington; Los Alamos, New Mexico; and Oak Ridge, Tennessee, were built by the federal government for the Manhattan Project, proved permanent, and are now company towns of the paternalistic variety.[53] Oak Ridge, Tennessee was a closed community which was equaled only by some mining communities in Colorado or Appalachia in terms of the control that management exercised over the lives of its occupants. Only management of Lowell, Massachusetts, came close to ordering its employees lives to the extent which Oak Ridge did to their staff.[54] Oak Ridge was, in most respects, a singularly, intrusively paternalistic company town.

Others were temporary settlements constructed by Kaiser for his shipyard workers. Among these were Vanport, Oregon, and a housing project constructed at Richmond, California. Kaiser's camps have the appearance of towns and were unlike most camps in that they included provisions for families as well as housing for employees. Day care was one of the benefits Kaiser provided to employees who built ships for him. Kaiser pioneered and refined the construction of prefabricated housing as part of the process he employed when constructing his camps.[55]

During the 1980s, the Iowa Beef Packing Company operated a trailer park in Holcomb, Kansas, as a camp for its employees, some of whom were illegal aliens. Turnover in the camp, because of wages and working conditions, as well as the hiring of illegal aliens, was very high. Its camp reprises the logging and mining camps of the nineteenth century.[56] Some firms now operate corporate campuses which have town-like, or at least camp-like, features. The Federal Express facility at Collierville, Tennessee, includes quarters for 1,500 as well as jogging trails and a library. The Google Plex located at Mountain View, California, includes sleeping pods for its employees.[57] Perhaps ever-longer commute times, if not engendering an era of company town construction, will make company camps even more common.

Privately owned and operated towns were once a common feature of the rural Pacific Northwest. Timber companies built towns out of necessity. Operations were often located in places that were remote. In Central Oregon, company towns existed for the same reason they existed elsewhere in the region, and they have tended to disappear for the same reasons they ceased to exist in other parts of the Pacific Northwest. Economic development, improved transportation systems, and the growth of neighboring communities have made them unnecessary. Yet some former company towns still endure. Gilchrist, Oregon, located in northern Klamath County, is such a place, though it has changed. This book will recount the history and the changes that this still existent former town has experienced.

Towns such as Gilchrist, company towns, came into being because there was a need for them.[58] The closest town might be many miles from where the timber was. The lack of adequate transportation made it impractical for the company's labor force to commute to and from the nearest town to the logging or milling site.[59] These towns did more than provide rented housing. The towns that timber companies operated in the Pacific Northwest were usually equipped with stores, recreational facilities, libraries, churches, taverns, restaurants, post offices, schools, and barbershops. Among company towns of the Pacific Northwest, banks and medical facilities were usually not provided. Sometimes the company that owned the town would operate the town's businesses and community services. Often the building would be leased to a private party who would make a living operating the local store or barbershop on a concession basis. Provisions for municipal services (including police protection, electricity, gas, water, fire protection, and school systems) were made in many different ways by the company that owned and built the town. These services were almost always available, but the manner in which they were provided and administered varied from town to town.[60]

The Pacific Northwest was home to several of the most recently constructed company towns. It is also the location of several towns which until the 1980s and 1990s continued to operate as company towns. Most company towns and camps in the Pacific Northwest were connected to mining or forest products. It is impossible to estimate the number of camps which companies operated in the Pacific Northwest. They were, by design, impermanent. One exception was Shevlin, a camp that was a de facto mobile town which existed from 1916 until 1950, as long as some company towns. Camps tended to have very high employee turnover rates. The camps of the Pacific Northwest needed three crews (one coming, one going, and one on the job) if they were to achieve full manning levels. Maintaining full manning, even during times of economic downturn, was difficult. The turnover in logging camps in Washington prior to World War I was 55 percent a month for an annual personnel turnover of 600 percent a year. The Simpson Lumber Company reported in 1947 that it needed 700 hires to keep its logging camp's 350 positions filled.[61] The camps were Spartan and located in remote locations. Men living in camps also tended to drink more than did men who were living with their families. The companies responded to this staffing problem by building towns which offered amenities that would induce their employees' families to live with them.[62]

The differences between a town and a camp weren't always rigidly maintained. At first blush, the difference was that camps were intended to be impermanent, had no provision for anyone other than employees, and provided few, if any, amenities for their occupants. There were camps, such as the one operated by Shevlin-Hixon, which differed from a company town primarily by being mobile. It was in all other respects a town. It possessed more or less all the amenities one would find in a company town. By 1936, the camp's houses all had electricity.[63] Shevlin's post office was established in 1931. The camp, which existed at various locations in Deschutes and Klamath counties, operated from 1916 until 1950. It had all the amenities one finds in company towns including a post office, stores, theater, school, and tavern.[64] It was a camp that functioned as a town.

Shevlin, Oregon: a camp that functioned as a town. Circa 1930s.
Collection of Deschutes County Historical Society

The Gilchrist-Fordney Lumber Company operated lumber camps in Mississippi. These camps differed from a town only in that their existence was intended to cease as soon as they were no longer in practical proximity to the timber that the loggers were felling. All houses in this camp had electricity. The camp was designed and constructed with a store and an infirmary, and with the expectation that the employees who lived in it would have their families with them. There were company towns with bunkhouses for single employees and camps, such as the one operated by the Gilchrist-Fordney Lumber Company, which never included bunkhouses.

Company towns in the Pacific Northwest began with Port Gamble, Washington. Port Gamble, founded in 1853 and located on the Kitsap Peninsula by the Puget Lumber Company, was the first company town established in the Pacific Northwest. The town survived as a company town into the twentieth century. It was transplanted from Maine. Port Gamble was built to resemble a New England village.[65] Company towns established in the Northwest numbered among the ones most recently established in the United States. They were the larger and most successful company towns built to date.[66] The ranks of the most recently constructed company towns are Gilchrist, Oregon; Holden, Washington; and Grisdale, Washington.[67] Gilchrist, Oregon, the most recently established of the company towns of the Pacific Northwest, is arguably the most successful of all company towns. Gilchrist was the company town with which was achieved all that successive generations of planners and business owners had attempted to accomplish with their towns. Holden, Washington, was the Pacific Northwest's only company town whose access to the outside world was limited to a water route. Gilchrist, Holden, and Grisdale are three company towns remembered with particular fondness by their current and former residents.

Pacific Northwest employers built company towns to recruit and retain married men because they, unlike bachelors living in camps, were generally stable and sober. The towns the companies built to attract married men, which would pass the scrutiny of their wives, had to include schools, stores, churches, and facilities for recreation.[68] Houses in these towns were often better than houses located in cities and renting for similar sums.[69] Almost without exception, rents charged by employers operating company towns in the Pacific Northwest were at or below market for similar houses. In many instances, the operation of a town was a proposition which lost money for the company. This was a factor which eventually helped bring about the end of many of the Pacific Northwest's company towns.[70] The rents charged for housing in the company towns in the Pacific Northwest remained consistently at or below prevailing market prices for comparable houses. During the 1890s, houses at Port Gamble, Washington, rented for $6-$7 per month. In 1918 the firm which owned Carbonado, Washington, rented houses to its employees for $7.50 to $16.50 per month. During 1918 employees residing in Black Diamond, Washington, owned their houses which they built on land rented from their employer at a dollar a month. Houses in Grisdale, Washington, during the 1940s and 1950s, rented for $20 to $30 a month. Comparable houses located in Tacoma, Washington, during the 1930s, rented for $30 a month and did not include utilities.[71] In 1991 houses in Gilchrist, Oregon, rented for $67 to $125 a month.[72] The rents the companies charged their employees included maintenance and often some or all utilities to include water, electricity, and garbage removal. A mill hand residing in Selleck, Washington, during the 1920s, who earned $3.50 to $4.00 per day, was able to send home $80.00 per month because the cost of living in the company town was so low.[73] The particular house an employee was able to rent typically was a function of family size and position held with the firm which owned the town.[74]

Stores operated in company towns in the Pacific Northwest significantly varied with regard to size, range of merchandise offered, and the relationship of the person operating it to the company which owned the building it was located in. Some employers operated all their town's retail businesses, while others more typically leased the businesses out to individuals who operated them as concessions. Some stores in company towns were sufficiently competitive to attract customers from adjacent communities.[75] The Merc, located in Potlatch, Idaho, was a three-store department store which sold an extraordinary variety of merchandise including automobiles. It was a regional shopping center which attracted customers from throughout the area it was located in. The Merc continued in business after Potlatch ceased to exist as a company town during the early 1950s, and went out of business after burning down in 1963.[76] The shopping center constructed by the Gilchrist Timber Company, the first of its type east of the Cascades and perhaps in all of Oregon, attracted customers from throughout the north end of Klamath County and the south end of Deschutes County. Stores located in the company towns of the Pacific Northwest tended to relax credit policies and even reduced prices for town residents during strikes and depressions so as to assure they at least had access to grocery supplies.[77]

The few Pacific Northwest company towns which did issue script did so in response to the absence of banks, consumer credit and to shortages of hard cash. In Gilchrist, Oregon, which never issued script, the lack of banking services was augmented by the post office, grocery store, and drugstore which cashed checks, sold money orders, and handled banking transactions by mail.[78] Pacific Northwest companies that did issue script always redeemed it for cash at face value.[79] The Henry McCleary Timber Company issued script to its employees as an advance against wages. It was accepted by the town merchants at face value, though the timber company did discount it by 10 percent when it was redeemed for cash by the merchants.[80] Script was the exception, not the norm, for the company towns of the Pacific Northwest. Script, when it was issued, disappeared as soon as some or all of the aforementioned became more readily available.

The companies who established company towns in the Pacific Northwest consistently included provisions for churches when constructing their towns. Houses of worship were expected by the women who lived in the town with their husbands who worked for the companies that built the towns. The mill owners were usually devout men, too.[81]

Mill owners who established company towns in the Pacific Northwest were frequently abstemious as well as devout. They made their company towns "dry" as a matter of conviction as part of an attempt to promote temperance among their employees. Alcohol was banned in Potlatch, Idaho, and Dupont, Washington. Alfred Anderson, owner of the Phoenix Logging Company, purchased much of the land adjacent to his town as part of an attempt to preempt the establishment of businesses which might sell alcohol near his town.[82] These attempts at prohibition were unpopular and unsuccessful. Most were first ignored, and then discontinued. Gilchrist, Oregon, and Shevlin, Oregon, both made provisions for the sale and consumption of alcohol as part of the social activities of these company towns.

Schools were another feature that companies which established towns in the Pacific Northwest went to great lengths to provide for the children of their employees. Long-Bell Lumber built, then donated to Longview, Washington, its first high school.[83] The first high school established in the north end of Klamath County was one of the structures erected when the Gilchrist Timber Company constructed Gilchrist, Oregon. Local children, prior to the arrival of the Gilchrist Timber Company, had to leave the region if they wished to attend high school. Schools were one of the focal points of social life in the company towns of the Pacific Northwest.

Social life in the company towns of the Pacific Northwest was more active than that of other small towns, because the companies usually subsidized clubs and sports teams as well as providing theaters and libraries.[84] The Gilchrist Timber Company built a bowling alley as part the club it constructed for all residents of its town. Provision was also made by the Gilchrist Timber Company for a place for the town's teenagers to gather. These activities reduced isolation among the inhabitants of towns, which were usually situated in remote locations, as well as facilitated the integration of new arrivals.[85] The arrival of television tended to undermine the active social lives which had been a feature of company towns in the Pacific Northwest. Residents of the town would stay at home rather than going to the theater, visiting neighbors, or participating in clubs or teams.[86]

During the 1920s, some of the company towns in the Pacific Northwest began to close for reasons including the advent of widespread automobile ownership and better roads.[87] Employees from closed company towns would move on to surviving ones. Employees, following the closure of the mill at Brookings, Oregon, during 1925 moved more or less as a single unit to Central Oregon to work for Shevlin-Hixon and Brooks-Scanlon. In 1939, after the destruction by fire of a company town named Pine Ridge, the planer crew relocated to Gilchrist, Oregon.

The Hoover-Roosevelt Depression bankrupted many firms whose towns were emptied when their mills went out of business.[88] By time the lumber market improved, the isolation, which as often as not was the reason mill owners had built towns for their employees, was no longer the factor it once had been. Following the Second World War, one by one, the company towns of the Pacific Northwest ceased to exist as company towns or else entirely ceased to exist.

Gilchrist, Oregon, was the Pacific Northwest's last company town. The Gilchrist Timber Company, through a combination of practicality and decency, achieved in the matter of town planning what governmental city planners have never managed and which progressive business types consistently failed at, Pullman, Washington, and Gary, Indiana, being among the most well-known examples of failed progressive paternalism. What the Gilchrist Timber Company achieved with Gilchrist was a perfection of employee housing practices already established for its logging camps by the Gilchrist-Fordney Timber Company. Its history, since it was a product of the Gilchrist family's leadership and management practices, begins with an overview of the background of the Gilchrist family.

Aerial view of Gilchrist-Fordney logging operations near Laurel, Mississippi, early 1930s.
Collection of Mary G. Ernst.

Gilchrist Oregon: The Model Company Town

Turpentine Camp near Laurel, Mississippi, early 1930s.
Collection of Mary G. Ernst.

CHAPTER II

The Gilchrist Timber Company: Laurel Mississippi and Before

*Gilchrist, derived from the Gaelic phrase, "giolla Chriost,"
meaning Servant of Christ, is a surname of Scottish origin,
having originated in Islay, the southernmost island of the Inter Hebrides.*

The leadership and management practices of the Gilchrist family are the reason Gilchrist, Oregon, was a singularly successful company town, why it became the model company town. The town, forest, and mill were the culmination, the perfection, of the Gilchrist family's six generations of involvement in the timber industry. The character of the individuals who established company towns was the reason some company towns were successes and others failures. Gilchrist was singularly successful because the Gilchrist family remembered and learned from the knowledge and experience they accumulated generation after generation in the timber industry to include building mills and constructing the operating camps and a town.

The Gilchrist family came to the United States from Ayershire, Scotland, by way of County Londonderry, Ulster. In 1730 Robert and William Gilchrist emigrated from Ulster to Chester, New Hampshire. They were part of the exodus of Scots-Irish from Ulster whose members settled on the frontier regions of the Thirteen Colonies in a band extending from New England to Georgia. This band began moving west even before the Thirteen Colonies achieved independence from Great Britain. William Gilchrist died without issue. Robert Gilchrist had six children one of whom, Alexander Gilchrist (born 1733), served in the Continental Army under the command of General Sullivan.

Alexander Gilchrist married Martha Shirley. This union produced eight children, including six sons, one of whom, Robert, served as captain with the Continental Army during the Colonies' war of independence. Another son, David (born 1778), married Hannah Kennedy.

From the marriage of David and Hannah came eight children. They comprised the third generation of the Gilchrist family born in the New World. Their fifth child, Albert, born May 9, 1816, married Abigail Corliss. It was this branch of the Gilchrist family which would establish Gilchrist, Oregon. Another son of David and Hannah, Alexander also entered the timber business after moving to St. Clare, Michigan, from Manchester, New Hampshire, where he was employed as a merchant.

In 1848 Albert Gilchrist moved with his family to Marine City, Michigan. He worked in the lumber manufacturing business before purchasing the Rust Brothers Mill. After the mill burned in 1856, he moved to Saginaw, Michigan, where he acquired a water-powered mill which he converted to steam power and fitted out with the most advanced equipment then available, which included a circular saw.[89]

Among Albert and Hannah Gilchrist's children was Frank W. Gilchrist (1845-1912). He was highly successful in sawmills, transportation ships on the Great Lakes, and sugar factories in the United States and Canada. He was a major partner in the Rust-Owen Lumber Company in

*Frank W. Gilchrist.
Collection of Mrs. Mary G. Ernst.*

*SS Frank W. Gilchrist.
Collection of Milton Hill.*

Wisconsin, the Three States Lumber Company, and the W. E. Smith Lumber Company of Illinois and later Tennessee and the Gilchrist Transportation Company.[90]

Frank W. Gilchrist's investments included water transportation, which he regarded as a business which would facilitate the more efficient movement of his lumber to market. The firm he established, Gilchrist Transportation, eventually grew into the second largest shipping company operating on the Great Lakes. The firm, at its zenith, operated a fleet of seventy vessels, which included steam barges and tugs. In the firm's hulls were transported bulk cargos to include grain, ore, lumber, and coal. The Gilchrist Transportation Company, by 1890, was building its own ships.[91] One ship in the Gilchrist fleet, an ocean-going steamer, was sold in 1916 to a New York firm. Following the sale, she was sunk on her first voyage under the flag of her new owners by a German U-boat.[92] It was a steam whistle from a Gilchrist-owned ship which the Gilchrist Timber Company used to signal the noon hour, shift changes, accidents, and events such as V-J Day.

In 1901 Frank W. Gilchrist chose Frank S. Dushau to serve as his "land looker," a position he held with the Gilchrist family for the rest of his life. The task he was assigned was to discover likely tracks of land, estimate the amount of timber on them, and then, if he deemed them worth acquiring, purchase them. Frank S. Dushau traveled to most every stand in the Union as well as in northern and western Canada.[93] In 1902 Frank W. Gilchrist dispatched Frank S. Dushau to Central Oregon. He began acquiring the timberland where thirty-six years later his employer's grandson, Frank W. Gilchrist, would establish Gilchrist, Oregon.

The prescience of the timberland purchases in Central Oregon in 1902 is all the more remarkable given that no railroad would come near the Gilchrist timber holding until the late 1920s. These purchases were also in line with the foresighted, long-term planning that was typical of the Gilchrist family during its six generations of involvement in the timber industry.

In 1907 Frank W. Gilchrist helped form the Gilchrist-Fordney Company to develop large tracks of timber near Laurel, Mississippi, primarily in Jasper and Smith Counties. The mill, following its reconstruction, covered thirty acres and was renowned for its safety features and technical innovations. The mill was capable of producing 140,000 board feet a day. Its annual output, 36 million board feet, was shipped to domestic and foreign markets to include shipyards located at Pascagoula, Mississippi.

For almost fifty years, Engine Number 204 served the Gilchrist-Fordney Timber Company, then the Gilchrist Timber Company. Engine Number 204 departed from the Baldwin Locomotive Works at Eddystone, Pennsylvania, for Laurel, Mississippi, on March 15, 1909. The locomotive was the third in Baldwin Class 10-34¼D, the first in the class built for a logging railroad, and also the largest of its type up to that time ordered for a logging railroad. It had a 2-6-2 wheel arrangement. Engine Number 204 was built for maximum power and strength. It had an engine weight of 142,100 pounds, of which 112,500 pounds was carried on the drivers. The locomotive's 20x24-inch cylinders, 48-inch drivers, and 160-pound per square inch steam pressure yielded 27,200 pounds of power for traction. Engine Number 204 burned coal. The tender carried 4,500 gallons of water. The locomotive came out to Oregon in 1938 where it served the Gilchrist Timber Company until 1955. The tender, now a snowplow, remains in service.

During the eighteenth and nineteenth centuries, the timber industry preceded the arrival of farmers. An aphorism of the era had it that "The plough followed the ax." Timber companies harvested timber from land which was then sold to agriculturalists who farmed it.[94] The expectation for timber companies in Mississippi, as well as the Pacific Northwest, was that logging practices would follow a similar pattern as they had in New England and the old Northwest. Railroad logging (the use of trains and temporary railroad to move timber out of the woods) which was very labor- and capital-intensive provided an additional incentive to continue the logging practices utilized in New England and the old Northwest. Putting down, maintaining, then taking up the tracks for temporary railroads was almost entirely accomplished by teams of laborers.[95] It was the internal combustion engine that made selective cutting economically feasible. Moreover, the way in which timber was taxed in Mississippi during the first decades of the twentieth century also provided an additional incentive to harvest all timber as quickly as possible.

Care for its employees was another hallmark of the Gilchrist Timber operations in Michigan and of

Trestle construction.
Gilchrist Timber Company papers, Klamath County Museum

the Gilchrist-Fordney Company, then the Gilchrist Timber Company. A case in point is insurance for employees. *The Notice,* dated February 1, 1912, the subject of which is medical care, insurance payments, and insurance terms, is noteworthy not only for the obvious reason (employee compensation included an insurance program and medical services), but the size of the fees associated with the program. Forty cents a week for coverage for a married man, even assuming he was earning two or three dollars a day, means that the relative cost of the insurance was less than the relative cost of insurance for a family nowadays.[96]

Frank W. Gilchrist died on December 13, 1912, at the age of 68 in Memphis, Tennessee. His career was best summarized in an obituary which appeared on the front page of *The Lumber Trade Journal:*

> Lumbering was natural to Mr. Gilchrist. His father, Albert Gilchrist operated a sawmill in New Hampshire. When his son was five years old the family moved to Michigan, settling at

NOTICE

INSURANCE--On entering our service, all employees are required to pay the sum of 15c from their first earnings, and at the beginning of each succeeding week, the same amount, to cover either of the following benefits in case of accident and injury:

1—If such injuries alone result within ninety days from the date of accident in the death of any such employee, this Company will reimburse the employee in a sum equal to TWENTY-SIX WEEKS half wages, computed at the rate per day received by such employee at the date of the accident, but such sum shall in no event exceed SEVEN HUNDRED AND FIFTY DOLLARS.

2—If such injuries alone immediately, continuously and wholly disable such employee from engaging in any work or occupation for wages, the Company will reimburse the employee in an amount equal to one half the injured's daily wages for the period of such total disability not exceeding TWENTY-SIX WEEKS for any one accident, but in no event shall such sum exceed SEVEN HUNDRED AND FIFTY DOLLARS.

No benefits accrue to any employee except for accidents received while actually in our employ.

MEDICAL ATTENTION.

For medical attention, in addition to the above, on entering our service all employees are required to pay the sum of 25c for married men, or 15c for single men from their **FIRST EARNINGS** and at the beginning of each succeeding week the same amount, to cover the cost of medical attention for themselves and family, if any; said medical attention to include all that may be required by the employee or his family, if any, excepting in surgery and obstetrics, and to cover personal services of the Company's physician and not to include drugs and medicinal supplies. This medical attention to cease when employee leaves Company's service, except in case he leaves on account of his own illness.

Employees injured in the discharge of their duty **MUST NOTIFY THEIR FOREMAN IMMEDIATELY**, or they will not be treated by the Company Physician, whose certificate is necessary to make a claim for disability.

COMPANY PHYSICIANS:

AT PLANT DR. J. H. COOK   AT WOODS DR. J. T. BAILEY.

GILCHRIST-FORDNEY CO.

JUNE 1, 1909.

Insurance Notice.
Collection of Mrs. Mary G. Ernst

Marine City, where the father again entered the sawmill business. As his holdings increased he started and operated another plant at Sand Beach. Among the white pine timber Frank W. Gilchrist grew up to vigorous young manhood. He went to school, and worked around the plant, gaining the foundation that enabled him in a later life to be interested in timber and lumber operations in a dozen states. Notwithstanding the importance of his interests, Mr. Gilchrist was a man of great modesty, who preferred a quiet life to one of ostentation.

Mr. Gilchrist has done much for Alpena. As a tribute to his worth and sincere sorrow on account of his loss, business was suspended on the day of the funeral, while during the hour that the last words were being said, the bells of the churches rung their mournful tones.[97]

Frank R. Gilchrist (1871-1917) began representing the Gilchrist family's interests in Laurel, Mississippi, following his father's death in 1912. He also continued acquiring timberlands in Central Oregon. By the late 1920s these holdings exceeded 60,000 acres, all but 5,000 of which were located in Klamath and Lake Counties. Ralph E. Gilchrist (1877-1936), youngest son of Frank W. Gilchrist, assumed control of the Gilchrist family's timber holdings located outside the South while Frank R. Gilchrist was actively involved in the operation of the Gilchrist-Fordney mill as well as quietly becoming a leading figure in the life of Laurel, Mississippi. He and his wife, Flora, spearheaded the establishment of the YWCA in 1913, and served as its first president.

The Gilchrist-Fordney mill's lumberyard was a readily visible manifestation of Frank R. Gilchrist's management of the mill. It was remarked upon by a contemporary reporter:

> . . . that such a vast sea of mill products can be stacked in such an artistic manner conserving to the utmost degree compatible with conveniences every available foot of yard space. So symmetrical are the hundreds of stacks of lumber that cover this faultlessly kept yard that each has the appearance of a perfectly proportioned building with graceful outlines. No more attractively kept lumber yard adorns the ground of any company than is to be seen at the Gilchrist-Fordney plant.[98]

Frank R. Gilchrist.
Collection of Mrs. Mary G. Ernst

The response in March of 1915 by the Gilchrist-Fordney Company's management to a depressed lumber market is an example of the conduct of the Gilchrist family when dealing with its employees. The mill, after years of operating six days a week, was forced to reduce its operations to five days a week. Gilchrist-Fordney management, one week later, decided to return to a six-day week, not because the market had improved but out of concern for its employees, particularly the ordinary laborers who would have been hard-pressed to make ends meet for themselves and their families on the wages they'd received for a reduced week. The company decided to allow its yards to fill with unsold lumber, to reduce the incomes of its owners, rather than to impose hardship on its employees.[99]

Frank R. Gilchrist's death in 1917 was unexpected by his family, business associates, and those in the Gilchrist-Fordney Company who had anticipated that he would live to provide the firm with leadership for many years to come. He died, following an operation, the morning of February 19, 1917. It was said of him in the *Laurel Daily Leader*:

> When Mr. Gilchrist came to Laurel he seemed to grasp the situation and understand the people here better than anyone who was not a native. For this reason he was universally liked by all with whom he came in contact. He was unostentatious in his manner and in his life. His gifts were large and numerous but few people knew of them. He was always ready to help a good cause and any movement for the benefit of the city.
>
> Mr. Gilchrist personally provided new quarters for the Young Women's Christian Association, and his wife was a ready founder of that institution . . . He contributed largely to the new Young Men's Christian Association Building and to various other institutions and charities.
>
> A pall of sorrow hangs over Laurel. At the big lumber mill the employees are shocked beyond words. His genial good nature had won him a warm place in the hearts of his employees, as well as all others who knew him, and all Laurel joins in morning his death.[100]

The following summer on July 9, 1918, Ralph E. Gilchrist, Frank R. Gilchrist's brother, was selected to succeed his brother as president, Joseph W. Fordney was re-elected as vice president, Harry E. Fletcher was elected treasurer, and Stewart M. Jones (1878-1935) was elected secretary and appointed as general manager of the Gilchrist-Forndey mill. Ralph E. Gilchrist and Stewart M. Jones continued the work begun by Frank R. Gilchrist of molding his son Frank W. Gilchrist (1903-1956) into the man would lead the Gilchrist Timber Company to Oregon in 1938 then manage all aspects of his operations there to include the mill, town and timberlands.

The logging camps operated by Gilchrist-Fordney camp presaged Gilchrist, Oregon. The Gilchrist-Fordney camps were temporary towns where loggers could bring their families. This attracted married men, who were typically more stable and sober than were their single counterparts. The presence of their families reduced turnover among the woods crews. The camps attracted families, specifically the wives, by offering amenities which easily competed with those available in towns. All fifty-six buildings which comprised Camp Allenton, constructed in 1930 at a cost of approximately $30,000, were plumbed and wired for electricity.

Dushau, named after Frank S. Dushau, occupied a 360-acre site. The houses, built on pier and beam foundations, were permanent bungalows of five or six rooms. Each house had running water and electricity, which set it apart from neighboring communities where hand pumps were the norm and electricity remained an exception. Elise Graham wrote of the Dushau in her recollection of life in the camp:

> The company provided its inhabitants with a house in Dushau. Most of them were small bungalows consisting of five or six rooms... All the houses in Dushau had running water which was a step up from those in the surrounding towns still operating with pumps and wells. Our houses had electricity long before the rural electric programs . . . Our small Mississippi town, although deserted now by the loggers and their families, will always remain alive with me. It is in this place I spent many happy times and received many of life's lessons that are with me even today.[101]

Dushau's public buildings included a large commissary, clubhouse, doctor's office, school, and a YMCA which did additional duty as a church and community center as well as provided space for a barbershop and a traveling dentist. The commissary buildings of Camp Dushau and Camp Allenton, as is the Gilchrist Mall, were shopping centers located under a single roof. The town's post office was also located in the commissary building. The construction and operation of these camps presages the construction and operation of Gilchrist, Oregon. Quarters for the logging superintendent and school teacher were located in the clubhouse. There was a house which was occupied by the doctor whom the Gilchrist-Fordney Company provided for its employees and their families. Visitors and single loggers lodged in a two-story boardinghouse.[102]

Elise Graham, in her memoir entitled *Dushau Days*, describes life in a lumber camp operated by Gilchrist-Fordney during the 1920s. The school commences operations on September 12, 1921, with a faculty consisting of three teachers including the principal. Grades 1-8 were taught in Dushau. Students attended high school in nearby towns. Movies were shown on Saturday nights at the YMCA.

Elise Graham described a near-idyllic, very close-knit and supportive community. She spoke of Christmas in Dushau with particular fondness:

> Christmas in Dushau brought the most excitement. The company always put up a big tree in the middle of town. It would be trimmed with manger light and each year Santa Claus came to visit every child in town. Our teachers would help make out our Christmas wish lists and the company would see to it that would Christmas wishes were fulfilled.[103]

Mrs. Frank R. Gilchrist would travel out to Dushau several days prior to Christmas to oversee and participate in the celebration with the Gilchrist-Fordney Company's employees and their children. Each year the children of Dushau put on a Christmas play which was staged at the YMCA.[104]

Late during October 1921, Dushau's residents petitioned the governor of Mississippi to charter the community as a village. Among individuals named in the petition for municipal offices were Benjamin V. Wright and Isom A. Ezell. Both these individuals would subsequently figure in the establishment of Gilchrist, Oregon.

Among the signers of the Dushau petition was James P. Applewhite who was trained as a civil engineer. From 1921, when he was hired by Gilchrist-Fordney to lay out railroads and build bridges until his death in Oregon in 1967, James P. Applewhite was a key employee of the Gilchrist-Fordney and the Gilchrist Timber Company.[105] Another resident of the Dushau camp who would also figure prominently in the history of the Gilchrist Timber Company and Gilchrist, Oregon, was William A. Carmichael. He was hired in 1927, just out of high school, as a bookkeeper. In 1930 he transferred from the camp to the Gilchrist-Fordney mill where he served as Frank W. Gilchrist's personal secretary, a position he continued to hold after the move to Central Oregon and the establishment of Gilchrist, Oregon.[106]

In 1910 Benjamin V. Wright (1875-1944) had been hired by the Gilchrist-Fordney Company to replace John F. Mahoney as logging superintendent. He was trained as a civil engineer. His combination of training as a civil engineer, coupled with this experience as logging superintendent, would prove particularly useful once he began working in Central Oregon as manager of the Gilchrist timber holdings located in that region. He was dispatched to Oregon in 1925 to assume the duties performed by Frank S. Dushau who had died during the summer of 1924. James P. Applewhite succeeded him as logging superintendent.

During the 1920s Frank W. Gilchrist (1903-1956), son of Frank R. Gilchrist, entered the employ of Gilchrist-Fordney. In the summer before what would have been his freshman year at Harvard, while receiving some tutoring for his first-year studies, he was rooming at the Moorman home in Gulfport, Mississippi. There he met and then fell in love with Mary Moorman. She was the daughter of the house. In 1922 when they eloped, she was sixteen and he was nineteen. Frank W. Gilchrist supported his bride by taking a position at the Great Southern Hotel as a night clerk.

His mother dispatched her brother-in-law, Ralph Gilchrist, to Gulfport to meet with his nephew. It was subsequently decided that Frank W. Gilchrist would begin his preparation for eventually assuming by management of the Gilchrist-Fordney Company by attending a business college in Grand Rapids, Michigan. While attending school in Grand Rapids, Frank R. Gilchrist (1924-1991), the first of the three children of Frank and Mary Gilchrist, was born on April 2. Frank W. Gilchrist, after completing his business studies, returned to take a position with the Gilchrist-Fordney Company as a timekeeper. Over the next several years, under the tutelage and mentorship of his uncle, Ralph Gilchrist, and Stewart M. Jones, he learned the various phases of operating a large pine sawmill through a process of on-the-job training. By the mid-1930s, he had become company secretary and treasurer. He had also developed into the leader who led the move from Laurel to Central Oregon, where he established the Gilchrist Timber Company, determined the management practices for the firm's timberlands, and founded Gilchrist, Oregon.[107]

Gilchrist Fordney, Laurel, Mississippi panorama.
Collection of Mrs. Mary G. Ernst

During the 1920s, while Frank W. Gilchrist was gaining the experience and mastering the skills which he would employ throughout his tenure as leader and general manager of the Gilchrist Timber Company and of Gilchrist, Oregon, the Gilchrist-Fordney Company hired several individuals who, along with their children, would play prominent roles as employees of the Gilchrist Timber Company as well residents of Gilchrist, Oregon. Forrest A. Hendry, born in Jasper County, Mississippi, in 1901 was hired as a saw filer. Edgar Shotts, born in Clarke County, Mississippi, in 1901, whose son eventually served as president of the Gilchrist Timber Company, was hired as a millwright. Curtis Breazeale and R. Jud Terrell were also hired during the 1920s by Gilchrist-Fordney Company, and then went on to careers in Central Oregon as employees of the Gilchrist Timber Company and to mark their marks as residents of Gilchrist, Oregon.[108]

During the late 1920s, trucks and roads began to supplement then eventually replace trains and tracks as the transport system Gilchrist-Fordney Company utilized to move logs from the woods to the mill.[109] By 1937, only trucks were used to move logs out of the woods to the Gilchrist-Fordney Company's mill.[110] Trucks, powered by internal combustion engines, and roads were a combination which made economically feasible the forest management practices for Gilchrist Timber Company was renowned. Railroad logging was capital-intensive and labor-intensive. Jim Childre, whose father, Rufus Childre, began his career with the Gilchrist-Fordney Company as a member of a track crew, recounted the following:

> They gave him the job and he went to work on the railroad. What they did was they had the ties, some of them they cut little spur lines. They didn't think they would be there for more than a little while. They just went out and cut poles out of small pine trees, topped them, knocked their limbs off, put them on their shoulder and carried them up and put them down on the rope bed. Then they laid the tracks on it. Maybe a summer is all they lasted and then they moved on. It wasn't a permanent roadbed. When they were done they just picked up the steel and left the ties there. The job consisted cutting and carrying that stuff. The good thing was at least dad had a chance for promotion. A fellow called Mr. Ralston, who also came to Gilchrist when they came west, was the foreman of that crew and Mr. Ralston used to tell dad, "Well, the only reason they hired you Rufus is because the mules died."[111]

The expenses connected with relocating trackers every time an area was logged created an incentive to harvest all timber accessible by a section of track before moving it. The Gilchrist Timber Company was the first mill in Central Oregon to have never employed logging railroads to move timber from the woods to the mill. Brooks-Scanlon, when it switched from logging railroads to roads and trucks following the Second World War, obtained information from the Gilchrist Timber Company pertaining to logging operations

employing trucks rather than trains to move logs out of the woods.¹¹²

Also influencing logging practices in the South and Pacific Northwest during this era was the assumption that logged land would become farmland. This had been what occurred after logging operations were completed in states of the old Northwest. Logging company created farmland by clearing away the timber. "Letting in sunlight" was a phrase from the early nineteenth century which described the process of expanding farmland by removing timber. Much of the logged land in the south and Pacific Northwest proved unsuitable for farming after the timber was removed. This discovery created another incentive to reforest logged lands, though it was one which, in the case of Mississippi was stifled by the then-existent taxation practices.

By 1927 Benjamin V. Wright had established himself in Oregon as overseer of the Gilchrist timber holding. He was engaged in an active correspondence with Ralph Gilchrist and Stewart M. Jones which included discussions of logging practices, to include sustain yield, and the detrimental effects that Mississippi's timber taxation policies had on forest management practices intended to maintain timber supplies for the long term

Mississippi's state government and local government attempted to maximize the money they took from Gilchrist-Fordney Company and other sawmills by taxing lands containing timber at ever higher rates. Stewart M. Jones, in a letter dated September 14, 1926, to Benjamin V. Wright, wrote:

I quite agree with you that the question of reforestation on the lands which are at present heavily timbered is useless and that to try to grow young trees on such land is simply to add to the hazard of carrying the standing timber.

I wish some arrangement of equitable taxation could be worked out. However, this is some job. The only way I can figure out we are going to beat the taxing authorities is to speed up production and get out of the business.¹¹³

Stewart M. Jones, in a subsequent letter to Benjamin V. Wright, dated September 16, 1927, wrote:

In our case, and I do not think our case is different from anyone else's, our taxes are five times as much on the timber we have today as they were in 1917, and we have between three and four hundred million feet less today than we had in 1917. The timber which we harvest each year is taken off the assessment roll but the "powers that be" increase the remaining timber to offset that portion taken off the roll. In other words, it looks now as though our taxes on standing timber the last year of our operation will be as high as they now are on our ten year's supply.

When you take into account all the taxes which corporations have to pay, as especially the lumberman, inasmuch as he has to buy all of his raw material in advance, it is a wonder that they make any money at all. I should say that with the present method of taxation in Mississippi a mill with twenty-five years of timber ahead is in a might bad fix. In other words I do not believe such a property could possibly operate and get its money back. I have made the statement frequently that I believe such a property would face bankruptcy before the end of the twenty-five years. On account of this the mills in this section are forced to push production at the highest rate of speed and sell the output regardless the intrinsic value of the product.[114]

Mississippi state and local taxation policies, besides creating an incentive to log timberlands as quickly as possible and to mill lumber without regard to optimal lumber yield from each log, also created disincentives for reforestation and selective timber harvesting.

> These taxation policies taxation policies made reforestation and selective timber harvesting costly and inefficient to the timber companies . . . Many mill owners upon deciphering the state's tax code initiated the uprooting of trees from recently seeded land.[115]

Edward Hines of the Hines Lumber Company attempted to allow the timber to regenerate on its cutover lands by leaving seed trees. An immediate consequence of his reforestation efforts was to have the cutover land he was attempting to reforest taxed as timberland.[116] Taxation assured the extinction of Gilchrist-Fordney as well as the other mills operating in Mississippi during the 1930s. For the Gilchrist family, who had timberlands in the west, relocation was possible. There was only the cessation of operations and unemployment for their employees for firms without the option of flight. Forty years later, the Gilchrist family and their employees would once again suffer the deleterious effects of ruinous taxation and onerous government regulations. Mississippians eventually began aggressively reforesting their state. The state is now 65 percent forested and its timberlands are managed to provide its mills with a steady, sustained supply of logs. Eighty years later the positions of Mississippi and Oregon have reversed. Mississippi once again has a vigorous timber industry, while that of Oregon is struggling to survive in spite of tax policies and regulations which are driving it towards extinction.[117]

By the summer of 1930, the timber near Dushau was nearing exhaustion. Preparation began for a new logging camp. Stewart M. Jones announced its location, near Mossville in southern Jasper County, and that it was the last camp which the Gilchrist-Fordney Company would establish. This last camp was named Camp Allenton, though it became known and remembered as Camp Allen.

Camp Allenton was similar to Dushau in that houses in both camps were plumbed and wired, had ceilings, had floors laid on subfloors, shingled roofs, and pier-and-post foundations. Once again the community had a commissary, community center, doctor's office, and school. In Camp Allenton, as had been the case in Dushau, family life was stressed and promoted by the Gilchrist-Fordney Company. Decorous behavior was expected of residents of Camp Allenton as had also been the case with Dushau.[118] What made the tenure of Camp Allenton different from that of Dushau was the knowledge that it was Gilchrist-Fordney Company's last and the effects of the Hoover-Roosevelt Depression, which had been triggered by the stock market collapse of October 1929, exacerbated by a succession of unsuccessful efforts by Hoover, then, on a larger scale by Roosevelt, which included tax increases, spending programs, government intervention, and expanded regulations.

During January 1931, Gilchrist-Fordney officials decided not to resume operations following the shutdown for annual repairs which had begun on December 2, 1930. Lumber prices had already fallen to levels where to operate the mill was to lose money. More than two hundred men in the mill and one hundred in the woods were left without work. Work on Camp Allenton was delayed. Approximately a hundred men received intermittent employment whenever the planing mill, shipping, or other parts of the mill were operated. The Gilchrist-Fordney Company also succored its employees by opening a canning plant which provided for them by seeing that its laid-off employees received food from a market which was located near the mill as well as generating some income for the company.[119] Mrs. Ernst described actions by parents (Mr. Frank W. Gilchrist) during the years of the Hoover-Roosevelt Depression to mitigate the lot of the less fortunate among Laurel's residents:

> I remember daddy (Frank W. Gilchrist) telling about they had sacks of food they gave the Em-

ployees every week. I can remember going down to the train station with my mother, where they packed turnip greens. The turnip roots were sold up north, but not the greens. So, we'd pick up the greens and mother would take them to the families to eat. They just cared and daddy took a lot of pride in things.[120]

Gilchrist-Fordney Company resumed operations on May 18, 1931. The mill had suspended operations for a period of five-and-a-half months. Company officials, when queried as to whether or not the permanent operations would continue, acknowledged that they hoped to do so, though they had no way of knowing, given that the Hoover-Roosevelt Depression continued to deepen.

During June 1931, Camp Allenton was completed. Only 56 of the planned 60 buildings were erected. The Dushau's families and equipment were shifted to Camp Allenton. On June 30, 1931, Dushau's post office was discontinued. Dushau's buildings were dismantled. The sense of community which had characterized Dushau continued on at Camp Allenton. Church services were conducted in the community whenever an itinerant minister visited. Community sings were popular. Performances by choral groups from neighboring towns were well attended.[121]

The results were bleak for the Gilchrist-Fordney Company when it closed its books on its operations during 1931. During the seven-and-a-half months the mill operated during 1931, it produced 22,503,669 board feet and sold 25,759,444 board feet which included approximately 3 million board feet which remained unsold from 1930's production. The company lost $29,000 on its operations during 1931.[122]

1932 proved worse than 1931. Lumber prices fell below the previous year's levels. Unsold lumber accumulated. By the end of June there was room for no more. Gilchrist-Fordney Company began a four-month shutdown which at last ended when the mill and woods crew resumed operations on November 1, 1932. An official of the Gilchrist-Fordney Company, when asked how long the mill would remain in operation said, "As long as we can operate." The wish of the management of the Gilchrist-Fordney Company was that the mill could continuously operate. What prevented this was that lumber stacked in the yard deteriorated over time; moreover, there was a limit to the amount of lumber which the yard could hold.[123] The Gilchrist-Fordney Company, when the books were closed on 1932, had posted a loss of $108,000 on sales of 23,250,439 board feet, 2,000,000 fewer board feet than was sold the previous year. Output for the mill during the eight months it operated during 1932 totaled 23,051,103 board feet.[124]

Franklin Roosevelt's six-day Bank Holiday began on March 6, 1933. During Roosevelt's Bank Holiday, depositors were denied access to their funds. Federal Reserve bank notes stopped circulating. Gilchrist-Fordney Company acted to offset the hardship created for its employees by Roosevelt's Bank Holiday. Script was printed, and then issued in one-dollar, two-dollar, and five-dollar denominations. All, with the exception of three dollars, were subsequently redeemed.[125] This was the only instance during its six generations in the timber business that a Gilchrist enterprise issued script to its employees.

During June 1933, the Gilchrist-Fordney Company deeded to the Club Women of Bay Springs, Mississippi, a one-acre tract of virgin longleaf timber. The donation of the land and timber, which is located only on Highway 15 between Laurel and Bay Springs, marked the beginning of the eventual reforestation of Mississippi and restoration of its timber industry.[126]

Stewart M. Jones, during the last week of July 1933, announced that wages paid unskilled laborers would increase by twenty-five cents a day. The wage increase applied to both mill and woods crews. It was the second wage increase granted by the Gilchrist-Fordney Company during 1933. Wages paid skilled laborers increased by ten to twenty percent. These wage increases more than offset wage decreases which conditions forced on the Gilchrist-Fordney Company the previous year. On August 7, 1933, the Gilchrist-Fordney Company placed its employees on a schedule of eight-hour days and a six-day week. They had previously been a schedule of ten-hour days and a six-day week. The length of the work week was then reduced from six days to five days. The employees continued to receive the same wages for five-day work weeks of eight-hour days that they'd received for a six-day work week of ten-hour days.¹²⁷ This was yet another example of the management practices with which the Gilchrists earned the loyalty and dedication of their employees.

Towards the end of 1933, the Gilchrist-Fordney Company responded to the ongoing shortage of cash which continued to afflict the United States by engaging in barter. Approximately fifteen car loads of lumber were exchanged for cotton, pecans, and hay. At one point the Gilchrist-Fordney Company held 450 bales of cotton. In another instance, enough lumber for the construction of a five-room house was traded for 5,000 gallons of syrup. The combination of barter and some lumber sales enabled the Gilchrist-Fordney Company to continuously operate throughout 1934. The Gilchrist-Fordney Company, throughout the years of the Hoover-Roosevelt Depression, bartered lumber for cotton, sweet potatoes, syrup, and other goods produced by the neighboring farmers. The Gilchrist-Fordney Company installed equipment for canning, and then invited the residents of Smith County to use the canning equipment to put up their excess produce for use during the winter months.¹²⁸

The following year, on February 13, 1935, Stewart M. Jones died of pneumonia. He was 56 years old. Laurel, Mississippi, and the Gilchrist-Fordney Company lost a stalwart man whose labors contributed significantly to the fortunes of the Gilchrist-Fordney Company and Laurel, Mississippi. He was succeeded by Frank W. Gilchrist as general manager.¹²⁹

One August 31, 1936, Ralph E. Gilchrist died. He was 58 years old. Ralph Gilchrist had served as president of the Gilchrist-Fordney Company since 1917, following the death of his brother, Frank R. Gilchrist. He was a mentor to Frank W. Gilchrist, his nephew. Moreover, he directed the management and expansion of the Gilchrist family's Central Oregon timber holdings as well as setting the course which would lead to the establishment of Gilchrist, Oregon. He was succeeded as president of the Gilchrist-Fordney Company by Harry E. Fletcher who was the firm's last president.¹³⁰

During 1937, the Gilchrist-Fordney Company's final year of operations, the mill produced approximately 26,218,100 board feet of lumber.

Ralph E. Gilchrist.
Collection of Mrs. Mary G. Ernst.

Shipments during the first seven months of 1937 totaled 24,225,093 mill board feet. Employment was provided to 450 men who worked in the mill or woods. The annual payroll totaled $550,000. A few minutes before 3 p.m. on July 28, 1937, the Gilchrist-Fordney Company milled its last log. James A. Richard, a sawyer who in 1907 had milled the Gilchrist-Fordney Company's first log, returned to cut the last log. The mill had run night and day during its final months of operation, milling the last of the timber which was being felled by the woods crew in Jasper County near Camp Allenton. The planing mill and shipping department continued to operate for several more months, which provided employment for approximately one hundred men. The office staff remained employed for even longer. On December 17, 1937, the millsite, buildings, and all machinery, save for Engine Number 204 and machine tools which were intended for use in Oregon, were sold to Oliver U. Addison for one dollar. He had served the Gilchrist-Fordney Company for many years as its office manager and purchasing agent. The sale was a sinecure, a reward, for his years of service to the firm. On December 31, 1937, the Gilchrist-Fordney Company was dissolved. Frank W. Gilchrist and Frank J. Foley were appointed as trustees who were responsible for disposing of the company's remaining assets. The assets included 17,690 acres of cutover timberland located in Smith, Jasper, and Jones Counties as well mineral rights for 16,784 acres located in the aforementioned counties.[131] One of the individuals hired by the Gilchrist-Fordney Company during its final years of operations was Rufus E. Childre. His son, Jim, recounted his father's efforts to obtain a position with the Gilchrist-Fordney Company:

> He went down there and he didn't have any dress shoes to wear so he put on a suit that he had to wear to apply for a job. He had to walk several miles to get down there; he didn't have any dress shoes so he borrowed his brother George dress shoes. Of course they were too big for him, he carried his shoes and once he got there he stopped to put on his shoes, and he washed his feet in a creek and went in and did the interview and they gave him a job. Then he went back out took his shoes off and went home. It was about 10 or 12 miles he had to walk.[132]

Rufus Childre moved with the Gilchrists to Central Oregon, and then went on to play a significant role in the management of the Gilchrist Timber Company's timberlands.

Stewart J. Gilchrist, namesake of Stewart M. Jones, returned to Laurel, Mississippi, where he established a law practice.[133] The Gilchrist-Fordney Company and the Gilchrist family remained fondly remembered decades after the last log was milled. Eighty years later, Mississippi's timber industry surpasses that of Oregon. Businesses now flee Oregon's confiscatory taxations and onerous regulatory burdens for Mississippi and other states in the South and Midwest.

Camp Allen Reading from left to right.
Collection of Lauren Rogers Museum.

Gilchrist Oregon: The Model Company Town

Close up view of loading crew in action.
Lauren Rogers Museum, Laurel, Mississippi

Gilchrist-owned ship.
Lauren Rogers Museum, Laurel, Mississippi

The Gilchrist Timber Company: Laurel, Mississippi and Before

Gilchrist-Fordney Main Line Engine and Train Crew
Lauren Rogers Museum, Laurel, Mississippi

Gilchrist-Fordney track laying in Jasper County, 1931
Lauren Rogers Museum, Laurel, Mississippi

Laurel Leader-Call, Laurel, MS
Lauren Rogers Museum, Laurel, Mississippi

The Gilchrist Timber Company: Laurel, Mississippi and Before

View of camp houses.
Lauren Rogers Museum, Laurel, Mississippi

Mary M. Gilchrist and Frank W. Gilchrist with their children (L to R): Stewart J. Gilchrist, Mary Geales (Gilchrist) Ernst and Frank R. Gilchrist. Early 1930s.
Collection of Mary G. Ernst.

CHAPTER III
1938-1941
The Move West and Building the Town

"Surely heaven must have something of the color and shape of whatever village or hill or cottage of which the believer says, This is my own."

— Light In August *by William Faulkner*

The establishment of Gilchrist, Oregon, resulted, in part, from Mississippi's tax laws on standing timber which created a burden on sawmill operators doing business in the state and which also stifled reforestation. The Gilchrists intended to remain in the lumber business. Doing so in Mississippi was not feasible. They already held 60,000 acres of timberland in Oregon in Klamath, Lake, and Deschutes Counties, so the decision was finalized to move to Oregon once the Laurel mill was cut out, then to begin to do business as the Gilchrist Timber Company, an entity which had been established in 1925.[134]

In 1902, when Frank W. Gilchrist first dispatched Frank S. Dushau to Central Oregon, Prineville was the principal town in Central Oregon. The region was largely uninhabited. It had few residents, most of whom were ranchers. The officers of both the Great Northern Railroad and the Union Pacific Railroad deemed the area unlikely to ever produce enough freight to warrant the construction into it of a railroad. Central Oregon in 1902 was the largest area in the whole of the United States still without a railroad.[135]

The Union Pacific constructed a feeder line, the Columbia Southern Railway, which reached Shaniko in 1900 which is where it stopped. The town is almost 150 miles from Gilchrist, Oregon, and is separated from it by the Ochoco Mountains. Edward Harriman had no interest in tackling the steep grades to the south of Shaniko. The town remained the Columbia Southern Railway terminus.

Frank S. Dushau began scouting the timberlands of Central Oregon for the Gilchrist family, while the ranchers of the area attempted to attract a railway to the area. It was not certain that railroad tracks would ever reach the region. Throughout the spring, summer, and into autumn, he traversed the region, first on horseback then later by automobile. His task was a solitary one that took him out in all types of weather. He cruised the region's timber which entailed traversing tens of thousands of acres on foot and camping out for extended periods. By 1918, based on his recommendations, the Gilchrists had acquired almost 60,000 acres of timber. Most of it was located in Klamath and Lake Counties. Even after James J. Hill built the Oregon Trunk Line, which reached Bend, Oregon in 1911 then stopped, the timberlands, acquired at the recommendation of Frank S. Dushau, remained without access to a railway. The Gilchrist, Oregon, timber purchases were an act of faith, a gamble, that eventually there would exist a way to bring the timber to market. Until then, for all the quality of the standing timber as well as the suitability of the area's terrain for logging operations, the value of the unharvested timber remained negligible.[136]

Frank S. Dushau died on July 6, 1924. He was succeeded in 1925 by Benjamin V. Wright who had previously served as logging superintendent of the Gilchrist-Fordney Company. B. V. Wright arrived in Oregon in 1925. He operated out of an office located in Portland, Oregon, in the Bedell Building until 1938, when Frank W. Gilchrist shifted the Gilchrist Timber Company's operations center to Gilchrist. He was responsible for expanding and managing the Gilchrist Timber holdings. He figured prominently in the founding of the Walker Range District, which still exists and is an association of timber owners who have banded together to manage their timber holdings, including providing fire protection. Eventually, his duties came to include tasks related to the establishment of the Gilchrist Timber Company in Central Oregon as well as the construction of Gilchrist, Oregon. He remained with the Gilchrist Timber Company until his death in 1944.

On February 27, 1925, the Gilchrist Timber Company was incorporated in Delaware with an office in Detroit, Michigan, and $557,000 in paid capital stock. The company's first directors, Ralph E. Gilchrist, Grace Gilchrist Fletcher, and Stewart M. Jones (who was also then serving as the Gilchrist-Fordney Company's general manager) were elected when the company met for its incorporation meeting. The Gilchrist Timber Company's other stockholders, in addition to the directors, were Gilchrist & Company, Ltd. (the Gilchrist family's holding company), A. R Owen, and Flora Smith Gilchrist (executrix of the estate of Frank Rust Gilchrist). On March 14, 1925, at the first meeting of the directors of the Gilchrist Timber Company, Ralph E. Gilchrist was elected president; with 1,911 shares, he was also the majority stockholder. Stewart M. Jones was elected vice president. The initial objective in organizing the Gilchrist Timber Company was to acquire the 55,122 acres of Central Oregon timberland that had been held in trust by Ralph E. Gilchrist.[137]

Interest renewed in the extension of the Oregon Trunk Line south of Bend during the 1920s. At the same time, the Southern Pacific Railroad began building a line which extended from Eugene, Oregon, over Willamette Pass then on to Klamath Falls, Oregon, where it joined with California and Northwestern Railroad, a subsidiary of Southern Pacific which had reached Klamath Falls from Weed, California, in 1909. During 1925, Southern Pacific was actively soliciting support for its line over the Willamette Pass. Ralph Gilchrist discussed Southern Pacific's efforts to solicit the Gilchrist Timber Company's business in a letter to B. V. Wright which was dated October 2, 1925:

> I have been of the opinion that our position should be one of being neutral, but, as you suggest, we may possibly have to come out and take a side. The difficulty with this is that the Southern Pacific has been very active in soliciting our support to their program, and in return have intimated that they would do whatever we might want in the way of Railroad building to our properties, while on the other hand the Hill people have done little or nothing in either soliciting our support of suggesting and promises. There may be something back of this that at you and I do not understand, but I think that we should be careful in volunteering to much to the Hill people as it might affect our position with them in the future. I hardly think we can volunteer anything to them until they have earnestly solicited our aid . . . The situation I would like to see develop is, have the Hill lines chase us and make promises and assurance as to the construction of their line before we actually take a position and volunteer anything to either side.[138]

The Southern Pacific completed its line from Eugene to Klamath Falls in 1926. Late the following year, the Great Northern Railroad at last received permission from the Interstate Commerce Commission (I.C.C.) to extend the Oregon Trunk Line from Bend to Chemult, where it joined Southern Pacific's line to Klamath Falls. In letters from B. V. Wright to J. P. Applewhite, dated July 24, 1926, and in others dated January 12, 1927, from B. V. Wright to S. M. Jones, details were provided of the regulatory obstacles raised by the I.C.C. to Great Northern's plan to extend the Oregon Trunk Line.[139] In 1927 Great Northern began building its extension of the Oregon Trunk Line. Construction was completed in 1930.[140] Both railroad lines touched Gilchrist timberland. Great Northern came within five miles to the west of where Gilchrist, Oregon, was established. Southern Pacific was fourteen miles to the south of it. Completion came just in time since by then the end of the Gilchrist-Fordney Company was more or less settled. The completions of extensions of Southern Pacific and the Oregon Trunk Line provided the Gilchrist Timber Company with an outlet to market for its lumber.

The Walker Range Fire Patrol Association was formed on May 31, 1927, by representatives of the Gilchrist Timber Company (including B. V. Wright), Ralph E. Gilchrist, the Fremont Land Company, and Shevlin-Hixon Company. The Walker Range Fire Patrol Association, which still exists, was one of the Gilchrist Timber Company's most enduring legacies. It was formed to preserve forest land, specifically to protect it from fire and the cyclical insect infestations that destroyed timber and increased the danger of fire. At first Walker Range's area of protection encompassed all the timberlands of its members in or adjacent to the Deschutes River Valley. In 1939 it expanded the area it protected to include the Deschutes and Fremont National Forests. Walker Range has proven singularly successful in preventing forest fires. The largest fire it ever had to fight was a 945-acre fire which occurred in 1990. The battle with insect infestations is an ongoing fight that continues to this day. The offices of the Walker Range Fire Patrol Association are located on the south end of Crescent, Oregon.[141.]

By late 1927 B. V. Wright was routinely receiving solicitations from firms offering equipment or services for the mill which, it was rumored, would soon start milling timber taken from the Gilchrist holdings. B. V. Wright explained to C. W. Willette of Seattle, Washington, in a letter dated October 4, 1927, that even though a railroad line near the Gilchrist timber holdings was under construction, until the rates the railroad would charge were known it was impractical to make any plans, much less go into the details of planning a mill.[142]

During 1934 B. V. Wright began working to establish clear title for the short line railroad, the Klamath Northern Railroad, which would eventually provide the Gilchrist Timber Company with access to Southern Pacific Railroad. On March 29, 1935, he filed a petition to vacate streets in the Crescent and Odell additions of Crescent where the track of the Klamath Northern Railroad would cross. In a letter dated June 26, 1936, from B. V. Wright to Ralph E. Gilchrist, fear was expressed that the principals of the Crescent Townsite Company would at last make their holdings pay by inflating the price of the lots needed by Gilchrist Timber Company for Klamath Northern Railroad's right-of-way. In the same letter, B. V. Wright described three possible routes for Klamath Northern Railroad, and then recommended the one which didn't require crossing property controlled by Weyerhauser or Shevlin-Hixon. In a related letter from B. V. Wright to Ralph E. Gilchrist dated June 29, 1936, B. V. Wright continued advocating connecting Klamath Northern Railroad to Southern Pacific Railroad, by noting that the route to Southern Pacific Railroad offered the option of also using Klamath Northern Railroad to haul logs to the mill, as well as transporting lumber to market.[143] A few weeks later, in another letter to Ralph E. Gilchrist, B. V. Wright reported that he had entered into negotiations with the Crescent Townsite Company, the object of which was to purchase lots for Klamath Northern Railroad's right-of-way.[144]

The site for the mill had been purchased by early 1935, though the decision to build the town and mill at that location wasn't finalized until early 1937.[145] Research and planning for the town continued during 1935 and 1936. In a letter from B. V. Wright to Ralph E. Gilchrist dated July 24, 1936, he reported that he was conducting fact-finding trips to company towns located throughout the Pacific Northwest. Wright reported that he had visited J. Neils' town at Klickitat, Washington. In the same letter, he also asked for more specific guidance before conducting further visits.[146]

Gilchrist Timber Company continued to manage, organize, and expand its timber holdings at the same time it was preparing to build its mill town and railroad. In a letter dated October 24, 1935, B. V. Wright reported to Ralph E. Gilchrist unsuccessful efforts by Shevlin-Hixon to eradicate the beetles which were killing its timber. In the same letter, B. V. Wright advocated logging, then milling beetle-killed timber as quickly as possible.[147] Several weeks later, in a letter dated November 15, 1935, B. V. Wright reported to Ralph E. Gilchrist that no progress was possible in the matter of proposed exchanges of timberland with Shevlin-Hixon, the purpose of which was to organize timber holdings into adjoining blocks, because the decision-makers were out of state.[148] In another letter to Ralph Gilchrist dated July 10, 1936, B. V. Wright discussed the acquisition of timberlands containing 2,710,000 board feet of timber[149] B. V. Wright, now in his sixties, continued to cruise timberland for the Gilchrist Timber Company as well as inspect property it had already acquired.

Ralph E. Gilchrist shaped the broad outlines for the Gilchrist Timber Company and its town. Both were very much creations of his vision. Harry Fletcher was given overall responsibility for planning the mill and its supporting infrastructure which included the town and the Klamath Northern Railroad. He was assisted by James P. Applewhite and Frank W. Gilchrist. Throughout 1936 and 1937, they made numerous trips to Oregon.[150]

On August 31, 1936, at the age of 58, Ralph E. Gilchrist died at his home in Alpena, Michigan. Harry Fletcher succeeded Ralph E. Gilchrist as president of Gilchrist Timber Company. He was responsible for completing the plans for Gilchrist Timber Company's operations in Oregon. Execution of these plans became the responsibility of Frank W. Gilchrist.[151] Throughout the next eighteen months he made numerous trips to Oregon. These trips soon changed from exploratory visits to ones whose purposes included negotiation, troubleshooting, and site inspections.

The site selected for the mill was located 50 miles south of Bend, Oregon, and was on the Little Deschutes River. This location was picked because it was at a place on the river where it was possible to erect a dam to form a millpond and provide water for the mill's boilers. B. V. Wright sent a letter dated November 20, 1936, to Peter Swan of Portland, the purpose of which was to inform him that a few days prior Frank W. Gilchrist and Harry Fletcher had decided to retain him to design the Gilchrist Timber Company's sawmill.[152] A preliminary sketch of the millpond was sent to Frank W. Gilchrist by B. V. Wright with a letter dated December 12, 1936. The pond was seventeen feet at its deepest point which was at the dam. The pond covered 50 acres and was 3,000 feet long. The embankment for the Klamath Northern Railroad, located on the pond's west side, did additional duty as a levee. Some filling was required on the northwest end of the bank where the mill was located.[153] B. V. Wright described having to clear trees in order to establish the site lines he needed to survey the site for the millpond. During the final days of 1936, B. V. Wright sent a letter dated December 22, 1936, to Frank W. Gilchrist in which he reported that negotiations were continuing with Southern Pacific and that he had to complete a series of surveys prior to March 1, 1937, when clearing was tentatively scheduled to commence.[154]

In a letter dated January 2, 1937, from B. V. Wright to Frank W. Gilchrist, he stated that he intended to have the preliminary surveys completed prior to the spring of 1937.[155] Frank W. Gilchrist, in a letter to B. V. Wright dated January 6, 1937, expressed his frustration with the failure of the Southern Pacific regarding its connection with the Klamath Northern Railroad:

> Company between the time we were in his office and the first of the year. I know it is your wish that were make the connection with the Southern Pacific, but, if they do not see fit to make us a proposal, maybe we had better contact the Great Northern.[156]

Two weeks later, in a letter dated January 21, 1937, from B. V. Wright to Harry Fletcher and Frank W. Gilchrist, B. V. Wright wrote:

> I had hoped to be able to give you something definite from the Southern Pacific long before this but there is nothing yet. A week ago last Monday, which is eleven days now, I jogged Mr. Kline on this and had a definite promise from him that their proposition would be in my hands within ten days.
>
> I called his office this morning and am told that he is out of the city but will be back tomorrow so will wait until I talk to him before doing anything definite. However, it seems to me that the Southern Pacific has held up this program entirely too long and that unless Mr. Kline does come with a proposition tomorrow, we should take our program up with the Great Northern and see what we can get that.
>
> I prefer, I admit, a Southern Pacific connection because it gives us quicker movement of freight from Portland or San Francisco into the plant and quicker movement of lumber out for the East. However, I do not feel that to make a connection with the Great Northern would

necessarily bar us making a Southern Pacific connection later when they find out they have slipped a cog.[157.]

B. V. Wright, in a letter dated January 29, 1937, to Harry Fletcher and Frank W. Gilchrist reported that he had at last received a letter from H. W. Kline.

> I am attaching copy of letter from Mr. H. W. Kline, general freight agent for the Southern Pacific, outlining their proposition regarding Railroad connections for our proposed plant. From this you will see that the way the Southern Pacific proposes to tie us to their line is by making our line a common carrier and taking a division of the freight rates, plus a possible reduction in the price of the steel to build our line.
>
> I have had Mr. Thompson check to see if the laws permit a Railroad company to give a division of freight rates where the spur line is not a common carrier, as to tell me the required procedure of building with the idea of eventually becoming a common carrier, in the event it was thought advisable to do so. Mr. Thompson's report is that a Railroad cannot give a division of freight rates to a private line like ours will be, and he suggests that the proper procedure would be to go ahead and build the line as a private carrier and when it seems best, to change to a common carrier, if that time should come, and I think there will be no trouble to do it that way. You will note that Mr. Kline suggests that procedure.
>
> In the discussion of this matter with Mr. Kline, I told him that there were reasons why we do not want a common carrier line through the area between our mill site and the Southern Pacific Railroad, at least for the present, that everything favors a Great Northern connection is a common carrier line is to be built.
>
> The reason, as I see it, is that a common carrier Railroad put through that area would completely block our chances to acquire the other timber we want in townships 24-8 and 25-8, and that we might find ourselves required to handle logs for shipment out of that area to mills on the Southern Pacific Railroad.
>
> I have apparently gotten Mr. Kline to see that his people should offer some other inducement to us to build to their line so he has written his superiors asking them to consider making us an offer for the Southern Pacific to build the Railroad, or share its construction, and make an agreement with us, giving up the option of paying them for the material that they put in this track (at a stipulated price) at some future date when we decide we want to make the line a common carrier, if we should decide this would be desirable, and to wire him their answer (he showed me this letter).
>
> Mr. Kline now sees that there is an advantage to us in a shorter line and less additional Railroad for logs if we tap the Great Northern, so it is up to the Southern Pacific to offset this disadvantage and give us as favorable conditions as the Great Northern will. So I rather expect he will come back to me with the question: "What will be satisfactory to you people?" Should it take this turn we should discuss it in person, I think. At least I should hear something more from Mr. Kline next week.
>
> I am convinced that we will need to make our line a common carrier after some of our present difficulties are ironed out. I doubt if the Southern Pacific will consider putting money in our connection without some definite way of being paid this money back other than by the freight from our plant. I think we will see that three cents per hundred weight on lumber to the East and a proper division of freight on local shipments will be so big that we will prefer to stand the necessary expense and hardship to operate our line as a common carrier.[158]

Rumors regarding the Gilchrist Timber Company's activities were abundant. Some gained credibility they did not deserve, such as the one that appeared an article in *The Bend Bulletin*. B. V. Wright, in a letter to Loyde Blakley of Bend, responded to his query which was based on the paper's erroneous story. B. V. Wright wrote:

> Replying to your letter of January 27th, the announcement you saw in the paper should never have been published as it was not authorized and is premature. We have not yet reached the stage where we know definitely what we will do and hence are not ready for any statements of this kind to be published.
>
> For your information, regarding the questions you ask, the chances are that when we do build, we will build more in line with the McCloud plant – that is, all the residences and

businesses at the mill village will be conducted by the company and while all those things will have to come in, the drug store feature will be part of the general merchandise program.[159]

The next day B. V. Wright answered yet another inquiry which had been based on *The Bend Bulletin's* story regarding the Gilchrist Timber Company's plans. He warned F. L. Newton of Sterling Electric Motors to wait for an announcement from the Gilchrist Timber Company and not to take seriously the stories printed in newspapers.[160] B. V. Wright reported in *The Bend Bulletin* the erroneous story about the Gilchrist Timber Company's activities to Harry Fletcher and Frank W. Gilchrist, furnished them with a copy of the article, informed them that the story had spread throughout the West Coast, and stated that he had already been inundated with inquiries which were based on the paper's baseless story. He attributed its origins to a talkative man named Stevens who met a newspaper reporter with an unfettered imagination who worked for an editor indifferent to the factual basis of his copy.[161]

The Gilchrist Timber Company had begun developing plans for sustained-yield forestry on its Oregon timberlands as part of its long-term plans for its Central Oregon business plan.[162] During the late 1930s, Oregon was hospitable to business. The state's tax and regulatory policies, coupled with the Forest Service's timber management policies, were conducive to sustained-yield forestry. The Gilchrist Timber Company's timberland management was without peer and endured until, once again, as had been the case in Mississippi, it was destroyed by taxation and regulation.

The duration of the Hoover-Roosevelt Depression and the tax and regulatory burdens imposed by the Roosevelt administration were factors in the speed with which the Gilchrist Timber Company accomplished the construction of its Central Oregon complex of mill, town, and railroad. In early 1937, West Coast mills were running at 38.28 percent capacity. The year before, the West Coast mills had operated at 61.12 percent.[163] The Gilchrist Timber Company proceeded prudently and with caution.

The Gilchrist Timber Company needed to complete the Klamath Northern Railroad before it could begin building its mill and town. It used the railroad to bring in materials and tools for both projects. B. V. Wright sent a telegram to H. W. Klein of Southern Pacific Railroad in which he reported that no steel had arrived with which to build track on the five miles which had already been graded, that this late delivery was slowing work on all the Gilchrist Timber Company's projects.[164]

During March 1937, Frank W. Gilchrist, his wife, Mary, and James Applewhite returned to Oregon to meet with officers of Southern Pacific Railroad, to visit sites for the mill and town, and to discuss the lumber market with officers of Brooks-Scanlon and Shevlin-Hixon. The officers of these timber companies (both located in Bend, Oregon) had hoped to purchase the Gilchrist Timber Company's holding, not have it as a neighbor. Gilchrist's reception when they met with officials of the United States Forest Service was no warmer. They already had established relationships with Brooks-Scanlon and Shevlin-Hixon. In time the Gilchrist Timber Company, Brooks-Scanlon, Shevlin-Hixon, and the Forest Service developed cordial relationships. Frank W. Gilchrist, his wife, and James Applewhite visited the Gilchrist Timber Company's holding. Here they discovered that 10,000 of the company's acres were infested with pine beetles and that 50,000 acres of adjoining federal and private lands were also infested with the timber-killing insects.[165]

Frank W. Gilchrist, by March 1937, had made numerous trips to the Pacific Northwest. He had visited more than 100 mills and in excess of 50 logging camps located throughout the region. Gilchrist Timber Company's directors decided, based on the information he and his subordinates had gathered, to construct a state-of-the-art mill of medium size with a capacity of not more than 60 million board feet per year. The directors also decided to build, in phases, a thoroughly up-to-date town which would include a commercial district. It was projected that the town might eventually grow to have a population of 1,500.[166]

During April 1937, B. V. Wright wrote a letter to Fred Peterson, Superintendent of the Klamath County School District. He urged the superintendent to develop plans for a larger school, one capable of accommodating the children of the employees of the Gilchrist Timber Company. At that time, the only school available was a one-room school that was located in Crescent in a structure that now houses the Baptist Church.[167]

Through May 1937, work continued on the Klamath Northern Railroad. James Applewhite, following the closure of the Gilchrist-Fordney Mill, was dispatched to Oregon to oversee preliminary construction of the Klamath Northern Railroad, mill, and town. On May 24, 1937, he was on-site surveying the route for the Klamath Northern Railroad.[168] Frank W. Gilchrist, in a letter to B. V. Wright dated May 24, 1937, informed him that Southern Pacific Railroad very much wanted the business of the Gilchrist Timber Company, that he was very pleased with their attitude. He also wrote, "I have very definite plans as to just what we are going to do out west and it will be some weeks before I know definitely what the plans are to be."[169]

Work continued on the Klamath Northern Railroad during June of 1937. B. V. Wright informed Frank W. Gilchrist, in a letter dated June 7, 1937, that the railroad's grade was one-and-a-half percent.[170] Frank W. Gilchrist informed B. V. Wright in a letter dated June 16, 1937, that the directors had decided that Klamath Northern Railroad would join with the Southern Pacific Railroad, not the Great Northern Railroad. In the same letter, he also notified B. V. Wright that it was the intent of the directors to complete the dam for the millpond and the Klamath Northern Railroad by April 1, 1938. Construction of the sawmill was scheduled to commence on April 1, 1938. On June 28, 1937, James Applewhite was in Crescent where he was working to resolve right-of-way issues for the Klamath Northern Railroad.[171]

Towards the middle of the month B. V. Wright wrote a letter to Frank W. Gilchrist, dated June 14, 1937, in which he informed his employer that the Forest Service had decided to stop selling timber from federal lands to Brooks-Scanlon and Shevlin-Hixon. The Forest Service required firms who purchased federal timber to practice sustained-yield forestry on their timberlands. Brooks-Scanlon and Shevlin-Hixon weren't, so they were ineligible for federal timber sales.[172]

The Gilchrist Timber Company awarded the

Frank Gilchrist and James Applewhite inspecting work on Klamath Northern Railroad. Collection of Mrs. Mary G. Ernst.

contract to build the Klamath Northern Railroad and the dam for the millpond to Kern & Kibbe. The contract for the construction of the railroad was for $74,530.74. The Gilchrist Timber Company furnished the contractors with the rails and fittings needed for the installation of the rails. The contract for the construction of the millpond dam was $19,168 plus the cost of grouting the rock formation on which the dam was erected. No price was agreed upon for the cost of the grouting, since it was impossible to determine the magnitude of the grouting work until the construction of the dam commenced. Kern & Kibbe dispatched their equipment to Gilchrist, Oregon, on August 3, 1937. Their employees began arriving on the jobsite on August 5, 1937.[173] A separate contract was entered into for the clearing the millpond site of timber, brush, and stumps. The cost for clearing each acre of the millpond's 50-acre area, including removal of the stumps, varied from $70 to $80 an acre.[174] Projected completion

Back of dam seen prior to filling of mill pond.
Stewart J. Gilchrist's photo album, Gilchrist Timber Company papers, Klamath County Museum.

of the clearing of the pond and most of the mill site was set for autumn.[175] James Applewhite was responsible for overseeing the work done by the contractors on the dam, millpond, and railroad.[176] By the August of 1939, when the mill commenced operation, Gilchrist Timber Company had spent in excess of $2 million building its mill, railroad, and town. It was the largest construction project undertaken by the productive sector in Oregon during 1938 and 1939.

During August and September of 1939, B. V. Wright continued to work to expand and consolidate the Gilchrist Timber Company's timber holdings. Negotiations continued with Shevlin-Hixon in the matter of land exchanges for the purpose of blocking their timber holdings.[177] B. V. Wright wrote a letter dated September 13, 1937, to H. A. Utley of Fawell Utley Realty Company, in which he noted that conflicting patents had been recorded for a property that Utley's firm was offering to sell to the Gilchrist Timber Company.[178]

The matter of the Highway 58 overpass, in retrospect, was a harbinger of what the future held for Oregon's timber industry as well as the rest of the state's productive sector. Klamath Northern Railroad crosses Highway 58, a two-lane road that departs from Interstate 5 near Goshen, Oregon, and then merges with Highway 97 approximately ten miles north of Chemult, Oregon. Much of it remained unpaved during 1938. One of the Oregon Highway Department's senior bureaucrats envisioned Highway 58 as a super highway that would stretch from Eugene, Oregon, to Klamath Falls, Oregon. A gated crossing for Klamath Northern Rail across Highway 58, identical to the gated crossing which still existed as of 2011 across Highway 97 near Wickiup Junction for Burlington Northern Railroad, was not consistent with the bureaucrat's vision for Highway 58. In 1938, the Progressives were advocates of the automobile foes of railroads. Klamath Northern Railroad's application to cross Highway 58 was barred by the Oregon Highway Department, unless Gilchrist Timber Company built either an underpass or an overpass to cross Highway 58.[179] Members of Central Oregon's productive sector rallied to the defense of the Gilchrist Timber Company. E. L. Isted, Shevlin-Hixon's general manager, wrote a

*Front of dam seen prior to filling mill pond.
Collection of Ike Bay.*

letter dated August 25, 1937, to N. G. Wallace, Oregon's Utility Commissioner, in which he argued in favor of granting Gilchrist Timber Company right-of-way without requiring the construction of an overpass.[181] The president of the Bend Chamber of Commerce wrote:

> Certain highway engineers are trying to insist that Gilchrists pay for either an underpass or an overpass which will naturally run into thousands of dollars. If, in our judgment, there were any danger to highway travel, we would agree with the highway engineers, but apparently they are using every effort to coerce the Gilchrist interests by bringing into the matter of controversy other government agencies. Information which we possess, leads us to believe that the Gilchrist interests have done everything reasonable to assure the highway engineers that this grade crossing would be entirely safe for highway travel. The fact that there would be only two trains a day of not over fifteen cars; that Gilchrists have agreed to stop each train at the highway and to furnish any sort of electrical stop signals that the highway engineers desire, leads us to the conclusion that the engineers are quite unreasonable, in view of the further fact the Gilchrists have agreed to put in such underpass as they require at a later date providing the grade crossing does prove dangerous.
>
> It is regrettable that outside capital coming into the State of Oregon should be continuously harassed as is generally considered it has been in the past. These people wish to and are making a very large investment of private funds, which seems to me justifies the encouragement of adjacent communities and the State itself, particularly when they are helping to increase the state's payrolls and from their past record, are known to be fair and just in the operations.
>
> It is little wonder, if this is to continue to be the attitude of some of our State Departments that the State of Washington and the State of California have developed so much more rapidly than our own state which have similar natural resources.[181]

The coercive power of the state prevailed. Gilchrist Timber Company built the overpass, even though it was only Oregon Highway Department

*Highway 58 Overpass, circa 1938.
Collection of Ike Bay.*

bureaucrats who wanted it. The construction of the overpass delayed the completion of the Klamath Northern Railroad as well as added thousands in additional costs, including a $900 expenditure for the purchase of girders from the Southern Pacific Railroad.[182]

During October of 1937, in Laurel, Mississippi, the last of the Gilchrist-Fordney Company's remaining inventory was prepared for delivery to buyers. It was anticipated that by the end of the month none would remain.[183] Frank W. Gilchrist selected machine tools from the Gilchrist-Fordney mill, and then shipped them to Oregon for use by the Gilchrist Timber Company. Engine Number 204 was selected for use by the Klamath Northern Railroad. Gilchrist-Fordney Company's other locomotives were sold.[184] Walter Smallwood (master mechanic for the Gilchrist-Fordney Company, then the Gilchrist Timber Company) and his crew rebuilt Locomotive Number 204. Throughout the next eighteen years, the locomotive would haul lumber out to Southern Pacific Railroad's main line then haul freight back to the Gilchrist Timber Company and Gilchrist. The locomotive, effectively, was remanufactured. Number 204's fuel supply was converted from coal to oil. Coal was not as readily available in Central Oregon as it was in Mississippi. Firing the locomotive's boiler with wood was certain to eventually result in a forest fire which might have destroyed much unharvested timber. Moreover, wood isn't as efficient a fuel source as is oil. Locomotive Number 204's tender was equipped with fire-fighting equipment, provided with new brass fittings and was then painted Gilchrist Brown. Gilchrist Timber Company was emblazoned on the sides of the tender with aluminum paint which was also used on the smoke box, stack, and for the striping and all other lettering. Engine Number 204, once Walter Smallwood and his crew had completed their overhaul, was all but a new engine.[185]

During the autumn of 1937, it was anticipated that construction of the mill would commence the following spring.[186] Filling cavities found in the rock formation slowed the dam's completion. B. V. Wright was advised in a letter dated September 10, 1937, for Boar & Cunningham Civil Engineers, that Kern & Kibbe had failed to explore a cavity found in the foundation rock near the dam's center. The civil engineers advised B. V.

1938-1941 – The Move West and Building the Town

Engine 204.
Collection of Mrs. Mary G. Ernst

Wright that no portion of the dam proper had been poured, that pouring had been delayed until the extent and number of the cavities had been determined. They further reported that the slab for the sluiceway had been poured, and that the concrete for the sluiceway piers had been poured to a sufficient height that it was now possible to divert water through the sluiceway.[187] Arrangements for the purchase of the rails and fastenings for the Klamath Northern Railroad had been arranged by the middle of September 1937.[188] B. V. Wright, in a letter dated September 13, 1937, reported to Frank W. Gilchrist that Kern & Kibbe was requesting delivery of the rails for the track, that they had attempted during the preceding four or five weeks to learn the width of the rails so that they could order the plates to fasten the rails to the sleepers.

In response to a query from the Stulman-Enrick Lumber Company in the matter of the placement of lumber, B. V. Wright answered in a letter dated October 13, 1937:

> It will be sometime in the early part of 1939 before we are in a position to offer any lumber for sale as our plant has not yet been started,

other than some Railroad work and some concrete work preparing a dam.[189]

Rail for Klamath Northern Railroad was purchased from the Hammond Lumber Company. The sixty-eight pound rail was taken from a defunct railroad line which the firm selling the material to the Gilchrist Timber Company had operated near Mill City, Oregon. Southern Pacific Railroad was engaged to move the rails from Mill City to the site where the Klamath Northern Railroad was under construction.[190] Horse teams were employed by the Deschutes Lumber Company of Mowich, Oregon, to skid logs from the Klamath Northern Railroad's right-of-way. By the end of October 1937, 449 logs already been removed. Completion of the work was slowed by a lack of horses.[191] Prior to the beginning of October 1937, Ora F. Blay had entered into a contract to clear the millpond site for $1,188.[192] Other sections of the dam's foundation was ready for final inspection by the end of October 1937. The contractor had reached solid rock and was clearing and preparing it for the pouring of the dam's concrete.[193] A contract for clearing the site for the Gilchrist

Railroad, dam and mill site, circa 1937-1938.
Stewart J. Gilchrist's photo album, Gilchrist Timber Company papers, Klamath County Museum.

Timber Company's mill was awarded to J. H. Haner on October 30, 1937. October 1937 concluded with B. V. Wright answering another query from a man interested in Gilchrist, Oregon. Benjamin V. Wright wrote in response to a letter from C. S. Starrett, who was interested in entering into an arrangement with the Gilchrist Timber Company for the town's drugstore concession: "However, the details of all this will likely be worked out during next year while the mill building, planing mill and sorting sheds are being built."[194]

By the beginning of November 1939, late deliveries of rail by the Southern Pacific Railroad were slowing the construction of the Klamath Northern Railroad. Frank W. Gilchrist wrote to B. V. Wright in a letter dated November 4, 1937: "I have a letter from Applewhite today in which he advises that the Southern Pacific has been very slow in delivering the rail to him and this is delaying his work considerably."[195] Benjamin V. Wright contacted Mr. H. W. Klein of the Southern Pacific Railroad. Two weeks later B. V. Wright reported to Frank W. Gilchrist that the Southern Pacific Railroad had begun delivering the rail the Gilchrist Timber Company had purchased and track, under the supervision of James P. Applewhite, had already been laid from the junction with the Southern Pacific Railroad near Mowich, Oregon, to the site where the trestle would cross Highway 58. In the same letter, he also cautioned Frank W. Gilchrist that he anticipated winter weather would soon slow construction of the railroad, and that it threatened to stop James P. Applewhite's plans to conduct a series of tests on the millpond's dam to confirm that it would hold back water."[196] The plans for the dam, Frank W. Gilchrist informed B. V. Wright, included a fish ladder and that he was to test the dam by holding some water in the millpond.[197] Frank W. Gilchrist wrote to Peter Swann in a letter dated November 5, 1937, that the location of the mill had been decided.[198] The Southern Pacific proposed to B. V. Wright during the final week of November 1937, naming the junction of the Southern Pacific Railroad and the Klamath Northern Railroad "Pumice," "Scoria," or "Cone" B. V. Wright recommended "Gilchrist" as the junction's name.[199]

During the final weeks of 1937, B. V. Wright

continued to respond to inquiries from individuals who desired employment with the Gilchrist Timber Company or who hoped to become one of the concessionaries who would operate the enterprises which would serve the inhabitants of the town the company was building. The magnitude of the Gilchrist Timber Company's project attracted attention and interest. It was an exception to the economic stagnation and retrogression which characterized the preceding eight years of the Hoover-Roosevelt Depression. On May 24, 1937, the United States Supreme Court upheld the Social Security tax in *Steward Machine Co. v. Davis*. Over the next seven months, the Dow lost thirty-six percent of its value and the unemployment rate reported by the federal government rose from 13.5 percent to 17.4 percent.[200] Gilchrist Timber Company's town, mill, and railroad offered the prospect of opportunities at a time when they were once again disappearing. B. V. Wright, in response to an inquiry from Charles H. Mack in the matter of a store concession responded in a letter dated November 12, 1937, by explaining that he anticipated that at least two years would elapse before the mill was in operation and that "at present we do not know what the plans for the store will be."[201] Benjamin V. Wright, in a letter dated November 16, 1937, informed Dr. I. I. Rosen of Camp Pori, Michigan, that a significant period of time would elapse before a decision was made in the matter of on-site medical services. He also wrote, ". . . our development will not be such that we will be ready for any service of this character until the 1st of May 1940."[202] George O. Updegraff of Modoc Point, Oregon, was interested in obtaining the concession to operate the pool hall and barbershop. B. V. Wright answered in a letter dated December 6, 1937, that it was too soon to determine who would operate the pool hall and barbershop. Benjamin V. Wright wrote, "Those things will come up when our organization is being established which will not be until the spring of 1939."[203]

Frank W. Gilchrist notified B. V. Wright in a letter dated November 8, 1938, that he was to close the office in the Bedell Building, Portland, Oregon, by December 31, 1937, that he should place all furniture and files (save for essential ones) in storage until offices were established at Gilchrist, Oregon, the following spring. He then confided to B. V. Wright ". . . As you probably know, this operation was decided upon mainly due to my recommendations . . ." Frank W. Gilchrist concluded the letter by writing:

> I am hoping that during January and February and possibly part of March, or until we open up offices, that you will be able to rest and possibly take a vacation, which you probably haven't had for some time and, if it suits your and Mrs. Wright's program, I am perfectly willing that you make arrangements to get off a month or six weeks. In other words, until offices are opened at our plant site or at Bend, I am hoping that you will be relieved of detail work and that you will get some relaxation.[204]

The names of the Gilchrist Timber Company's town and the junction of the Klamath Northern Railroad with the Southern Pacific Railroad was the subject of a letter, dated December 14, 1937, from Frank W. Gilchrist to Benjamin V. Wright, in which he wrote:

> We have decided to name the junction "Gilchrist" and the town "Ralph." I am writing Mr. Klein today with reference to naming junction. Until I hear from him that it is satisfactory for us to name the junction "Gilchrist," we will not make any further plans about naming the town "Ralph," as we do not want the town named "Ralph" unless the Southern Pacific agrees to our name for the junction.[205]

The quality of the rail received by the Gilchrist Timber Company was proving unsatisfactory and was slowing completion of the railroad.[206.] The onset of winter weather and accumulating snow was also slowing work on the Gilchrist Timber Company's mill, town, and railroad.

Hollis Johnston of Portland, Oregon, was given the commission during the latter half of 1937 to design Gilchrist to include its houses and business district. He was a 1920 graduate of the University of Oregon who had majored in architectural design.[207] Prior to receiving his commission from the Gilchrist Timber Company, other than a designing a camp for the Bonneville Power Administration, Hollis Johnston had no experience designing communities though he was a highly renowned architect who had executed numerous commissions

*Gilchrist under construction, circa 1938-1939.
Collection of Oregon Historical Society.*

for individual buildings. The town he designed for the Gilchrist Timber Company was the product of the guidance he received from Frank W. Gilchrist and the firm's other principals. Gilchrist, Oregon, was the perfection of the designs, ideas, and management practices the Gilchrist family had developed while operating successive camps near Laurel, Mississippi, such as Dushau and Allenton. Hollis Johnston, after executing his commission for the Gilchrist Timber Company, designed other communities including Columbia Villa. None were as successful as Gilchrist, Oregon.

Hollis Johnston produced a design for a town of 1,500 that included provision for schools, retail businesses, bank, medical facilities, post office, library, and professional services such as doctors and lawyers. He designed a shopping center, with provision for parking, which was a refined and enlarged version of the commissaries that the Gilchrist-Fordney Company had included when building their logging camps. He designed a theatre and separated the business district from the residential area. Provision was made for landscaping which included maintaining a forest setting by leaving many trees. Hollis Johnston proposed providing the houses of Gilchrist with steam heat, which would have required providing each house with a furnace and boiler or building a steam plant then piping it to each house. The town was located on the east side of Highway 97, with the business district closest to the highway and a succession of parallel residential streets above it. Gilchrist, Oregon, as was also true of the Gilchrist-Fordney Company's logging camps, was designed, by reason of its isolation, for self-sufficiency and to assure the comfort and dignity of its residents. The entire town was designed and built in a style known as Norwegian Modern.

Ultimately it was the forest, specifically the manner in which it was planned to harvest it, that determined the size of the town.

The shopping center, subsequently named the Gilchrist Mall, was a new idea at the time of its construction. It was the first structure of its type east of the Cascade Mountains and was probably the first of its kind built in the United States. Housed under the roof of the shopping center

1938-1941 – The Move West and Building the Town

Boarding House, circa 1938-1939.
Stewart J. Gilchrist's photo album, Gilchrist Timber Company Papers, Klamath County Museum.

Bunk houses, circa 1938-1939.
Stewart J. Gilchrist's photo album, Gilchrist Timber Company Papers, Klamath County Museum.

were a grocery store, post office, barbershop, beauty shop, drugstore, liquor store, bowling alley, library, and a private club for employees of the Gilchrist Timber Company as well as its subsidiary operations and concessionaires. Contained within the club were a bar, lounge area, dance floor, pool table, and a meeting room. The shopping center also included space for a department store. On the shopping center's upper floor was a space which was made available to the town's churches. The movie theatre was located across the street from the shopping center's northeast corner. The businesses were operated as concessions.

Hollis Johnston completed and submitted his designs for the town's houses during the final weeks of December 1937. He submitted floor plans for houses ranging in size from one bedroom to four bedrooms. All the houses in Gilchrist, as had also been the case with the camps operated by the Gilchrist-Fordney Company, were plumbed and wired for electricity. Gilchrist, Oregon, was the first town in Oregon to have all its structures plumbed and wired for electricity at the time of its establishment. Gilchrist was also the first town in Oregon to have a rotary dial telephone system. Electricity for the town was generated by the Gilchrist Timber Company's mill. Gilchrist, Oregon, was the model company town. It was known, without irony, at the time of its completion as "The Wonder Town." Its residents resided in houses which were superior to much of the housing stock available in neighboring communities. The rents paid for these houses were below the prevailing market rates for comparable structures.

The first houses built in Gilchrist were located on streets south of the school and Gilchrist Mall, the town's central area. They were finished in 1939. Houses were subsequently constructed as needed in 1941 and 1946-1949.[208] Rainbow Circle, a cul-de-sac located on the north end of Gilchrist, was built not long after the end of the Second World War. Its name came from the fact that for many years the houses located on it were the only ones in Gilchrist which weren't painted Gilchrist Brown.

Located on the west side of Highway 97, on the eastern shore of the millpond, several large buildings were constructed which were intended to serve as a motor court hotel (motel), though they were never used for that purpose. These structures, along with the boardinghouse and the bunkhouses (temporary structures), were among the first of Gilchrist's buildings completed.

Hollis Johnston, after completing his commission for the Gilchrist Timber Company, wrote the following to J. C. Hazen, Associate Editor of *The Architectural Forum*:

> The town of Gilchrist was built in the primeval forest as an industrial town, serving the logging and sawmill operations of the Gilchrist Timber Company. There is a planned business district, school and other necessary public buildings in addition to about one hundred houses.
>
> The town is designed with a wood architecture theme and there is a unity of expression run-

ning through all the buildings, although they have been signed, at the same time, with appropriate variety.

> To my mind, the most important element in the design of this little community is the owner's foresight and desire to make a comfortable place for people to reside. It is the company's belief that workmen who are content have a much better attitude toward the company. In any case, people who live comfortably and decently are inclined to be good citizens.[209]

The Gilchrist Timber Company established Gilchrist, Oregon, at a time when many companies with towns, commencing during the 1920s, began disposing of them as no longer necessary or worth the effort and expense of maintaining and operating.[210] Frank W. Gilchrist, as observed by Hollis Johnston, judged that the isolation of the mill's location coupled with the management practices the Gilchrist family had successfully employed for several successive generations, warranted going his own way rather than imitating the practices of other businesses in the matter of building, then operating a town for its employees.

One of the consequences of the leadership and management practices of the Gilchrists, employed in the building and operation of their camps, then town, was that they achieved, more or less as a by-product of their policies, much of what businessmen of the nineteenth and early twentieth centuries, who were also of Progressive sensibilities, tried and usually failed to achieve. Company town owners who attempted to impose Progressive ideas such as compulsory temperance for their employees consistently engendered resentment.[211] The Gilchrists included a liquor store and a bar in the town's club when they built Gilchrist. They did not attempt to remake their employees.

The Gilchrists maintained their town and camps, took pride in them, and did all that befitted a responsible landlord. In turn they expected, and received, from the families who rented their property the care, which included keeping yards mowed, that befitted an honorable tenant. What was expected of the employees of the Gilchrist Timber Company was industry, diligence, honesty, and honorable conduct in their dealings with each other and their creditors. In exchange, the Gilchrist Timber Company provided the successive generations of its employees with the ability to earn for themselves a secure, comfortable, and very solid middle-class life. Perhaps at the heart of the Gilchrist's leadership and management practices was a vestigial memory of the best aspects of the lairds of all those generations before on Islay Island.

During the first week of January 1938, Benjamin V. Wright wrote to Frank W. Gilchrist that the closing of the Portland, Oregon, office had been completed and that its furnishings had been placed in storage, pending transportation to Gilchrist the following spring when it was expected the Gilchrist Timber Company would open its Central Oregon office. Benjamin V. Wright said that he had not yet been able to dispose of his company car. He reported, "Business is in worse condition in Portland perhaps than in any other American city at present due to the mills and factories being almost all closed for the past four months by the union fight, AFL vs. CIO." In the same letter, he said that he anticipated receiving within a few days the abstract for the Klamath Northern Railroad's right-of-way.[212]

Weather during February 1938 slowed work on the town, mill, and railroad. Frank W. Gilchrist, in a letter dated February 21, 1938, to Benjamin V. Wright stated that, based on weather conditions, he was changing the start date for the mill's construction from the 1st of April to the 15th of April. In the same letter he wrote:

> I contemplate having Jud erect the saw mill with a small crew of men, and do it rather leisurely as the times do not warrant fast construction. I want you to have charge of building and managing the town in its entirety. We are gradually getting our lay-out for the town completed, and I hope to have things in readiness so that you will be able to go forward with this as of April 15.
>
> To start with, we will want to build a boarding house and possibly a tourist camp and these projects probably will be done by contract, but the rest of the town I hope to be able to build without contracting the same. All these plans I will go over in detail with you when I see you in Portland the latter part of March, but just thought I would give you a line-up of what I

expected you to do and you can be thinking the matter over so that we will be able to discuss it when I see you.[213]

Benjamin V. Wright received notice from Frank W. Gilchrist that the Gilchrist family had decided to name the town "Ralph" and that in the near future he should contact Mr. Henderson of the postal service to learn what steps were required to create a post office with that name.[214] In a subsequent letter to Benjamin V. Wright, also dated February 21, 1938, Frank W. Gilchrist said that he had written Mr. Klein of Southern Pacific Railroad to confirm that the connection of Klamath Northern Railroad to Southern Pacific Railroad had been completed and that oil was available from Southern Pacific roundhouses for Engine 204 which would soon depart Laurel, Mississippi, for Gilchrist, Oregon.[215] Benjamin V. Wright confirmed on March 1, 1938, that he would contact Mr. Henderson to arrange for establishing the Gilchrist Post Office.[216]

Frank W. Gilchrist wrote to Benjamin V. Wright on March 9, 1938, that the work on Engine Number 204 had been completed, that he anticipated departing for Gilchrist on March 18, 1938, and that he expected to have eighteen or twenty men on the job by April 1, 1938.[217] During the winter of 1938, Curtis Breazeale, formerly foreman of the Gilchrist-Fordney Company's green chain and dry kiln operations, loaded three boxcars with machine tools and office furniture. The tools and furniture were previously utilized by the Gilchrist-Fordney Company. Also loaded in the boxcars were household goods belonging to individuals who had previously been employed by the Gilchrist-Fordney Company and had decided to move to Central Oregon to join the Gilchrist Timber Company.[218] By the middle of March 1938, preparations were completed for the departure of Engine Number 204 and its three boxcars for Central Oregon. On March 15, 1938, B. V. Wright informed Frank W. Gilchrist that three to four feet of snow covered the tracks of the Klamath Northern Railroad, that he judged the 1st of April as two weeks too soon for the men coming out to Gilchrist from Laurel to begin working.[219]

Engine Number 204 departed Laurel, Mississippi, on the morning of March 20, 1938. The train traveled on the Southern Pacific Railroad from New Orleans to San Bernardino, north through the San Joaquin Valley to Klamath Falls, and then on to the junction of Southern Pacific Railroad and Klamath Northern Railroad.[220] On the morning of April 11, 1938, Engine Number 204 passed through Los Angeles. Mr. McPhelan of Southern Pacific Railroad reported that he anticipated that the train would arrive at the junction of Southern Pacific Railroad and Klamath Northern Railroad in approximately one week.[221] The train laid over for the night at Fresno, California. Throughout the trip, Engine Number 204, because of its colors, attracted considerable attention. On the 16th of April, the train at last reached the tracks of the Klamath Northern Railroad.[222]

Former Gilchrist-Fordney employees left Laurel for Gilchrist prior to the departure of Engine Number 204 for Central Oregon. Among those first to travel west to assist with the construction of the town and mill was Robert J. Terrell, mill superintendent, who was accompanied by Dan F. Denham (millwright), John N. Pryor (carpentry foreman), and Will Curry. The Shotts family departed at approximately the same time as did Robert J. Terrell. An auto accident delayed the arrival of Terrell and Denham eventually reached Gilchrist. John Pryor died in the accident. Curry returned to Laurel following the accident, and then decided not to go west to Gilchrist.[223]

The next group of Gilchrist-Fordney employees to depart Laurel for Gilchrist included Walter Rigdon (blacksmith and welder) and Alva Hendry (saw filer). Alva Hendry was a former member of the Gilchrist-Fordney Company's baseball team. He was the father of F. A. Hendry and grandfather of Rob Hendry and Phil Hendry, all of whom went on to careers with the Gilchrist Timber Company.[224] Shotts arrived first, on March 25, 1938; Rigdon and Hendry arrived on March 28, 1938.[225] Not long afterwards they were joined by Walter Smallwood, who continued to serve as master mechanic, plus Rufus Childre and Curtis Breazeale. Rufus Childre traveled west in a car that he'd modified to include an improvised kennel which housed dogs belong to a co-worker who was traveling west by train. Jim Childre, son of Rufus Childre, reported that his father was stopped while traveling through Los Angeles on Sunset Boulevard by members of the Los Angeles Police Department who were astounded by the sight of his rolling kennel with its barking occupants. Rufus Childre, Jim Childre said, was lost and told the police officers that all he wanted to do was put Los Angeles behind him.

> They were stopped in LA by the cops because they had the dogs. They were on Sunset Strip with all these dogs barking. The cops pulled them over and said, "Alright country, where do you think you're going?" Dad's temper, he flared up and said if you tell me how to get out of this damn town I'll tell you one thing, I'll never come back. He never went back to LA. They finally got over the Grapevine. In 1938 Hotels then weren't the way they are today. You had the tourist courts and places where you camped out.[226]

Rufus Childre, who walked ten miles carrying borrowed shoes for his initial interview with the Gilchrist-Fordney Company, became the Gilchrist Timber Company's forester. He oversaw the implementation of Gilchrist's program of sustained-yield forestry and discovered William Steers who was his successor.[227] The move from Laurel, Mississippi, to Central Oregon by the Gilchrists with their employees and their families was another chapter in the migration of the Scots-Irish to rural Oregon. The importance of the Scots-Irish is neglected since the state's histories are usually written by individuals who were a part of, or else in sympathy with, the Yankee families who settled in the Willamette Valley in towns such as Portland or Salem.

What the initial contingents who arrived from Laurel found a construction site and Crescent, Oregon, a small crossroads town a mile to the south. Crescent consisted of perhaps one hundred residents plus a store, small hotel, one-room school, post office, and livery stable which also served as a service station for automobiles. Housing was in very short supply. The Shotts family lodged in the Crescent Hotel for the next three months. Jim Childre said that some Gilchrist Timber Company employees camped out on a meadow west of Crescent, along the banks of the Little Deschutes River, while the town's houses were completed.

> Mom and I came out here in April of 1938 after Dad got a cabin. That's the reason we came out is because dad was able to acquire the cabin. We lived on the other end of the cabin from Mr. and Mrs. Smallwood. People were camped; see there were no houses, so people were camped in the meadows at Crescent. There were some cabins in a place called Rosedale, which doesn't exist anymore. There were some cabins there in Crescent. There was the old hotel; there were some rooms you could sleep in.

> The Mohawk was there and what we called for years Al's Tavern. Those two places have been there ever since I can remember in one form or another. To get to Crescent, mother and I, if you had a car you could drive down there, there was just a path that followed the highway and you could walk down to the store. We would walk down there on the weekends to get an ice cream cone, which was our weekend outing. Eventually some other people began to get cars that were reliable and began to go to Bend on Saturday and Sunday.[228]

During April 1938, the Gilchrist Timber Company's work force increased to 150 men who were supervised by Jim Applewhite. Construction of the mill, located on the northwest side of the millpond, commenced after the first permanent structure, a machine shop which housed the machine tools transported from Laurel in the boxcars pulled by Engine Number 204, was completed. Edgar Shotts served as mill construction foreman, while Jud Terrell recovered from the injuries he had sustained in an automobile accident. Employees of Kern & Kibbe, as well as its subcontractors, worked alongside the arrivals from Laurel, Mississippi, who were the nucleus of the Gilchrist Timber Company. They worked in late-winter weather, clearing snow then grubbing stumps and digging foundations. Frank W. Gilchrist conducted operations out of the Pilot Butte Inn, located on Wall Street in Bend, Oregon, during April before returning to Laurel to bring his family out west to Gilchrist.

The construction crews took their meals in a boardinghouse (now the offices of The Ernst Brothers) and lodging in two-man bunkhouses which, following completion of the town, were sold off to individuals located throughout Klamath and Deschutes Counties who used them as woodsheds, tool sheds, and cabins.[229] Benjamin V. Wright reported to Frank W. Gilchrist in a letter dated

April 25, 1938, that Mr. Sullivan was to take over the operation of the boardinghouse. He reported that Mr. Sullivan wanted to use chairs rather than benches, since they were easier to handle, which simplified cleaning the boardinghouse. The boardinghouse served three meals a day, six days a week, with no meals offered on Sundays.[230] Sullivan and his crew began operating the boardinghouse on June 6, 1938.[231] He was preceded as boardinghouse operator by Alice Rintala and A. J. Dahl. Jim Childre described the boardinghouse and the bunkhouses during the period prior to the completion of the town:

> There was no town site, they were working on it. Trees were being cut, the store was not built. Where the real estate office is now was a cookhouse. Then they built a bunch of little cabins. There were 40 or 50 little cabins right there that were between the cook house and the highway. This was where all the single men stayed. Each cabin had two bunks and a tin heater. It was a tin stove. There was an open-face cabinet on the walls you could put canned goods or whatever, a chair and a bunk bed. It was very sparse even by 1938 standards. There were no houses finished. They were being built. The boarding house served meals. A lady named Dagney. She was a Norwegian woman who was the cook. She was a very large woman. She cooked three meals a day: breakfast, lunch, and dinner, or supper as they called it. There was a commissary where you could buy a few things.[232]

During June 1938 more families of the men who had already come west from Laurel, Mississippi, continued to arrive. The Rigdon and Hendry families arrived on or about June 1, 1938. The Albert Carmichael and Isom Ezell families arrived not long afterwards.

Benjamin V. Wright, throughout the spring and into the summer of 1938, was flooded with inquiries from individuals seeking employment or to obtain concessions to operate the town's businesses. On May 9, 1938, he wrote to J. J. Polin, who had applied for a store concession:

> There will be no store at our mill site this year other than a little commissary that will be run in connection with the mess hall. I do not know what our permanent arrangement will be for the store set-up but hope to get that worked out in some definite shape during the year. We will not put in a store until next year however.[233]

In a letter to Frank W. Gilchrist, dated June 1, 1938, Benjamin V. Wright wrote, ". . . I will likely have moved over to Crescent by Tuesday of next week and will start as quickly as possible on house construction." He continued in the same letter with a discussion of heating options for the houses. He explained that circulating heaters would cost $135 per house, while a steam system with radiators would cost $405 per house and require the construction of basements.[234] Another possibility mentioned was a steam-heating system that would have involved piping steam from the mill's powerhouse to each house in the town. The following day on June 2, 1938, Benjamin V. Wright reported to Frank W. Gilchrist that the contract for plumbing the town's houses was awarded to William Montgomery of Bend, Oregon.[235]

B. E. "Ed" Hill, after arriving at Gilchrist from Laurel, worked to build the reservoir for Gilchrist's water supply and the mill where he would work from 1939 until he retired in 1981. He described how much of the work was accomplished using hand tools and blasting powder. "All those dry kilns over there are cement. We'd build ramps that went up how ever high the kiln walls were then we'd push cement in wheelbarrows up the ramps to pour the walls."[236]

On July 18, 1938, after returning to Laurel to conclude business, Frank W. Gilchrist came back to Central Oregon with his family. They traveled by car from Laurel to New Orleans, then by Southern Pacific Railroad from New Orleans to Chemult, Oregon. Frank and Mary Gilchrist traveled with their three children (Frank Rust, Stewart Jones, and Mary Geales); Mary had her dog, Doc, with them. Also accompanying them on the train was Will Thompkins, Alice Williams, Cherry Smith, Alf Holmes, Nellie Holmes and James Applewhite who was very close to the Gilchrist family and was godfather to Stewart and Mary Geales. They arrived in Chemult the morning of July 23, 1938, then traveled by car to Gilchrist for lunch before proceeding to Bend where, for the next six weeks, while the construction of their house was finished,

*Mill under construction. Mill pond prior to filling. Circa 1938-1939.
Collection of F.A. Hendry.*

they resided at the Pilot Butte Inn. Each day, until their house was finished, Frank W. Gilchrist and his family traveled to Gilchrist. He would oversee the work on the town, mill, and railroad, consulting with his staff and making decisions. Mr. and Mrs. Gilchrist had lunch with either the Ezelles or Carmichaels while their children ate lunch at the boardinghouse.[237]

The reason the Gilchrist Motor Court was not operated as a hostelry was that Mary Gilchrist was so taken with one of the buildings and its setting that she decided it, after remodeling, should become their house. From the back of it, one looks across the millpond, sees the mill and the forest beyond it, then, off in the distance, Odell Butte and the east slopes of the Cascades. Mrs. Mary Geales Gilchrist Ernst and her sons continued to reside there as of the date of this book's writing. Another one of the motor court's buildings became James Applewhite's residence. Benjamin V. Wright and his family, until their house was completed, occupied yet another of the motor court buildings.[238]

Work continued on the mill, town, and railroad through the summer of 1938. Thomas Burgess reported to Benjamin V. Wright that there remained 16,000 to 18,000 board feet of timber awaiting removal from Klamath Northern Railroad's right-of-way.[239] F. A. Hendry, son of Alva Hendry, described the summer of 1938 as a sort of extended camping trip that both very much enjoyed:

> I thought it was the greatest place in the world. I thought, man I'm in heaven now because the trees were still there, the Ponderosas. The Gilchrist millpond was empty, it was just a little Deschutes River running down through it and we could catch fish. I just thought it was great.[240]

On or about September 1, 1938, just prior to the start of the school year, the Gilchrist family moved into their house. The Gilchrist School, though already under construction and which would, upon completion, house grades K-12, was not finished until September 1939. The Gilchrist children and children of the members who were building Gilchrist attended school approximately a mile south in Crescent in a building that as of the date of the writing of this book housed the Baptist Church. The four-room school building was packed to overflowing with students. The elementary school students occupied two rooms, another room was used by junior high students, and the fourth room was occupied by the high school students. The year 1938 was the only one when Crescent had a high school. Bill Terrell, son of R. J. Terrell, was its only senior. He was the only high school student who graduated from the Crescent school.[241]

Mary Geales Gilchrist Ernst said of her first year as a resident of Gilchrist:

> If we were in trouble in school, the teachers made us copy pages from Oregon History and learn the state song. Our parents had to come to school to explain that when we answered "Yes Ma'am" we were not calling her an old maid. It was hard for the Oregonians to learn we just said those things as respect.
>
> Growing up in Gilchrist was an education and was fun. There were very few (14) children at first and we had to find things to entertain ourselves. We did things like chase cows in the meadow and go on long hikes and picnics. On Saturdays some of us got to go in the car to Bend to the picture show while whoever took us went grocery shopping for everyone. We had no stores that first year.[242]

F. A. Hendry remembered attending the Crescent school while Gilchrist was under construction:

> One thing I remember about that school, there was no running water, there was a hand pump outside there and prime it and pump it to get water. All of us kids at noon when we had our lunch we would just walk out into the woods, in the snow and stand around out there and eat our lunch, probably build a fire. That's the part I remember about that old school was going out lunch, building a fire, and going out into the snow.[243]

The initial phase of the construction of the mill, town, and railroad was accomplished by late September 1938. The Gilchrist Timber Company's employees wished to move into their houses prior to their completion. B. V. Wright was overseeing the town's construction while also working with the employees of the Southern Pacific Railroad with whom he had established an amiable relationship to replace defective rails which had been included in the material he had purchase from them the previous year.[244] Frank W. Gilchrist stated to Benjamin V. Wright:

> The people are anxious to move in the houses and I know you are doing all possible to finish them up just and-as soon as you can.
>
> After due consideration, I have decided not to let anyone move into the house until the house is fully completed and the workmen have moved out.[245]

Benjamin V. Wright received the preliminary rent schedule from Frank W. Gilchrist on November 10, 1938. Two-bedroom houses were rented for $24.25 per month, three-bedroom houses for $26.25, and four-bedroom houses for $28.25. Utilities, trash collection, and street cleaning were included. There was an additional charge of $1.50 per month for households using electric iceboxes which were then great users of electricity. There was an additional charge of $1.50 to $2 per month, depending on the size of the house, where oil heaters had been installed. Residents of Gilchrist were expected to provide a satisfactory can or box for trash and to place it where it was readily accessible by the trash hauler.[246]

All the houses and commercial buildings in Gilchrist, with the exception for several years of those located on Rainbow Circle, were painted Gilchrist Brown with whimsically inspired Norwegian patterns for trim. Every five years every building in Gilchrist was repainted by Keith Cottington of Klamath Falls. Using a single color simplified repainting the town.[247] Since houses varied in size and were not all built to a single design, Gilchrist always more closely resembled a neighborhood with strict conventions regulating the appearance of its buildings (Sunriver, Oregon, is an example of such a community) than it did the standardized institutional appearance typical of government-built and operated housing projects as well as some company towns.

Record low temperatures were reported on December 17, 1938. The *Klamath Falls Herald and News* also reported that the commissary and post office had been painted Gilchrist Brown with green trim and that some of the Gilchrist Timber Company's employees had decided to spend Christmas back in Laurel.[248] Replacing the Klamath Northern Railroad's defective rails continued to occupy Benjamin V. Wright's attention during December 1938. M. L. Jennings of Southern Pacific Railroad, in a letter dated December 22, 1938, to Benjamin V. Wright, confirmed that the most recent batch of replacements he had been sent was satisfactory. The previous batch received has been described by Wright as being of scrap quality.[249]

In Gilchrist, as had also been the practice in Dushau, a community Christmas tree was erected. The high school students set it up then decorated it. It was reported by the *Klamath Falls Herald and News* that for Christmas of 1938 the children of Gilchrist were asking for skis and ice skates.[250]

Early in January, the *Klamath Falls Herald and News* reported that a fire truck had been delivered to Gilchrist on December 31, 1938. The same story also reported that the millpond was slowly filling, that Frank W. Gilchrist had hosted a lunch for his employees, that a skating rink with a warming hut had been erected, and that Buchler Construction Company had begun clearing the twelve acres that the Gilchrist Timber Company had donated as the site for the town's school.[251]

During the spring of 1939, the powerhouse was nearing completion. Its boilers had been installed and the smoke stack was rising. The Gilchrist telephone exchange, as soon as it went into operation, attracted much attention too:

> Oregon's newest telephone exchange was placed into service Wednesday at Gilchrist, the new and rapidly growing city 46 miles south of Bend. The telephone exchange will be operated by Pacific Telephone and Telegraph Company.
>
> The telephone central office at Gilchrist is the new community dial type, recognized as the most modern and up-to-date for a town the size and location of Gilchrist. Approximately

Mill pond after filling.
Gilchrist Timber Co. Papers, Klamath County Museum.

> 30 telephones are connected with the new Gilchrist telephone office.
>
> All local calls are to be dialed, the telephone numbers having three digits. Long distance, information and other miscellaneous calls will be handled by direct circuits to Bend and such calls are made by dialing "operator."[252]

It was the first of its type in Central Oregon. Gilchrist was also the first town in Oregon to have an entirely dial telephone at the time of its establishment.

The Gilchrist Timber Company's project (town, railroad, and mill) was a $2 million undertaking. It was the largest project undertaken by the productive sector east of the Cascades during 1938-1939, or anywhere in Oregon. The arrival of the Gilchrist Timber Company in Central Oregon was one of the few reasons for optimism in a region which, as was the case for all of the United States, was enduring the tenth year of the Hoover-Roosevelt Depression. The national unemployment rate, in spite of Roosevelt's promised results from his spending schemes, high taxes, and massive borrowing was at 17.4 percent in 1938.[253] The Gilchrist Timber Company was building and hiring. It was doing so with its own money, not spending money taken from other people, as was the case with the money Roosevelt used to fund his schemes. The Gilchrist Timber Company's projects, particularly the town, were unique in their own right as well as because they were occurring at a time when no end seemed near for the Hoover-Roosevelt Depression.

Klamath Falls Herald and News reported the

progress made in the construction of Gilchrist in an article the paper published on April 21, 1939:

> Extensive development activity in the north end of the county was described by Jack Almeter, manager of the Oregon Employment service offices after a two-day trip as far north as Bend.
>
> Fifty houses, no two alike, have been just completed at Gilchrist, new town near Crescent at the scene of the Gilchrist Timber Company's impressive development. These are from one to four bedroom houses, attractive and modern in every respect, Almeter said.
>
> The local man learned that construction of another 50 houses will start soon.
>
> A shopping center at Gilchrist combines numerous community services. A store which all types of merchandise is sold, club rooms and community hall are included.
>
> Present plans, Almeter learned, call for starting mill operations in the fall. The mill is still under construction. The dam has been partially closed and has backed up a large lake.
>
> Buckler Brothers are pressing work on the new school at Gilchrist. Footings were being poured when Almeter was there.
>
> The Gilchrist townsite is being carefully landscaped and development proceeds. Streets are wide, and trees are left standing wherever possible. A fire protective system has been installed, including water pipes and a fire wagon.[254]

Gilchrist was also Oregon's first town to be established with a system of water piped to hydrants for the purpose of firefighting. The Gilchrist Timber Company developed and enforced policies, the purpose of which was to preclude the occurrence of house fires in Gilchrist. As of the date of the writing of this book, only once has never been a house fire in Gilchrist. The Smallwood House, located on Nob Hill and originally built for the Buchholz, was destroyed by fire during the mid 1950s. House fires in Bend, La Pine, Crescent, and Chemult are routine occurrences.

By the spring of 1939, Rufus Childre and his family had moved into their house. Jim Childre reported that his father had been selected to move into the first house completed in Gilchrist. The house was located on the west side, north end, of the lower street, just south of Ernst Brothers, offices, and was the first house on that side of the street.[255]

The opening of the businesses in the Gilchrist Mall was an event which was looked forward to by residents of Gilchrist as well as those of neighboring communities. Stores operated in company towns, particularly in the Pacific Northwest, attracted customers from neighboring communities. The Potlatch Mercantile is an example of a company store that served an entire region as well as employees of the company that had brought it into existence.[256] The grocery store opened on June 15, 1939. It was initially operated by Toddhunter. The barbershop was leased by W. F. Coxen. Audrey Keihn was the first person to lease the beauty shop. The restaurant was leased by W. J. Cameron. C. H. Barrell leased the drugstore. It was noted that all buildings in the town, including the shopping center, were all state-of-the-art and that the furnishing and fittings of the businesses in the shopping center were the best available.[257]

The Club was operated by the Gilchrist Timber Company solely for the use of the employees of the Gilchrist Timber Company and of the businesses operating in the town of Gilchrist. Club members paid dues of $1.25 a month if over the age of 15 and $.25 a month if fifteen or younger.[258] Jim Childre, whose father operated The Club during the Second World War, described manually setting pins at The Club's bowling alley.[259]

Construction of the Gilchrist School had progressed far enough that, by the time businesses in the Gilchrist Mall were opening for business, the shingling of the school's roof was nearing completion. The school, built at a cost of $65,000, housed grades 1-12. It was laid out with two wings coming off a central administrative area and a combined gymnasium and auditorium located on the east side of the building. The Gilchrist Timber Company built an apartment complex to provide housing for the school's teachers.[260]

Six more houses were completed during June 1939. Construction of another unit of houses, this one located north of the school, commenced on or about June 19, 1939.[261]

Aerial view of Gilchrist, 1939.
Photo album of Stewart J. Gilchrist, Klamath County Museum.

Gilchrist service station, circa 1940.
Collection of Milton Hill.

1938-1941 – *The Move West and Building the Town*

Gilchrist Mall, circa 1940.
Collection of Milton Hill.

Gilchrist Mall, 1939.
Collection of Mary G. Ernst.

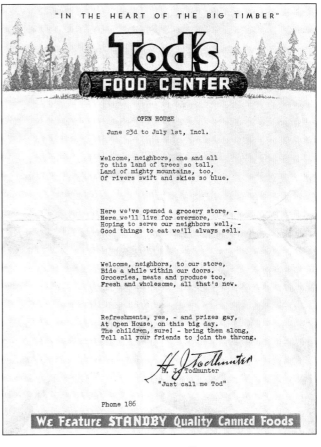

Grocery store flyer.
Photo album of Stewart J. Gilchrist, Klamath County Museum.

Gilchrist Oregon: The Model Company Town

Gilchrist Drug Store, circa 1940.
Collection of Mary G. Ernst.

Interior of Gilchrist Pharmacy, circa 1940.
Collection of Milton Hill.

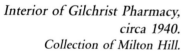

Gilchrist Theatre with school in background, circa 1940.
Collection of Milton Hill.

1938-1941 – The Move West and Building the Town

The mall in 1940.
Collection of Oregon Historical Society.

B.V. Wright house, Gilchrist, 1939.
Collection of Ike Bay.

Gilchrist house, circa 1940.
Collection of Ike Bay.

Gilchrist, Oregon in snow.
Klamath County Museum.

1938-1941 – The Move West and Building the Town

Gilchrist Oregon.
Klamath County Museum.

Gilchrist, Oregon in snow.
Klamath County Museum.

Gilchrist Oregon: The Model Company Town

Homes at Gilchrist.
Klamath County Museum.

Our house, Gilchrist, Oregon, 1938.
Collection of Mary G. Ernst.

1938-1941 – The Move West and Building the Town

*Gilchrist School, circa 1939-1940.
Collection of Oregon Historical Society.*

The Gilchrist Community Church moved towards organization when on July 21, 1939, the Reverend Charles Brown received into membership thirty residents of Gilchrist and nearby communities. The charter members included Mrs. Charles Brown, Mr. and Mrs. Edgar Brown, W. I. Bunnell, Mr. and Mrs. Henry Baron, Mr. and Mrs. W. A. Carmichael, Mr. and Mrs. I. W. Freeman, Mr. and Mrs. Lee Grant, Mr. and Mrs. Henry Gulley, Henry Maddock, Mr. and Mrs. Walter Rigdon, Mr. and Mrs. Oren R. Sample, Mr. and Mrs. C. E. Shotts, Mr. and Mrs. R. W. Speakman, Mr. and Mrs. E. B. Taylor and Billie Taylor, Mr. and Mrs. B. V. Wright, and Mr. and Mrs. R. B. Ward.[262] Benjamin V. Wright remained active in the Gilchrist Community Church, subsequently the Methodist Church, until his death in 1944.

The Gilchrist School opened in September of 1939 with a student body of 94 elementary students and 93 high school students. The high school graduated its first class, consisting of three students. Gilchrist remains the only school in Klamath County north of Chiloquin. Students came to it from as far away as Fort Rock, Oregon. They boarded in Gilchrist or Crescent with the school's teachers. Most came from Crescent, Mowich, Chemult, Odell Lake, Crescent Lake, Beaver Marsh, and Crater Lake Junction as well as from the surrounding ranches. Gilchrist School activities such as attending basketball games during the winter months became a staple of life in Gilchrist and its neighboring communities. Gilchrist High School has produced veritable dynasties of state champion cross-country teams, basketball teams, and exceptional track teams.

The first and second grade students of Gilchrist Elementary School built a model of Gilchrist, Oregon, on November 28, 1939. They named the streets, drew a map of the streets and then sent it to Frank W. Gilchrist, along with an invitation to inspect their model. He accepted the invitation, then visited the classes and inspected their model of Gilchrist. He commented favorably to them on what he saw.[263]

The Gilchrist Mill, eighteen months after construction started, commenced operations on the

Mill and dam, circa 1939.
Collection of Mrs. Mary G. Ernst.

morning of Monday, October 16, 1939. During the preceding year-and-a-half, the Gilchrist Timber Company had spent $2 million but generated not a dime of income. The country remained mired in the Hoover-Roosevelt Depression. The following January, the national unemployment rate still stood at 14.6 percent.[264] Poland had been invaded six weeks prior to the date the Gilchrist Timber Company commenced milling lumber. The world was at war though the United States was not yet one of the declared belligerents. Conditions were less than ideal for the undertaking of such an enterprise. Only when the mill went into operation was Frank W. Gilchrist able to prove the merit of his decision to come west to Central Oregon, then to spend more than $2 million to build a mill, railroad, and town.

A throng of spectators was on hand to watch the Gilchrist Timber Company mill its first log. Mrs. Mary Gilchrist described the event in her diary:

> Started running the mill this morning. Frank, the children and I went to the mill at 6:30. Mary Geales and Stewart went out in the duck boat to at least watch the logs go up the chain. It was a thrilling experience, and inspite of the fact that the air compressor broke down, then the carriage, everyone had smiles on their faces that just wouldn't come off. Young Frank blew the whistle at 10 a.m. and the first log was cut.[265]

The mill cut 40 million board feet during its first year of operation.[266] Gilchrist Timber Company, other than during World War II when the federal government imposed production goals, always set the upper limits of its production to a level that would not exceed the sustainable capacity of its timber supply.

The opening of the Gilchrist Timber Company's mill and the construction of its town was reported in the *Klamath Falls Herald and News* with a full-page article which was illustrated with photographs of the mill, town, and school.[267] In the article, Gilchrist was once again cited as the "wonder town." The project was news and a reason for optimism, for an entire region was in need of it.

Gilchrist Timber Company's mill was very

Interior of mill, circa 1939.
Stewart J. Gilchrist's photo album, Gilchrist Timber Company Papers, Klamath County Museum.

much the state of the art at the time of its completion. All the mill's equipment, with the exception of the shotgun carriage which was steam-driven, was powered with electricity. Filer & Stowell Company of Milwaukee, Wisconsin, furnished the nine-foot band head rig, an eight-foot band resaw, a bull edger, and a trimmer. The mill was pegged together. Not a single nail was employed in its construction. Sixteen steam kilns were built to dry the lumber. The concrete was poured by teams of men who pushed wheelbarrows loaded with concrete up ramps which grew higher the closer the project came to completion.[268] Two large planing machines were used to finish the lumber. Finished lumber was usually stored in sheds before being moved to the loading area for shipment to customers.[269]

The mill operation was very efficient. Portions of each log (bark and sawdust) that didn't become lumber were used by the powerhouse as fuel for steam to power the mill and dry lumber. Trimmings and edging were chipped, then sold to paper companies.[270]

Once construction of the mill was completed, Dan Denham, Alva Hendry, Walter Rigdon, B. E. Hill, Rufus Childre, and many of the other residents who came west with the Gilchrist Timber Company went on to stay with the Gilchrist

Ground Level Pond.
Collection of Mrs. Mary G. Ernst.

Timber Company for decades as well as residents of the mill's town. Benjamin V. Wright moved into Gilchrist's finest house which he occupied until his death in 1944. He was active in management of the town as well as woods operations. Jim Applewhite who, following the mill's completion, became general superintendent, had overall responsibility for the mill's operations. Edgar Shotts was the sawmill's superintendent. Alva Hendy was the head saw filer. Dan Denham was chief millwright. Curtis Breazeale was foreman in charge of the green chain, dry kiln, and dry shed. Jud Terrell was the mill's maintenance foreman. Walter Smallwood served as the Gilchrist Timber Company's master mechanic. Walter Rigdon was employed as blacksmith and welder, as he had been by the Gilchrist-Fordney Company. All were Mississippians who, with the exception of Jud Terrell, had similar positions to the ones they had held at the Gilchrist- Fordney Company.[271] Many of the Gilchrist Timber Company's employees had, during the course of their service with the Gilchrist-Fordney Company, been residents of Dushau. The central cadre of men with their families who had already known each other for decades, coupled with the Gilchrist family's leadership and management practices, as well as the quality of the town they built for their employees, were what made Gilchrist the model company town.

The planer crew, though not manned predominantly by veterans of the Gilchrist-Fordney Company, was a cohesive body of men who had worked together prior to entering the employ of the Gilchrist Timber Company. In 1939, before the Gilchrist Timber Company commenced operating its mill, a fire destroyed the Forest Lumber Company and Pine Ridge (located approximately eight miles north of Chiloquin, Oregon) which was a town the company had established for its employees. The mill's planing crew, led by Shorty Anderson, their foreman, entered the employ of Gilchrist Timber Company as a single body and in the same capacities as they had held with the Forest Lumber Company.[272]

Other alumni of the Gilchrist-Fordney Company who continued to serve with Gilchrist Timber Company included William T. Sherman, Engine Number 204's engineer. The Gilchrist Timber Company's front office staff included Albert Carmichael. He served as office manager, sales manager, and Frank W. Gilchrist's personal secretary. Oren Sample was employed as assistant manager. Sample, though never an employee of the Gilchrist-Fordney Company, was from Laurel, Mississippi, so he was aware of the Gilchrists and already acquainted with many of their employees. Isom Ezell kept the Gilchrist Timber Company's books and would later manage the town's grocery store. John Anding was the Gilchrist Timber Company's first paymaster.[273]

Gilchrist Timber Company's woods crew also included a core of men who had not only been employed by the Gilchrist-Fordney Company but had also been residents of Dushau. Ervin Griffin and Robert "Rob" Ward both worked for the Gilchrist-Fordney Company, then came west to build Gilchrist and had lifelong careers with Gilchrist Timber Company.

Robert Ward entered the employ of the Gilchrist-Fordney Company in 1926 at Dushau. Both

1938-1941 – The Move West and Building the Town

Mr. Alva Hendry, circa 1939.
Collection of F.A. Hendry.

Interior of Power House, circa 1939.
Stewart J. Gilchrist's photo album, Gilchrist Timber Company papers, Klamath County Museum.

```
CHRISTMAS PROGRAM
GILCHRIST COMMUNITY CHURCH
THURSDAY EVENING
DECEMBER 21, 1939


1.  SONG:      "JOY TO THE WORLD"                          Congregation
2.  SONG:      "THE FIRST NOEL"                            Congregation
3.  PRAYER:                                          Mrs. Charles Wright
4.  READING:                                              Virginia Garner
5.  SONG:           Mrs. Carmichael's & Mr. Bunnell's Classes
6.  READING:                                                  Lloyd Hale
7.  OFFERING:
8.  SONG:      "NIGHT OF NIGHTS"                         Miss Tae Knight
9.  PANTOMIME: "THE CHRISTMAS STORY"                     Gilchrist Choir
10. DISTRIBUTION OF GIFTS TO CHILDREN:                       Santa Claus
11. CLOSING PRAYER:                                        Mr. B. V. Wright
```

Christmas Program, December 1939.
Stewart J. Gilchrist's photo album, Gilchrist Timber Company papers, Klamath County Museum.

CLASS ROLL

LaRue Bradshaw   Evelyn Rigdon
Lorena Closson   George Thompson
       Bobbie Ward

CLASS MOTTO—"It isn't the gale, but the set of the sail, that determines the way we go"
CLASS COLORS—Blue and White
CLASS FLOWER—Rose

Bobbie Ward

The Class of

Nineteen Hundred Forty

Gilchrist High School

Announces its

Commencement Exercises

Friday evening, May tenth

at eight o'clock

High School Auditorium

Graduation Announcement, Class of 1940.
Stewart J. Gilchrist's photo album, Gilchrist Timber Company papers, Klamath County Museum.

1938-1941 – The Move West and Building the Town

*Alva Hendry, winter of 1939-1940.
Collection of F.A. Hendry.*

Griffin and Ward came west to Gilchrist from Laurel during the spring of 1939. Their families joined them a few months later during the summer of 1939. Griffin worked in the woods in various capacities including as a log truck loader. Ward rose through the ranks of the Gilchrist Timber Company, serving from 1947-1967 as head of the Walker Range Fire Protective Association.[274]

Dowell E. Garner, though not a former employee of the Gilchrist-Fordney Company, was also a Southerner, from Arkansas, who had moved to Bend, Oregon, to take a position as a sawyer with either Brooks-Scanlon or Shevlin-Hixon. He left their employ to work for the Gilchrist Timber Company, first helping to build the mill and town, then working on the Klamath Northern Railroad as a brakeman.[275]

The population of Gilchrist and the staff of Gilchrist Timber Company were homogenous. Their common experiences as Southerners and, frequently, as employees of the Gilchrist-Fordney Company, coupled with the management practices and leadership provided by the Gilchrists, were paramount factors that made Gilchrist, Oregon singularly successful

A Christmas program, the first Christmas observed in Gilchrist since the opening of the mill and its school, as well as the first since the town's houses were completed, was conducted by the Gilchrist Community Church on December 21, 1939.[276] The town's residents were housed and employed. It was a merry Christmas that included a distribution of gifts to the children as had been the practice in Dushau.

Frank W. Gilchrist, in a letter dated January 11, 1940, congratulated Jack N. Bryant on passing his architect's examinations, and then discussed plans for the expansion of Gilchrist:

> With reference to our work here, it is my purpose at this time to build the Samples a house this summer and also the Todhunters, and possibly one or two other houses for some of our employees, which houses will be above the average rent house. In addition, we will probably build twenty or twenty-five rent houses to take care of those employees who are now on our waiting list.[277]

In the same letter Frank W. Gilchrist also noted that business during the mill's first month of operation had been all that had been expected. Prices were holding and in some cases had advanced. There was reason for some optimism.[278]

The Gilchrist Theatre commenced operations on May 1, 1940. The first movie it showed was "Strange Cargo," a film which starred Clark Gable and Joan Crawford. Other movies screened during its first month of operations included "Northwest Passage," starring Spencer Tracy and Robert Young, and "The Road To Singapore" starring Bing Crosby, Bob Hope, and Dorothy Lamour.[279]

On Friday, May 10, 1940, at 8 p.m. in the high school's auditorium, Gilchrist High School conducted the commencement ceremony for its first senior class, graduating five students: LaRue Bradshaw, Lorena Closson, Evelyn Rigdon, George Thompson, and Bobbie Ward. The motto of the Class of 1940 was, "It isn't the gale, but the set of the sail that determines the way we go."[280] The motto was singularly suitable for a class that graduated during the eleventh year of the Hoover-Roosevelt Depression, nine months after the invasion of Poland, and little more than eighteen months before the attack on Pearl Harbor. The Class of 1941

*First Crew on the First Day.
Collection of Mrs. Mary G. Ernst.*

included Frank R. Gilchrist who attended Oregon State College at Corvallis (now known as Oregon State University) for a year, before leaving school to learn to fly in preparation for his service during the Second World War in the Pacific Theater as a pilot who was assigned to USS *Belleau Wood* (CVL-24).

Gilchrist Timber Company, with the graduation of Gilchrist High School's first class, began the practice of offering summer employment to the sons of Gilchrist Timber Company employees who were attending Gilchrist High School or enrolled in college. This de facto scholarship program for the children of Gilchrist Timber Company employees continued as long as the Gilchrist Timber Company existed. It was eventually expanded to include daughters such as Char Hendry, daughter of F. A. Hendry and granddaughter of Alva Hendry.

Klamath Northern Railroad, during the first eight months after the Gilchrist Timber Company commenced operations, operated as one of the mill's departments. This brought in no revenue on freight hauled which was remedied by incorporating the railroad as a separate entity, one that earned the first cut of the fees for freight. On July 2, 1940, Klamath Northern Railroad was incorporated then officially began to do business on January 1, 1942. During the first years of its operation, Klamath Northern Railroad operated three days a week, on Mondays, Wednesdays, and Fridays. Engine Number 204 hauled out to Gilchrist Junction ten to twelve lumber-laden boxcars, then brought back empty boxcars and the occasional tank car of gasoline for Crescent Oil Company. These fuel shipments were discontinued after shippers turned to trucks. It wasn't possible to turn around Engine Number 204. No turntable had been constructed. The locomotive always faced towards Gilchrist Junction, and always traveled backwards on the return trip to the mill. Engine Number 204 was also fitted with a snowplow. The locomotive's tender, as of the writing of this book, still serves the Klamath Northern Railroad as a snowplow.[281]

Gilchrist Timber Company's timber holdings, by the time the mill commenced operations, had grown from approximately 60,000 acres to approximately 86,000 acres. The Gilchrist-Fordney Company during the final years of its operations had switched from using trains to move its logs into its mill to using trucks for the same purpose. Trucks proved more efficient and less expensive than had logging trains. A network of unpaved roads was built which allowed logging crews access to Gilchrist Timber Company's holdings.[282] The logging roads also allowed Gilchrist Timber Company employees, inhabitants of neighboring

1938-1941 – The Move West and Building the Town

communities, and the children of both groups access to the woods for recreational purposes. The use of Gilchrist Timber Company lands by locals for recreational purposes was informal, regulated by custom, and extremely popular.

In the early months of 1940, Frank W. Gilchrist and the directors of the Gilchrist Timber Company might have been able to breathe a sigh of relief had another World War not been clearly in the offing. Building the mill in the midst of the Hoover-Roosevelt Depression was a considerable gamble which required spending $2 million on an investment that wouldn't generate a cent of income for several years. Lumber prices remained low, though there was just enough demand to justify continuous operations. The mill's success and the success of the town is a tribute to the planning of Frank W. Gilchrist and his uncle, Ralph E. Gilchrist. It also says much regarding the quality of their lieutenants, men such as James Applewhite, Albert Carmichael, and Benjamin V. Wright, as well as the yeoman service rendered by Gilchrist Timber Company's rank-and-file employees. Frank W. Gilchrist and Ralph E. Gilchrist had judged correctly. They had triumphed. The Second World War and its aftermath denied Frank W. Gilchrist an opportunity to pause to savor his accomplishments.

Gilchrist High School Band, 1939-1940.
Collection of Mrs. Mary G. Ernst.

Junior Class, 1939-1940.
Collection of Mrs. Mary G. Ernst.

1938-1941 – The Move West and Building the Town

High School Play, 1940.
Collection of Mrs. Mary G. Ernst.

Student Council, 1939-1940.
Collection of Mrs. Mary G. Ernst.

Gilchrist Oregon: The Model Company Town

Basketball Team, 1939-1940.
Collection of Mrs. Mary G. Ernst.

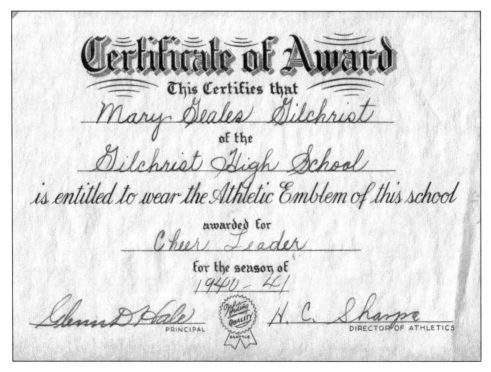

Mrs. Ernst's Cheer Leader Certificate.
Collection of Mrs. Mary G. Ernst.

1938-1941 – The Move West and Building the Town

8th Grade Class, 1939-1940.
Collection of Mrs. Mary G. Ernst.

Pine Room exterior, 1939.
Collection of Klamath County Museum.

THE CLUB

ORGANIZATION

THE CLUB shall be an organization for and by the employees of Gilchrist Timber Company, as well as for the employees of the various business enterprises located in the town of Gilchrist.

Membership to THE CLUB shall be restricted to persons as above stated and shall be governed by the payment of monthly dues, as hereinafter provided, the amount of which shall be $1.25 for members above the age of 15 years and 25c for members below the age of 15 years, all dues payable to the Secretary of THE CLUB monthly in advance.

Membership to THE CLUB shall entitle the individual, upon payment of the proper dues, to entrance in the club and use of the club lounge and card room only. Use of the facilities of the club shall be allowed the members only upon payment of the proper fee as stipulated by the governing Board of THE CLUB.

The operation of THE CLUB shall be in charge of a Board of Directors composed of twelve members of THE CLUB, six of whom shall be men and six of whom shall be women, such directors to be elected by members in good standing of THE CLUB to serve for a period of six months, without Compensation.

The Board of Directors, from its own number, shall elect a President, a Vice-President and a Secretary-Treasurer, who shall serve without compensation and whose duties shall be as follows:

PRESIDENT: It shall be the duty of the President to preside at all regular meetings of the Board of Directors and to call special sessions of the Board whenever he deems it necessary, or upon request of the members of THE CLUB. It shall be the further duty of the President of the Board of Directors to generally supervise the operation of THE CLUB but he shall have no power other than that conferred upon him by the Board of Directors.

VICE-PRESIDENT: It shall be the duty of the Vice-President to assume the duties of the President a such times as the President is unable to serve.

SECRETARY-TREASURER: It shall be the duty of the Secretary-Treasurer of THE CLUB to attend to the collection of dues, and to furnish the Manager of THE CLUB, on or before the first day of each month, with a complete list of the eligible members of THE CLUB for the ensuing month, and to keep the Manager informed at all times as to any changes in the eligibility of members. It shall be the further duty of the Secretary-Treasurer to receive all funds of THE CLUB and to attend to the disbursement of same, and to present to the Board of Directors, at each regular session, a detailed and accurate statement of the financial status of THE CLUB.

The Board of Directors of THE CLUB shall meet in regular session once each month on a date which is agreeable to all members of the Board.

The Board of Directors shall have authority to employ a Manager of THE CLUB, whose duties it shall be to supervise the use of the facilities of THE CLUB by its members, and to see that the club rooms are kept in good order at all times. The Manager shall admit to the club only members who are in good standing, as shown by the report of the Secretary of THE CLUB, but he shall have no authority to admit anyone not shown on the list furnished him by the Secretary. The Manager of THE CLUB shall be allowed to accept payment of dues by members of THE CLUB but payment of dues to the Manager will not constitute admittance to THE CLUB until such dues have been turned over to the Secretary and the Secretary has properly notified the Manager in accordance with the provisions hereinabove stated.

The Manager of THE CLUB shall have jurisdiction over all members of THE CLUB while they are inside the club rooms and shall have authority at all times to evict any member whose conduct is, in the opinion of the Manager, boisterous, rude or objectionable and not in keeping with the standards of THE CLUB. When it is necessary for the Manager to evict any member of THE CLUB, it shall be the duty of the Manager to then report his action to the Board of Directors who will, at its next regular session, take action on the membership of the party so evicted. Until such action is taken by the Board, the membership of the offending party shall stand suspended and he shall not be entitled to entrance to the club rooms or use of its facilities. Boisterous, rude or objectionable conduct will not be tolerated on the part of any member and this regulation shall be rigidly enforced by the Manager of THE CLUB. In the event it becomes necessary for the Manager to evict any member of THE CLUB, there shall be no refund of dues during the term of suspension from THE CLUB.

As hereinabove stated, the monthly dues entitle the members to the use of the club lounge and card rooms only. It shall also permit them the privilege of inviting out-of-town guests to enjoy the facilities of the club rooms. However, under no circumstances will abuse of this privilege be tolerated by the management of THE CLUB. That is to say, the continuous inviting of guests, or the inviting of an extraordinary number of guests at any one time will be a violation of this rule and such a violation shall immediately be reported to the Board of Directors by the Manager of THE CLUB and the Board shall immediately take drastic action. It is, of course, understood that the use of the bowling alleys, billiard tables and any other facilities of THE CLUB for which a charge is made will carry the same charge to guests as it does to regular members.

As hereinabove stated, the dues entitles members of the club to the free use of the card tables in the card room, but it is expected that no one member or group of members will monopolize the use of the card room under this privilege.

CHARGES FOR USE OF FACILITIES

BOWLING ALLEYS: There shall be a charge of 10c per person per game, or three games to one person for 25c, for the use of the bowling alleys. The use of the bowling alleys shall be extended to members 15 years and over, who are able to properly handle the bowling balls without injury to the alleys. All bowlers wil be expected to use the alleys in strict accordance with the rules. That is to say, no deliberate fouling or lofting (bouncing) of the balls will be allowed. Any flagrant violations of the rules in connection with the use of the bowling alleys shall be immediately stopped by the Manager of THE CLUB and such violation shall be reported to the Board of Directors for proper action.

BILLIARD TABLES: There shall likewise be a charge of 5c per person per game for use of the billiard tables and the same general rules shall apply to the use of these tables as apply to the use of the bowling alleys and such rules are set forth in the preceding paragraph.

There shall be served to club members, and/or their guests, **in the lounge only**, beer and other cold drinks, as well as food through an arrangement with the management of the restaurant. All such sales shall be for cash only, the receipts of which shall be received and kept accurately by the Manager of the club and turned over to the Secretary-Treasurer of the Board of Directors at such times as he sees fit to call for same.

Should any members in good standing of THE CLUB desire to rent or lease the club rooms for one night for some special occasion, this may be arranged by giving the Manager of THE CLUB five (5) days notice. It shall not be the policy of the management of THE CLUB to lease the rooms to any one member on Friday, Saturday or Sunday nights.

It is the hope of the management that THE CLUB will be enjoyed by its members but, at the same time, it is expected that the members will have pride in THE CLUB and its facilities, and see that it is kept in as good condition as it now is reasonable wear and tear excepted.

Gilchrist, Oregon
July 1st, 1939.

Collection of Mary. G. Ernst.

1938-1941 – The Move West and Building the Town

Bowling Alley, circa 1940.
Collection of Klamath County Museum.

Interior of The Club, circa 1940.
Collection of Klamath County Museum.

Gilchrist Oregon: The Model Company Town

Logging operations, 1939.
Gilchrist Timber Company Papers, Klamath County Museum.

1938-1941 – The Move West and Building the Town

Gilchrist Timber Company log truck.
Gilchrist Timber Company Papers, Klamath County Museum.

Gilchrist Timber Company burning slash.
Gilchrist Timber Company Papers, Klamath County Museum.

*Aerial view of Gilchrist Mill.
Collection of Mary G. Ernst.*

*Premilinary sketch of
Gilchrist Theatre.
Oregon Historical Society.*

1938-1941 – The Move West and Building the Town

Townsite drawing.
Gilchrist Timber Company Papers, Klamath County Museum.

Gilchrist Oregon: The Model Company Town

Architect's house drawings.
Collection of Mary G. Ernst.

1938-1941 – The Move West and Building the Town

Architect's house drawings.
Collection of Mary G. Ernst.

Architect's house drawings.
Collection of Mary G. Ernst.

1938-1941 – The Move West and Building the Town

Architect's house drawings.
Collection of Mary G. Ernst.

*Architect's house drawings.
Collection of Mary G. Ernst.*

CHAPTER IV

1941-1946

World War II and the Strike

"In our youth our hearts were touched with fire.
We have shared the incommunicable experience of war;
we have felt, we still feel, the passion of life to its top."

— *Oliver Wendell Holmes, Jr.*

Gilchrist Timber Company, when 1940 began, was an orderly place where years of work, millions in capital outlay, and decades of planning were coming to fruition. The state of Gilchrist and the Gilchrist Timber Company was a counterpoint to national and international events which were already intruding. The national unemployment rate at the beginning of January 1940 was 14.6 percent.[283] Three months before, the Hoover-Roosevelt Depression had entered its twelfth year. What Roosevelt did during the approximately eight years since winning his first term as president was to implement expanded versions of the programs which had been tried, then failed for President Hoover, to double-down on his previous failures. Then, after they failed yet again, he blamed the failures on the productive sector which he was hobbling with regulations and bleeding with confiscatory taxes. His various expensive programs of temporary make-work jobs, coupled with his class war rhetoric, were what he had used to win reelection in 1936 for himself and other members of the Democrat Party. By 1938, Roosevelt and his programs had grown increasingly unpopular. The Republican Party began to recoup their previous losses. For Roosevelt, the war, arguably undeservedly, redeemed his reputation. It provided him with a rationale for his third and fourth terms. Roosevelt, if nothing else, was an accomplished politician. He realized he had to change his tack.

On May 26, 1940, Franklin Roosevelt delivered a speech in which he committed the United States to preparing for war and to supplying the Allied nations. Belgium, Holland, and Luxembourg had been conquered by the National Socialists. France would soon fall, too. Spending on defense was now lower than it had been during Roosevelt's first term. Roosevelt had set the United States on a course which made the Second World War, as well as the involvement of the United States in it, all but inevitable. He had, however, done nothing to prepare the country's military for it. The United States Army consisted of 140,000 men who were scattered from the Philippines to the Panama Canal Zone and across the United States in remote camps and posts. All branches of the service lacked vehicles, aircraft, fuel, arms, and ammunition with which to train. The few ships whose construction had been authorized were built more as an opportunity to use part of the naval budget to create patronage opportunities, to buy votes with jobs, for the Democrat Party. Roosevelt sought to correct the effects of his policies of the previous eight years by turning to the productive sector and to the individuals he had spent his first two terms maligning for the failures of his policies and programs.[284] For the next six years, this change in policy would shape the activities and fortunes of the Gilchrist Timber Company and its employees. It sent some employees and sons of employees off for several years away from home, while sending a few off to their deaths. For a few months afterward, the full import of Roosevelt's May 26, 1940, speech was not felt by the Gilchrist Timber Company and its employees. Gilchrist and the Gilchrist Timber Company carried on much as they had before.

Albert Carmichael, at the end of December 1940 wrote a letter to James P. Applewhite in which he discussed the current state of the mill and its prospects for the coming year. He reported that Frank W. Gilchrist and many of the mill's employees were out sick. During December, the mill had shipped 137 cars of lumber which was averaging a sale price of $24 per thousand board feet. He anticipated shipping more lumber than was being cut, which would deplete inventories. Ice on the millpond had yet to slow the mill's operations. Albert Carmichael attributed the slowing of orders to a need by their customers to reduce their stock on hand prior to the levying of inventory taxes. He closed the letter by noting that the mill was still shaking down and that he thought prospects for a better year during 1941 were realistic.[285]

Gilchrist Timber Company continued to discover, and then correct problems involving its equipment. Frank W. Gilchrist, in a letter to J. A. Denton of Portland, Oregon, wrote that keeping saws on the planer shed's band ripsaws was proving a challenge.[286]

Two days later Albert Carmichael wrote to the *Bend Bulletin* to correct an erroneous story which the paper had published, the subject of which was Gilchrist's population. He explained by while the population of the town had been 378 when the 1940 Census was conducted, it had subsequently grown to approximately 500 following the completion of new houses which were located north of the school and shopping center.[287] A few days later, Albert Carmichael responded to a letter from John Heriza in the matter of the performance of Bill Burke. He explained that Bill Burke had conducted his affairs irresponsibly and that he had been dismissed after his wages had been twice garnished, which was a violation of the company's rules and customs.[288] Across the Atlantic things were going badly for the Allies.

During a meeting in Klamath Falls of the Western Pine Association, anti-trust actions by the federal government, which were leading to increased legal fees to defend against unwarranted actions, were discussed. War orders were starting to arrive which offset the decline in orders from buyers belonging to the productive sector.[289]

On March 6, 1941, Albert Carmichael wrote to Frank W. Gilchrist, who was back East on business, to report on Gilchrist Timber Company's recent activities as well as the results of a meeting of the Western Pine Association. Carmichael mentioned meeting a former resident of Laurel during that meeting who remembered the Gilchrist-Fordney Company, had heard much of Gilchrist, and wished to tour the town and mill. He said he took him back to Gilchrist for a tour. Albert Carmichael said that during February 140 cars, containing approximately 3,980,000 board feet, were shipped, that the average sales price was approximately $26 per thousand board feet. He reported that business had fallen off since his last letter, that he had shipped 61 cars but only booked 31. Albert Carmichael said that he regarded the decline in orders as a temporary matter. He noted that the mill's inventory of milled lumber was low, so the decline afforded an opportunity to replenish it. No accounts were past due. Carmichael then noted that the winter weather had relented enough to allow logging crews to return to the woods. He also reported on domestic and town matters:

> The Gullys and Mrs. Ezell returned last Wednesday. They all look fine and seem to have had a wonderful vacation. I am sure that they enjoyed every minute of it.
>
> Your children are all just fine. Young Frank is away with the Gilchrist High basketball team this week for the tournament. They were runners-up at Lakeview earlier in the week, which won for them an invitation to Ashland to compete in the finals, and they went down there yesterday. Understand that Chiloquin was to be their opponent last night, and I have heard how they came out.[290]

Plans for the expansion of Gilchrist were the subject of the letter Frank W. Gilchrist wrote to Jack W. Bryant on March 15, 1941: ". . . I am anxious to get started as soon as possible with our building program for the townsite for this summer."[291]

Two days later Frank W. Gilchrist received a letter from Mrs. Catherine Bauer, secretary of the

California Housing Association, in which she had written about her recent visit to Gilchrist: "I wonder if you could tell me how it came to be such an exceptionally fine lumber town." Frank W. Gilchrist, in a letter dated March 17, 1941, answered by explaining only that Hollis Johnston of Portland, Oregon, was his architect.[292]

Gilchrist Timber Company continued to attract Mississippians who came west on the basis of referrals. James Applewhite wrote to Mr. Horner Temple of Verba, Mississippi, offering him a position in the woods on Ervin Griffin's crew. The position paid $0.67 an hour for a forty-hour week, which was on the lower end of the Gilchrist Timber Company's wage scale.[293]

During the middle of May 1941, the Klamath County District Attorney demanded that Gilchrist Timber Company pay a licensing fee for the pool tables located in The Club. Frank W. Gilchrist explained in his response that The Club was available only to dues-paying employees of the Gilchrist Timber Company and its concessionaires, that it was not open to the public, that it was a nonprofit enterprise, and that the fees charged for the use of the table were sufficient only to cover expenses connected with the operation and maintenance of the pool tables.[294]

On May 22, 1941, Frank W. Gilchrist asked Hollis Johnston to submit a plan for the exterior of the Gilchrist Theatre. He wrote, "It looks like we have waited long enough and the you should have something definite to submit to use at this time which you think will materially help the appearance of our theatre building from the exterior." Hollis Johnston subsequently submitted a plan which was carried out.[295]

By the first week of June 1941, effects of the preparations for the entry of the United States into the Second World War were beginning to have a noticeable effect on the Gilchrist Timber Company. Albert Carmichael wrote to Frank W. Gilchrist, who was then in Memphis, Tennessee, on business. He began by noting that Joe Bertrand, who had been reported missing on the previous Sunday, had been found in the millpond, dead, the following morning at 7:15 a.m. Drowning was the cause of death. His funeral was conducted in Bend, Oregon, the morning of June 14, 1941. Albert Carmichael reported that he had booked 41 cars for the week and had shipped 35 cars. Expenses for May 1941 were $15.50 per thousand board feet, as compared with $14.87 per thousand during April 1941. He attributed the higher cost per thousand to rising wages. The average selling price per thousand for the mill's output during May 1941 was $25.23. During April 1941, the average sales price for the mill's produce was $25.20 per thousand. For the year to date, it was $25.71 per thousand.[296] Regarding the town, Albert Carmichael, in the same letter, reported:

> The construction in the townsite is going along in good shape. We got the plans for the Sample's basement and they excavated his basement with a dragline this week, and will start building the forms Monday. They have the first floor of Buchholz's house framed, and will frame the second story next week. I have had the furnace man and the roofing man from Bend here figuring on the jobs. Roofing is up $0.75 per square, installed over the time when my house was built, which I figure is about in line. He is going to roof Vine's house for $202.50 and we placed an order for sufficient roofing to cover all four houses, with the understanding that we could cancel part of the order if, for any reason, we didn't built four houses. The furnace man is going to install Vine job for just a few dollars more than his price on my house, which I think is a very good price indeed. I have an appointment to see Mefferd, the plasterer, tomorrow morning and get his figure on that part of the job. The plumbing fixtures have been ordered so that they will be here in plenty of time.
>
> I have a letter from Hollis Johnston this morning with reference to decorating the theatre. The cost is $955.00 so suppose he will go ahead with that work without delay.[297]

A week later Albert Carmichael reported that framing of the second floor of the Buchholz house had commenced and that the forms were in place for Sample's basement. The balance of the plans for the Sample house had been received. Work on that project could proceed without delay. The work on the Club's floor was reported to Frank W. Gilchrist as having been completed. Albert Carmichael also said that he expected the theatre's decorating crew to arrive the following week. That project, as of June 20, 1941, had not been started.[298] He noted that the demand for lumber was brisk though prices remained unchanged.

The mill's departments, James Applewhite wrote to his brother in a letter dated June 23, 1941, were all operating satisfactorily. He asked his brother to send him butter-bean seeds, that the local seed companies didn't stock them and claimed to have never heard of them.[299]

The Selective Service System was in operation and affecting the residents of Gilchrist, Oregon, by late June 1941. F. H. Heilbronner, an official of the Selective Service, Local County Board Number, wrote a letter to Albert Carmichael, dated June 23, 1941, in which he confirmed a telephonic conversation which occurred three days prior on June 20, 1941. He confirmed in writing that the draft board, with supplies, would arrive on June 27, 1941, to set up, and then would commence conducting registration for the draft on July 1, 1941.[300]

Gilchrist Timber Company, in spite of the obstacles created by Roosevelt's additional controls and increased taxes, justified by him as necessary for the war effort, continued the Gilchrist-Fordney Company's practice of aiding its neighbors which was a custom of the Gilchrist family that predated their relocation to Laurel, Mississippi. On June 27, 1941, Frank W. Gilchrist wrote to the Reverend J. M. B. Gill of Lakeview, Oregon, that the Gilchrist Timber Company would donate to his church the siding, per his specifications, which he had previously requested.[301]

Consumer credit was not so readily available during the early 1940s as it was during the first decades of the twenty-first century. Included in the Gilchrist Timber Company's papers was a copy of a payroll deduction agreement for the installment purchase of furniture from George Caldwell. The purchaser, on July 30, 1941, authorized the deduction of ten dollars every two weeks, payable to George Caldwell from his pay.[302]

Hollis Johnston wrote Frank W. Gilchrist on July 12, 1941, to report that Mrs. Frohman, the painter who had applied the theatre's decorative trim, would return the first of the following week to work on that of the Gilchrist Mall.[303] Frank W. Gilchrist, in a letter dated July 16, 1941, acknowledged receipt of Hollis Johnston's letter dated July 12, 1941, and stated that he wanted Mrs. Frohman to freshen up the Gilchrist Mall's trim. He then moved on to new business. He asked Hollis Johnston to obtain data for the grocery store's refrigerator unit, which he reported he was being pressed for by the store's tenant. Frank W. Gilchrist said he was interested in hearing about Tom Taylor's proposed layout for the rock entrance to the drive leading to his house.[304] Three weeks later, on August 7, 1941, Frank W. Gilchrist was once again corresponding with Hollis Johnson in the matter of the Gilchrist Theatre. He informed him that the theatre's floodlight had arrived without its rim, that the lack of the rim was delaying the light's installation. Frank W. Gilchrist concluded the letter by writing in the matter of Mrs. Froham's work on the theatre, "I think the work which has been done on this building has improved its looks greatly."[305] On August 22, 1941, Frank W. Gilchrist sent to Hollis Johnson a check for $650. The sum was to pay off the balance due Mrs. Froham for the work she had done on the Theatre and Mall.[306] The total she received for both projects was $850, a not- inconsiderable sum in 1941. Frank W. Gilchrist mentioned that he would like to meet with Hollis Johnston the following Monday or Tuesday to discuss other projects he had in mind. Hollis Johnston continued to execute commissions for Frank W. Gilchrist for several years to come, including providing a design for his office.

By August of 1941, the demand for lumber, specifically government orders, made it impossible for Gilchrist Timber Company to accept new orders from fellow members of the productive sector. Frank W. Gilchrist, in response to a plea from the Davis Lumber Company, explained that Gilchrist Timber Company was currently unable to accept new orders because all of its production had been already allocated.[307]

Gilchrist, Oregon, attracted the attention of people who wanted to live there or learn about it even before it was completed. Its completion did nothing to abate the inquiries from people who wanted to live there or visit it. During October 1941, Bruce Blahnik of San Francisco, California, wrote a letter to Albert Carmichael in which he said that after visiting his brother, Jack Blahnik, who was already an employee of the Gilchrist Timber Company and resident of Gilchrist, he had developed a desire to enter the employ of the Gilchrist Timber Company and to move to Gilchrist. Bruce E. Blahnik said that he desired a position as a bookkeeper, but that he would accept any position offered for a chance to live in Gilchrist.[308] Hollis Johnston wrote to Frank W. Gilchrist, in a letter dated November 12, 1941:

> The class in architecture at the University of Oregon intended to pay Gilchrist a visit, and I understand that they have set the date for this weekend. This will probably be in charge of Mr. Eyler Brown and one of the instructors, and I have taken the liberty of suggesting to him that he look you up on arrival.[309]

In the letter's final paragraph, he asked Frank W. Gilchrist to point out to Eyler Brown the houses which had been completed, incorporating changes made to Hollis Johnston's designs by Benjamin V. Wright which deviated from his designs.[310]

Later during October 1941, a fire started in the Gilchrist Theatre's projection booth when the film in the projector spontaneously combusted. The film stock used during the early 1940s was inherently unstable. The fire was entirely contained within the projection booth. Buster Osborne, the projectionist, escaped without injury. New projection and sound equipment of the most up-to-date sort available was installed by Frank W. Gilchrist, after it was determined that equipment damaged in the fire would prove satisfactory if repaired. He also had additional safety devices installed in the projection booth. The Gilchrist Theatre reopened on November 1, 1941, with a screening of "Unfinished Business" which starred Irene Dunne and Robert Young. It was noted in the announcement that the Gilchrist Theatre now had the finest projection equipment on the West Coast.[311]

Albert Carmichael, in spite of the expanding workload brought about by meeting war-related production requirements, continued to make time to aid the Gilchrist Community Church. On December 3, 1941, he was writing letters to publishers requesting information pertaining to the hymnbooks he was interested in purchasing for the Community Church's Sunday School.[312]

Most of the lumber the Gilchrist Timber Company shifted during World War II was shipped by railroad boxcar. Car shortages were a chronic problem throughout the war years. Frank W. Gilchrist wrote to James Applewhite later during December 1941. He noted that the car shortage continued and that because of it the planing mill had been down since the preceding Saturday. The plan, he wrote, if cars became available, was to run day shift the following week on a forty-five hour schedule and night-shift on a forty-hour schedule.[313]

By the end of 1941, the effects of Roosevelt's war production scheme had begun to tell on the Gilchrist Timber Company. Frank W. Gilchrist wrote to James P. Applewhite during the last week of 1941 in the matter of purchasing a piece of equipment the Gilchrist Timber Company needed to meet its portion of the production targets the federal government had imposed on the timber industry:

> We bought an Adams road grader and thought we would get immediate delivery of it, but find that our priority number is not sufficiently high for them to release it. We have signed all kinds of papers and made all kinds of affidavits and we are hoping to get the machine within the next few days.[315]

The grader wasn't delivered within a few days. Albert Carmichael wrote one week later in the matter of the grader:

> We had our first experience last week with Form PD-1, application for preference rating. We filled out the whole blank are spending a couple of days deciphering it and Howard-Cooper, from whom we purchased the road grader, advised us that they thought it would go through and that we would get better than an A-1-7 rating, which would secure the machine. As a matter of fact, they are so sure that it will go through they have released the machine to use. It is supposed to be delivered today, although it hasn't arrived yet.[316]

In the same letter Albert Carmichael noted that on the night of December 31, 1941, the temperature dropped to 23 below zero, and then only warmed up to seven above zero the following day. The mill's operations were curtailed by the difficulties involved in obtaining the loading equipment. The week before Christmas was almost entirely lost for want of boxcars. Only 134 loads were shipped out during December because of the car shortage. A motor for the edger burned out the preceding Saturday. A 75 horsepower substitute for the 100 horsepower motor which had burned out was all that could found, after frantic calls were placed to suppliers up and down the West Coast. Also mentioned was that price controls on lumber were to go into effect on February 1, 1942, and that the government planned to acquire one-and-a-half billion feet of lumber. More and more of the Gilchrist Timber Company's operations, its ability to acquire the materials and tools it needed to fill its orders, depended on the decisions of bureaucrats.[317]

The Gilchrist Timber Company, during the Second World War, was particularly successful in its efforts to promote the sale of bonds. Bond drives involved the entire community including the students attending Gilchrist's schools. Frank W. Gilchrist, less than six weeks after the attack on Pearl Harbor, wrote the staff of the Department of the Treasury's Defense Savings Program. He notified them that Benjamin V. Wright was already aggressively promoting the sale of bonds and stamps to Gilchrist Timber Company employees as well as to the employees of its concessionaries and subsidiary operations such as the Klamath Northern Railroad.[318]

Labor shortages were another chronic problem the Gilchrist Timber Company experienced throughout the war years. The timber company found it necessary to go farther afield to find employees and to apply less rigorous standards when screening them. H. H. McCall was notified on February 20, 1942, that there were currently open positions in the woods for two sets of fallers and that these positions, which required the fallers to furnish their own tools, paid $1.035 an hour.[319]

Jack N. Bryant, in a letter dated April 6, 1942, which accompanied sketches for houses Frank W. Gilchrist had requested of him the previous fall, discussed a plan for an upper street with lots for ninety houses. The street, which was never constructed, would have been located above the school. He asked Frank W. Gilchrist if the war had changed his plans for the town's expansion, since the system of rationing and priorities which had already been imposed by the federal government would make it difficult, if not impossible, to obtain plumbing and hardware for the houses. Jack N. Bryant concluded his letter by mentioning that he'd seen a notice in a Portland, Oregon, newspaper that James Applewhite had joined the United States Navy, that he was leaving the employ of Lytel and Shorett to take a position as an architect with the firm of Graham and Painter, which was engaged in war work for the army. He wrote, after discussing James Applewhite's enlistment in the United States Navy, that he had attempted to enlist in the navy a few months previously but had been rejected for service because of a hearing loss he had sustained to his left ear many years before.[320]

F. A. Hendry described the response by the residents of Gilchrist to the call for volunteers to serve in the armed forces as well as the labor shortage which existed during the war years:

> Well, one thing I remember about that was the ones old enough, headed down to the recruitment office and they were going to enlist if they could, if they were old enough and could get their parents to sign for them. Everyone was going into the service. I remember the last year I was in high school. I would go to the mill to work the night shift, I must have been sixteen. I'd go over to the mill and work the night shift and get off sometime in the middle of the night and then get up in the next morning to go to school. I was working the night shift at the mill and going to school at the same time. They were having a hard time getting people to work. Everyone was going into the service, all the able bodied men.[321]

Numerous men from Gilchrist, including principals of the Gilchrist Timber Company such as James Applewhite, volunteered for service. He served as a member of the United States Navy. He was commissioned, and then served throughout the Pacific Theater with the SeaBees. Others were drafted. Harry F. Garner, who had joined the Gilchrist Timber Company on November 6, 1939, enlisted on December 26, 1941. Ragner Hermanson entered the employ of the Gilchrist Timber Company on May 16, 1938, and then enlisted on May 5, 1942. W. Wyatt Ward enlisted on March 12, 1942. He had started with Gilchrist Timber Company on June 8, 1939. John M. Warren, who had been hired by Gilchrist Timber

Company on August 3, 1939, enlisted on April 6, 1943.³²²

Among the sons of the Gilchrist Timber Company and future employees of the Gilchrist Timber Company who entered the military service during the Second World War was Frank R. Gilchrist, who joined the United States Navy, then served as a pilot in the Pacific after completing flight training. The day he turned twenty-one he was providing air support for troops fighting on Okinawa. He was assigned to USS *Belleau Wood* (CVL 24). Stewart J. Gilchrist, after graduating from Gilchrist High School as a member of the Class of 1943, also served in the United States Navy as a line officer. Wayne H. Ernst served in Europe as a member of the United States Army. He rose to the rank of Technical Sergeant and won a Bronze Star for his service in the Philippines. Charlie Shotts, who graduated from Gilchrist High School with the same class as Frank R. Gilchrist, served in Europe during the Second World War as a member of the United States Army. He earned a battlefield commission as a 2ⁿᵈ Lieutenant.³²³ F. A. Hendry, son of Alva Henry, enlisted in the United States Navy in 1943, then went on to serve on a communications ship which took part in the

James Applewhite.
Gilchrist Timber Co. papers, Klamath County Museum.

Left to Right: Chuck Morris, Frank Gilchrist, Bill Terrell and F.A. Hendry
Collection of F.A. Hendry.

Battle of Okinawa. Both F. A. Hendry and Charlie Shotts worked for the Gilchrist Timber Company prior to enlisting. Bill Terrell, son of R. J. Terrell, was commissioned a lieutenant in the United States Army. Chuck Moris flew with the Army Air Corps. Robert and Arthur Sherman, sons of William T. Sherman, both enlisted in the United States Navy. They went on to serve throughout the war. Robert Sherman was off Normandy Beach, serving as a member of an LST's crew, the morning of June 6, 1944. Seventy-two men, by July 31, 1944 (approximately one year prior to the war's conclusion), had entered the armed forces. This number equaled roughly half the staff that the Gilchrist Timber Company needed for its wartime operations.[324]

The Second World War produced a military presence in Central Oregon. Camp Abbot, located where Sunriver Resort is currently located, was established on December 4, 1942. The camp's purpose was to train combat engineers and to function as a combat engineer replacement center. It was, at the time of its establishment, one of only three combat engineer training centers located in the United States. During March of 1943, the first trainees arrived. The camp was dedicated on September 3, 1943. Training cycles were seventeen weeks long. Each group of trainees consisted of approximately 10,000 soldiers. More than 90,000 combat engineers underwent training prior to June 1944 when the camp closed. The final phase, three weeks in duration, was a field exercise. Soldiers maneuvered through Central Oregon, including on Gilchrist Timber Company property. Plans were made, though never carried out, for the construction of a military airport on Gilchrist Timber Company land.[325] A weather station was another facility which was planned for construction near Gilchrist but never built.

The labor shortage which existed throughout the war affected Gilchrist Timber Company's hiring practices. Women were hired to work in the mill. Mrs. Ernst talked about some of the women who worked for the Gilchrist Timber Company as well as some other activities which took place as a part of the war effort:

> Annie Estes worked there. Happy Anderson, which was Dan Anderson's wife, worked there. Everybody tried to get through. We folded bandages for the Red Cross, and knitted socks and hats for the Red Cross, whatever needed doing, you did.[326]

The war also resulted in the hiring of men who worked for the Gilchrist Timber Company but weren't a part of it as were the men and their families who came west from Laurel during the late 1930s. By the spring of 1942, searching for manpower had become a routine part of the Gilchrist Timber Company's operations. Joe Webb of Mowich, Oregon, was offered a position as a car loader and was also informed that there was work for his brother Bob on the green chain.[327] Raymond Hosleder of Prineville was offered a job on the green chain. Glen I. Talley of La Pine was also offered a job on the green chain.[328] W. R. Cabaniss of Klamath Falls was offered a position with Gilchrist Timber Company because Mr. Maddor had been drafted into the Army Air Corps.[329]

Wages, at least to the extent possible under Roosevelt's wage-and-price control schemes, rose. By mid-1942, the green chain paid $0.80 an hour for a forty-five hour week. The same position, in 1939, paid $0.67 an hour. Car loaders were paid $0.85 an hour for a forty-hour week. A power house operator earned $0.98 an hour and worked a forty-hour week. Lumber graders earned $1.03 an hour.[330] Summer work was the subject of a letter Frank W. Gilchrist wrote to Herbert Penny, a college student of Eugene, Oregon, on May 18, 1942.[331]

Gilchrist's expansion was stopped for the duration of the war. Frank W. Gilchrist, early during April 1942, wrote a letter to Jack N. Bryant in which, in response to a letter dated April 4, 1942, he had previously received from Bryant, said that the plans for the town's expansion were on hold for the war's duration. House construction in Gilchrist didn't resume until the latter half of 1946.[332]

During the war years, the Gilchrists managed to continue carrying on with their custom of community support. On May 1, 1942, Frank W. Gilchrist sent one hundred dollars to Klamath Falls to support the county's Scout and Camp Fire programs.[333]

Unionization was one of the effects of change in hiring standards due to the labor shortages that existed during the Second World War years. No union ever won a majority of votes. When the International Wood Workers of America, an affiliate of the CIO (an organization which eventually proved notorious for the presence of International Workers of the World alumni, communists, and communist fellow travelers in the ranks of its membership and leadership), won an election conducted during May 1942, it did not win with an outright majority. Of the 177 employees who were eligible, 15 chose not to vote, 22 supported the AFL, 56 voted for no union, and 84 favored the CIO. Ninety-three of the 177 employees eligible did not vote in favor of representation by the CIO International Wood Workers of America.[334] Regulations imposed by the Roosevelt administration during the 1930s biased labor relations in favor of union organizers, even when a firm's employees did not desire their representation. In consequence thereof, a union, which never enjoyed the support of a majority of Gilchrist Timber Company's employees, was able to collect dues from all of them, even the ones who had never desired its representation. The exigencies of war-time production engendered a temporary change in the composition of Gilchrist Timber Company's work force, and of the standards used when hiring employees, which came to a head approximately three years later.

During the war years, the Gilchrist family and Gilchrist Timber Company were very generous in their support of the United Service Organization (USO). A drive conducted throughout Klamath County during the summer of 1942 raised $8,600 of which $606.76 was donated by employees of the Gilchrist Timber Company. Contributions were received from 174 of Gilchrist Timber Company's 190 employees. H. R. Maguire, Chairman of the USO for Klamath County, wrote in a letter to Frank R. Gilchrist:

> May we offer our sincere thanks and congratulations to you and the 174 employees of the Gilchrist Timber Company, who came through in such a splendid manner. If this same spirit in willingness to cooperate will spread throughout the county, we will have little trouble in reaching our goal.[335]

Throughout the war, government bureaucrats worked at cross-purposes. They demanded production from the producers of wealth such as the Gilchrist Timber Company then, through a system of rationing, made it impossible for them to obtain the raw materials and tools which were necessary to produce the goods the government demanded of them. Henry J. Kaiser, whose Liberty Ships and Victory Ships transported the material with which the Allies defeated the Axis, had to occasionally resort to black-market suppliers in order to obtain the steel he needed to build the ships the government ordered from him, because his ration of steel was smaller than the quantity needed to produce the ships he was required to deliver.[336] The federal government threatened, unless its orders were filled, to take over the timber industry. Many of Roosevelt's "New Dealers" had wanted to do exactly that, so the war provided them a pretext to create a centrally controlled economy, such as Hitler and the National Socialists had imposed on Germany, and the one that Stalin and the Communists had established in the Soviet Union. Frank W. Gilchrist described in a letter to the directors of the Gilchrist Timber Company the federal government's threat of takeover unless its orders were filled. In the same letter, he recounted how labor shortages and the lack of sufficient quantities of supplies and equipment, all created by the federal government's intervention in the economy, made it ever more difficult to fill the orders the government demanded. The mill needed a Caterpillar tractor. He explained that obtaining a new one was out of the question and that to date he'd yet to find a used one. Frank W. Gilchrist then reported that he was no longer able to fill orders for the mill's regular customers.[337]

Frank W. Gilchrist wrote a letter of recommendation dated August 1, 1942, for Hollis Johnston in which he commended him for all aspects of the service he had provided during the design and construction of Gilchrist, Oregon: "I can unhesitatingly recommend the services of Mr. Johnston to anyone who is in need of a man of his qualification and consideration of which might be shown him will be appreciated" Hollis Johnston, on the strength of his work involving the construction of Gilchrist, Oregon, was seeking further commissions involving the construction of communities.[338] He did succeed in obtaining commissions to design then construct other communities, though none proved as successful or as long-lived as did Gilchrist, Oregon, which still exists. The others, which were government housing projects, decayed into squalor, and then were demolished.

Later that summer tires were needed for emergency vehicles which served both the mill and town. Recapped tires were not an option for use on emergency vehicles. Frank W. Gilchrist, in a letter to Don B. Drury dated August 7, 1942, explained why new tires were needed for the emergency vehicles which served the town and mill, then concluded the letter by asking Drury to return the certificates if he couldn't supply the tires.[339]

The frantic search for a Caterpillar tractor continued throughout August 1942. Frank W. Gilchrist wrote a letter dated August 7, 1942, to M. E. Kenfield of the Kenfield Lumber Company in which he expressed the hope that the deal they were negotiating for the sale of a tractor would go through.[340] M. E. Kenfield responded with a letter in which he wrote that the tractor offered would require extensive modifications in order to perform the tasks that the Gilchrist Timber Company would require of it.[341] A week later Frank W. Gilchrist wrote to Charles M. Cooper of W. E. Cooper Lumber Company. He acknowledged receipt of Mr. Cooper's letter, then described some of the types of equipment, bulldozers in this instance, that he needed in order to produce the lumber the federal government expected him to deliver.[342] Five weeks later, used equipment was located. Three used tractors, including a D-8 bulldozer, were purchased from Valley Tractor and Equipment Company of Los Angeles, California, for $16,000. The bill of lading noted that all the machines were in need of overhaul and refurbishing.[343]

Gilchrist Timber Company needed manpower to produce the lumber the federal government demanded of it, for Roosevelt's arguably belated and often ham-handed war effort. Many of Gilchrist's residents, including Frank R. Gilchrist's sons, volunteered, then served with honor and distinction throughout the war. Others chose to wait for a draft notice, and then went on to acquit themselves honorably. Still others elected to apply for deferments so that they could remain behind to participate in the production of the materials the armed forces of the United States needed with which to prosecute the war. Employees of Gilchrist Timber Company were eligible to apply for deferments, based on their status as employees of a company which was active in an industry, the timber industry, which was vital to the war effort. Assisting in the preparation of deferments was yet another administrative chore imposed by the federal government on the Gilchrist Timber Company during the Second World War.

Albert Carmichael, in a letter dated August 29, 1942, reported to Frank W. Gilchrist in the matter of four employees whose deferments had come up for review:

> Doc Warren was just in the office and that his present deferment expires on September 5th instead of the 15th as was your understanding.
>
> I have prepared a 42A for Doc which I enclose herewith. If you want to file it, you may sign it and send it back to me in the enclosed envelope and I will forward it to Klamath Falls. I also enclose a letter to Mr. Heilbronner to accompany the affidavit. Sorry to trouble you with this but I thought we had better do it so as to have it in before the present deferment expires and Doc is called.
>
> The Selective Service Board advised us this morning on the following deferments:
>   Lee Snider has been placed in Class Tentative I.
>   Arthur Sherman has been deferred for 60 days only.
>   Norvill Anderson has been deferred until January 1, 1943.
>
> This will help some but isn't what I had hoped we would get.[344]

Other requirements imposed by the federal government as part of the war effort included fingerprinting all Gilchrist Timber Company employees. The Protection Inspection Program's regulations were the reason for this action. Albert Carmichael wrote an inquiry to Art Burnside & Company in the matter of the possibility of purchasing a fingerprinting set.[345] The system of rationing and price controls did nothing to increase the production of the materials needed to win the war, but did make it necessary for the Gilchrist Timber Company and other members of the productive sector to expend time and resources preparing and then submitting forms demanded by government regulators. Albert Carmichael explained in a letter that the Gilchrist Timber Company sent to all its customers:

> In order to facilitate the matter of securing certain supplies and repair parts which are vital to the operation of our plant, we are required by certain of our suppliers to establish and maintain from month to month the percentage of our products which are being manufactured and used in the National Defense. To establish this percentage, we are enclosing here within a letter, addressed to this Company, on which we have listed the shipments which we made for your account during, 1941, on which we will appreciate it if you will indicate the percentage of each shipment which was used for National Defense, giving us, if possible, the Contract Number and/or the Priority Rating.
>
> Inasmuch as this information must be maintained from month to month, it will be appreciated if, on future orders which you place with us, you will mark such orders "Defense" or "Non-Defense" and show, if possible, the priority rating or defense contract order number.[346.]

Tire shortages plagued businesses engaged in defense work throughout the Second World War. Earl Reynolds of the Klamath County Chamber of Commerce wrote a letter to Frank W. Gilchrist dated September 22, 1942, in which he described an effort the Chamber was making to obtain an larger tire ration for Klamath County's sawmills.[347] The effort was unsuccessful. Gilchrist Timber Company and the residents of Gilchrist spent the war years scrambling for tires. Occasionally, when they left their cars and trucks unattended on the streets or in Bend and Klamath Falls, their tires were stolen.

Frank W. Gilchrist frequently became directly involved in efforts to recruit employees to replace the constant trickle of men who left the Gilchrist Timber Company to serve, either as volunteers or draftees, throughout the Second World War. He wrote to Albert S. Rayner of Hattiesburg, Mississippi, to offer him a job. The offer, besides wages, included training for the position and the offer of a house in Gilchrist, either a one-bedroom house for $22 a month or a four-bedroom house for $30.25 a month.[348] Access to company houses at below-market rents remained a popular benefit the Gilchrist Timber Company offered its employees throughout the company's operations in Central Oregon.

The threat by the federal government to take over timber production continued into the final quarter of 1942. Albert Carmichael, on October 24, 1942, wrote Frank W. Gilchrist to report that while the federal government was not currently planning to take over mills producing pine lumber, it was planning to take over the operation of mills producing fir lumber.[349] Another consequence of temporary standards which existed during the Second World War was that there were residents of Gilchrist who occasionally needed a reminder as to the standards expected of them as tenants. Frank W. Gilchrist, in a notice dated October 10, 1942, and addressed to all residents of Gilchrist, wrote:

> It has come to our attention that trash, tin cans and other rubbish and debris has been carried out and disposed of in places adjacent to the Village of Gilchrist, other than the garbage dump.
>
> As you know, we maintain garbage disposal service for our Village, at no cost to the tenants, and we respectfully request that in the future, if you have things to dispose of, you either take them to the garbage pit, or leave them at the proper place at your home so that when the garbage is -collected it will be taken away and properly disposed of.
>
> It has further come to our attention that green timber has been cut from the property of the Company for wood purposes. Please, in the future, do not cut any green timber for wood under any circumstances and, before going into our woods to cut wood, please call at our office to see Mr. B. V. Wright, and secure from him the proper permission to enter our woods and have him advise you with reference to what timber to cut.
>
> We will appreciate your usual cooperation with the above requests.[350]

A War Saving Flag presentation ceremony was conducted at the foot of the Gilchrist Timber Company's flagpole on Saturday, October 17, 1942. Two War Savings flags were presented to

Saving Bond Flag presentation.
Stewart J. Gilchrist's photo album, Gilchrist Timber Company papers, Klamath County Museum.

Frank W. Gilchrist and Anne Estes, the Gilchrist Timber Company first woman employee, by J. Verne Owens of the Klamath County War Savings Committee in recognition of the level participation of the residents of Gilchrist and the Gilchrist Timber Company in a War Saving Bond drive. Owens reported that 186 of the Gilchrist Timber Company's 190 employees had enrolled in a payroll deduction plan for bond purchases. The extent of their purchases equaled 11.5 percent of the mill's payroll.[351] The article also mentioned that Gilchrist remained known as the "wonder town," because it was still the most thoroughly up-to-date and modern town in the region.

Gilchrist Timber Company received notice on November 30, 1942, that an agreement effective January 1, 1943, had been entered into with Oregon Physician's Service. They, under the provisions of the new agreement, would receive full medical and hospital coverage for illness and off-the-job injuries. The families of employees were provided insurance coverage under the provisions of the agreement, which was automatic for all employees. The premium was $1.20 every two weeks and was collected through payroll deductions, unless an employee filed a rejection slip.[352] Insurance coverage for employees of the Gilchrists had been customary at least since 1912.[353] For other employers, making insurance available to their employees was a benefit which they had not previously offered, which occurred because the federal government's scheme of wage and price controls prohibited them from offering higher wages.

Late during 1942, the United States Army started discharging older soldiers who had secured positions with employers who were engaged in production for the war effort. Frank W. Gilchrist wrote a letter dated December 30, 1942, which confirmed that he had been offered Russell Dieterich, an older soldier who had applied for discharge to enter the employ of a firm engaged in war production, a position with Gilchrist Timber Company.[354] Gilchrist Timber Company, as did every other employer during the Second World War, went farther and farther afield in an unrelenting quest for employees and materials with which to continue producing the materials that the United States needed with which to conduct its war effort.

Frank W. Gilchrist, during the first week of January 1943, reported to the federal government that the Gilchrist Timber Company had no camps or railroads. He informed them that during 1942 the mill had produced 49,150,000 board feet of lumber which was valued at $1,560,000. The Gilchrist Timber Company at the end of 1942 provided 215 men and women with employment. Its payroll for the year just ended totaled $485,000.[355]

A letter dated January 6, 1943, which was written to F. A. Hoagland of La Grande described Gilchrist Timber Company's woods operations and life in Gilchrist, Oregon, during the first weeks of 1943. Fallers were hired in pairs. They were each paid $1.14 per thousand board feet felled. The fallers were expected to buck the logs and to furnish their own tools. F. A. Hoagland was further informed that fallers, as employees of Gilchrist Timber Company, were eligible to live in Gilchrist, though no houses were currently available. It was emphasized in the letter that all houses in Gilchrist were plumbed, wired, and of recent construction. The rent for the houses ranged from $22 a month for the smallest to $30.25 for the largest. Employees of Gilchrist Timber Company could purchase mill waste for fuel with which to heat their houses for $2 a load.[356]

Benjamin V. Wright, in a letter to Robert E. Graham dated January 7, 1943, wrote that Mary C. Maddox had resigned as postmistress for Gilchrist's post office and that she had selected Mrs. Charles C. Maddox as her successor.[357]

Federal agencies demanding information almost identical to that which had already been furnished to other federal agencies was another unremitting feature of the Gilchrist Timber Company's operations during the Second World War. On January 25, 1943, Frank W. Gilchrist reported to Headquarters, Northern Security District, that the mill consisted of a powerhouse, sawmill, dry kilns, planing mill, lumber storage shed, and a garage. One hundred percent of the mill's production went to the war effort. The mill, as of the date of the report, was filling orders of the Denver Medical Depot located in Denver, Colorado, and for the Naval Torpedo Station in Newport, Rhode Island. The mill employed 225 men and women, all of whom had been fingerprinted. Frank W. Gilchrist returned an additional form, which was not completed, with the explanation that it did not apply to the Gilchrist Timber Company since the mill wasn't engaged in the production of aircraft.[358]

Frank W. Gilchrist and Albert Carmichael provided James P. Applewhite with constant and detailed correspondence, the subject of which was the activities in Gilchrist and of the Gilchrist Timber Company. On February 10, 1943, Frank W. Gilchrist wrote to James P. Applewhite that during the preceding four weeks Gilchrist had experienced the worst weather since the Gilchrist Timber Company commenced operations in Central Oregon. Five feet of snow had fallen. Klamath Northern Railroad had been closed for a week. In the woods, logs were buried under a layer of snow so deep that it wasn't feasible to locate, much less bring them into the mill. The weather reduced production during January to 3 million board feet. During the preceding week, the mill had only been able to operate two five-hour shifts. Frank W. Gilchrist reported that the mill had just been able to operate two seven-hour shifts and that he hoped to resume operating two eight-hour shifts by February 22, 1943. The weather's closing of the woods, by curtailing the mill's operations, was reducing the supply of mill waste which was the source of fuel for the Gilchrist Timber Company's powerhouse. The powerhouse generated electricity for both the town and the mill. Frank W. Gilchrist noted that the myriad of taxes imposed by the federal government and state government was taking almost all that the mill earned. He mentioned that the War Labor Board had yet to provide a decision with regard to a request to increase wages which Gilchrist Timber Company had submitted on September 1, 1943. Employees, Frank W. Gilchrist wrote, were frozen in place, that only the U.S. employment agencies were authorized to allow men to leave. Frank W. Gilchrist observed, ". . . When a fellow wished to leave and is forced to stay, his work is not very satisfactory."[359] The letter concluded with news of Rufus Childre. He had recently gone to Portland to have a goiter removed and was not expected to fully return to work for several months. Frank W. Gilchrist then reported family news:

> Frank seems to like his work at Susanville. He does not have much military control as yet but after a few more weeks, he will go to Saint Marys, where he will take strenuous training.
>
> I am trying to get Stewart an appointment to Annapolis but so far I have not succeeded. If I do not get him an appointment, he wants to go into the same division that Frank is in.[360]

During March 1943, personnel shortages remained the subject of Frank W. Gilchrist's correspondence. Frank W. Gilchrist wrote in a letter to A. B. Lytton that positions in the planer mill were currently paying $0.825 per hour but would soon rise to $0.90 per hour.[361] Toward the middle of March, Rob Ward was assisting Edgar Shotts. He was reported as doing well in his new capacity.[362] On March 27, 1943, Frank W. Gilchrist sent a telegram to O. U. Addison of Laurel, Mississippi, in which he informed him that a blocksetter for the night shift was urgently needed. The position paid $1.13 an hour for a forty-eight hour week. Gilchrist Timber Company would pay the traveling expenses of the man hired to fill the position.[363] During the first week of April 1943, Frank W. Gilchrist, in response to further intervention by the federal government in the operation of his plant, wrote to W. C. Anderson Planing Mill Foreman:

> Pursuant to the President's Executive Order, it is mandatory that this Company place all Departments on a 48-hour work week. In accordance with this Order, therefore, beginning Monday, April 5th, the Planing Mill will go on a 48-hour week basis and to accomplish this the following changes are necessary:
>
> The Moulding Machine, Rip Saw and Second Planing Machine will be discontinued. A swing crew of five men will be created to work the Planing Mill and also on the Dry Chain.

Stewart J. Gilchrist and Mary G. Gilchrist Ernst. Collection of Mrs. Mary G. Ernst.

> The wages for this swing crew will be based on the scale for the job which they are doing.[364]

The concessionaires who operated the businesses located in Gilchrist were not bound by the federal government to their enterprises. The concessionaire who operated the Gilchrist Restaurant abruptly departed when another opportunity presented itself. Frank W. Gilchrist entered into negotiations with Maurice H. Ashton who was interested in operating the Gilchrist Restaurant. The prospective concessionaire wanted the use of a house included as part of his agreement in the matter of the restaurant. Frank W. Gilchrist, in a letter dated April 6, 1943, explained that while operating the restaurant made him eligible to rent a house in Gilchrist, the use of one was not included as part of the agreement to take over the operation of the restaurant. Renting a house in Gilchrist involved a separate agreement.[365]

Frank W. Gilchrist, as had his forefather and as did subsequent generations of the Gilchrist family, made a routine practice of assisting his employees through rough patches. This custom sometimes included deferring rent and using his personal funds to make interest-free loans to Gilchrist Timber Company employees. On May 5, 1943, he wrote a letter to K. W. Rolinson, in the matter of a schedule for the gradual repayment of back rent as well as a loan he had made personally to the employee.[366]

The lack of sufficient manpower did not make it easy for Gilchrist Timber Company during the spring and summer of 1943. The Gilchrist Timber Company was barred by the federal government from competing for labor on the basis of higher wages. What it could offer, in addition to insurance, was the rental of houses in Gilchrist at rents which were below the prevailing rate. Albert Carmichael, when offering a position to Virgil Sickels, made a point of emphasizing that the rental of a company house was a benefit which would increase Sickel's disposable income. He further explained to Virgil Sickels that payment of money to the union was compulsory since the Gilchrist Timber Company was now a closed shop.[367] On June 22, 1943, Frank W. Gilchrist was in correspondence with Henry Kieper who had previously been employed by the Gilchrist Timber Company from December 2, 1942, until April 12, 1943, when he was drafted. Kieper was applying for separation from the United States Army so that he could return to work for the Gilchrist Timber Company. Frank W. Gilchrist explained that though the mill was currently short four edgermen, which was making it very much a challenge for the mill to operate at the capacity it needed to mill enough lumber to fill its defense orders, he cautioned that approval of Kieper's request was not certain.[368] During the middle of July 1943, Frank W. Gilchrist reported to Gilchrist Timber Company's board of directors with regard to the mill's chronic labor shortage. In his letter, dated July 13, 1943, he wrote:

> I wish to advise that we were invited to Eugene on last Tuesday, July 6th, to meet with the Conciliation Service, the War Production Board, the War Man Power Commission and the union representative.
>
> In order to get the matter out of the hands of the various agencies, none of whom seem to be the least bit sympathetic to industry, and back into the hand of management and the Standing Committee of the Local Union, I took the position that we would be willing to start on a two shift basis, provided the men were available.
>
> We have, as you know, been down for two weeks now, which has put us somewhat behind with our shipments. However, our order file was in such shape that we have not been traced for shipment of any orders and, if we are able to keep operating, we will soon have our shipments up to date again.[369]

Frank W. Gilchrist reported in the same letter to the Gilchrist Timber Company's board that to date forest fires had not been a problem. He said, "It is my understanding that the army expects to hold maneuvers in our territory for the next two or three months, and that 100,000 men will be brought in to take part in them."[370]

On August 11, 1943, Frank W. Gilchrist hosted a meeting at his home of members of the Klamath Falls and Bend Chambers of Commerce. They met at Gilchrist to develop consensus about the post-war reconstruction of the highway from Weed, California, to The Dalles, Oregon. The road which then existed was paved though it was also narrow and winding. It went around hills rather than through them as did the road following its reconstruction during the early 1950s. Prior to reconstruction, the trip from Gilchrist to Bend, weather permitting, required an hour-and-a-half to complete. During the war years, when the speed limit on Highway 97 was 35 miles per hour, the trip required almost two hours.[371] The time following reconstruction, weather permitting, was reduced by half. Gilchrist became less isolated once reconstruction was completed.[372]

During the middle of August 1943, Frank W. Gilchrist wrote a letter to James P. Applewhite in which he informed him that the mill was currently running smoothly, though manning remained an unremitting source of concern. He also reported that Stewart J. Gilchrist was currently attending classes at the University of California while waiting for the navy to call him to active service.[373] The following month, in a letter to the directors of Gilchrist Timber Company dated September 4, 1943, Frank W. Gilchrist reported that during the preceding month the mill was operating two ten-hour shifts. The mill produced 2,939,150 board feet of lumber at an average cost of $35 per thousand board feet.[374] During May 1941, the production cost per thousand board feet was $25.23. Production costs were rising in spite of federal controls on wages and prices. The federal government paid the Gilchrist Timber Company a price that it regarded as fair for the lumber it received from them.

During the middle of September 1943, Frank W. Gilchrist wrote to L. L. Tannehill of Valsetz, Oregon, to offer him a laborer position with the Gilchrist Timber Company. The position paid $0.90 per hour for a sixty-hour week with time-and-a-half for all hours worked in excess of forty hours per week. He was also offered a two-bedroom house which was rented at below-market rates, which would leave him with more income after paying his living expenses.[375] What was not explained in the letter was why he was writing to the resident of another firm's company town who was, presumably, already in its employ. That he wrote the letter suggests that it was sometimes possible to obtain dispensations from the federal labor boards whose wartime regulations bound employees working for war industries to their current positions.

While the war progressed, the Gilchrist Timber Company managed to continue its tradition of community support. Albert Carmichael received a letter dated October 6, 1943, from L. Parker Martinez of the Modoc Council, Boy Scouts of America, Klamath Falls, Oregon, whose subject was future Boy Scout activities in Gilchrist.[376]

Frank W. Gilchrist's letter dated November 11, 1943, to James Applewhite, who now held the rank of Lieutenant Junior Grade, provided him with an overview of Gilchrist, the mill, and the Gilchrist family. The mill was running two ten-hour shifts. The employees seemed content. They had elected to work on Armistice Day so the mill was operating on what would have otherwise been a holiday. The mill's equipment had come to suffer chronic malfunctions. All of it, including vehicles, was routinely overworked. Repair parts were scarce and additional vehicles were all but impossible to obtain. All orders were, directly or indirectly, government orders connected in various ways with

Mary G. Gilchrist Ernst, Frank W. Gilchrist and Buss. Collection of Mrs. Mary G. Ernst.

the war effort. A shortage of car loaders was slowing the shipment of orders. The weather, though winter was not far off, continued to cooperate so woods operations had not yet been stopped or curtailed by it. The army had conducted maneuvers on Gilchrist Timber Company land. Frank W. Gilchrist reported that he was satisfied with the condition he found it in after they had departed the area. He closed the letter by saying that Frank R. Gilchrist was attending flight training in Pensacola, Florida, and that Stewart J. Gilchrist had passed his physical for the navy.[377]

Frank W. Gilchrist informed J. W. Kerns of Klamath Falls that Gilchrist was less than two-thirds complete.[378] There were no definite plans as to when construction of the town would resume. It wasn't something that demanded much attention given the requirements and limitations imposed by the war effort.

By the end of 1943, cooperation between the

Gilchrist Timber Company, Brooks-Scanlon, and Shevlin-Hixon had become routine. The mills shared personnel and equipment. The cooperation was brought about by the war effort. The apprehension with which seven years before Brooks-Scanlon and Shevlin-Hixon had met the arrival of the Gilchrist Timber Company was set aside.[379] Federal regulators during part of the war years desisted from investigating cooperation among businesses as something potentially criminal in nature. Gilchrist Timber Company supplied two car loads of lumber to a box factory, located in Bend, Oregon, and engaged in the production of ammunition boxes to complete an order which Brooks-Scanlon and Shevlin-Hixon were unable to completely fill.[380] Cordial relations continued among the mills after the Second World War ended. Each had their particular sphere and they had common interests such as the protection of their timberlands from forest fires.

During 1943 the Gilchrist Timber Company's mill, Frank W. Gilchrist reported to his board of directors, produced 40 million board feet of lumber. He reported that demand remained strong, though consisting entirely of orders connected directly or indirectly with the war effort. He further cautioned that he expected wages to rise though the ceiling on lumber prices remained in effect, which could yield a lower return on their investment during 1944.[381]

During early during February 1944, a rumor spread though the mill that the Gilchrist Timber Company would no longer request draft deferments for its employees. Frank W. Gilchrist stated in a memorandum addressed to all Gilchrist Timber Company's employees:

> This is to assure you that it has been the policy of the company for some time to request draft deferments for its employees as, with the present manpower situation, all employees are essential to the operation of the plant, and, as you know, numerous employees have been granted deferments.[382]

During April of 1944, though V-J day was sixteen months in the future, thoughts returned to the future and peace. The question now was when, not if, the Allied powers would defeat those of the Axis. Frank W. Gilchrist wrote to Mr. W. G. Simpson of the *American Lumberman* to remind him that the Gilchrist had been in the lumber business for more than one hundred years, that they would resume normal operations as soon as the war-related restrictions were lifted.[383] Jay M. Allen wrote a letter to Frank W. Gilchrist in which he stated his desire to settle in Gilchrist and declared that he had wanted to do so since September 2, 1941, when he first saw the town.[384]

On April 29, 1944, the Gilchrist Timber Company's board of directors first discussed and then laid the groundwork for the policy of conservation and sustained-yield timber management, which would remain one of the hallmarks of Gilchrist Timber Company for the rest of the company's existence.[385] The forest management practices which grew out of that meeting supplied the mill with a sustainable supply of timber that might have produced indefinitely had external (political) factors not been compounded by changes within the Gilchrist family not intervened. Over the next few years, Gilchrist Timber Company's system of sustained-yield timber management was developed, implemented, and refined. During the mid-1920s, Benjamin V. Wright had been a proponent of sustained-yield forest management. Rufus Childre, then William Steers managed the Gilchrist Timber Company's timberlands. They provided the mill with a steady supply of logs from what was the Pacific Northwest's most remarkable tree farm.

The objective was to assure that the mill was permanent which, in turn, since the Gilchrist Mill was the reason for the Gilchrist town, would assure it permanence, too. The principals of Gilchrist Timber Company, through contacts within the Western Pine Association, were introduced to, and then quickly adopted, a technique known as Single Tree Management. The aforementioned timber management technique, coupled with the purchase of timber from adjacent federal timberlands, made Gilchrist Timber Company's timberlands a self-sustaining tree farm.

The basic unit for single-tree management was a sixteenth of a section, known as a "forty" because it consisted of forty acres. Frank Dushau, when he began acquiring timberland in Central Oregon for the Gilchrist family, did so in forty-acre parcels. Benjamin V. Wright carried on purchasing timberlands in forty-acre blocks, then lived to see

PROOF of ad to appear in the Dec. 12, 1942, issue of the American Lumberman, 431 S. Dearborn St., Chicago, Ill.

Christmas Greetings
to Customers and Friends Everywhere

A Christmas Tribute to Our Employes:

We are proud to announce that in recognition of the co-operation of our employes in the bond sales program this company has been presented with the "Minute Man" Flag.

100% of our present employes are subscribing to the purchase of U. S. Defense Bonds under the payroll deduction plan. Total subscriptions approximate 11½% of our payroll.

Out of a total of 200 men employed by our company, 44 have joined the armed services.

We believe that this is a record of which any company might well feel gratified—and we take this means of publicly expressing our appreciation of this fine spirit of Americanism on the part of our personnel.

GILCHRIST TIMBER CO.
Gilchrist, Oregon
Manufacturers of
Ponderosa Pine

Saving Bond Flyer.
Stewart J. Gilchrist's photo album, Gilchrist Timber Company papers, Klamath County Museum.

the beginning of the forty into the basic unit for the management of Gilchrist Timber Company's timber holdings. The logging superintendent and company forester, under single-tree management, culled the timber. Trees of varying age, as well as trees which were wind-damaged or diseased, were harvested. The remaining trees achieved faster rates of growth. After forty years the Gilchrist Forest was producing more timber of a better quality than had been the case when the application of the technique had commenced.[386] The level at which the forest was capable of producing a sustainable quantity of timber was a significant factor in the size of the mill and the number of shifts operated. It was a determinant in the size to which Gilchrist would grow. Hollis Johnston planned for a town of 1,500. It was never necessary to built Gilchrist to that size.

During the same period as when the change in forest management practices was approved, the directors of Gilchrist Timber Company also approved a change in the firm's leadership. Harry Fletcher was replaced by Frank W. Gilchrist as company president who also continued to serve as general manager of the Gilchrist Mill.[387]

The lumber the Gilchrist Timber Company produced for the war effort went into structures located on bases, forts, and camps as well as into ammunition boxes. Lumber produced by Gilchrist Timber Company was utilized in the construction of the B-29 Super-Fortress Bomber. George N. Comfort wrote in a telegram he sent to the Gilchrist Timber Company on June 14, 1944:

> Now it can be told. Stop. Your lumber has contributed to the successful development and construction of Super-Fortress Bomber B-29. Stop. Best wishes and congratulations to every member of your organization helping to bomb Japan yesterday.[388]

Bond drives were an important factor in financing the Second World War, in part because they involved the civilian population of the United States in the war effort. In a memorandum dated June 13, 1944, addressed to the mill's foremen, Frank W. Gilchrist informed them that the goal for the Gilchrist Timber Company for the Fifth War Loan was $13,275, that to achieve this goal each employee would need to purchase an additional one hundred dollar bond.[389] Forms were included with the memorandum. Two weeks later, in a memorandum addressed to all Gilchrist Timber Company employees which was dated June 26, 1944, Frank W. Gilchrist reported bond subscriptions to date by department, stated that the mill was short of its goal, then reiterated the importance of the mill meeting its target.[390] The Gilchrist Timber Company eventually exceeded its target for the Fifth War Loan. In a letter dated December 14, 1944, to the Oregon War Finance Committee, Frank W. Gilchrist reported that the Gilchrist Timber Company had exceeded its goal by two thousand dollars.[391]

A school board election for the Gilchrist School was conducted towards the end of June 1944. Benjamin V. Wright reported the election results to Fred Peterson who was Klamath County's superintendent of schools. Board members present were B. V. Wright, Mrs. O. F. Blay, and Albert Carmichael. The board was called to order then nominated C. E. Shotts. His nomination was seconded by Mrs. O. F. Blay. He received twenty-nine votes. Mr. Ferguson and his wife, who had also been nominated, received one vote each. Mr. Percy Dixon was elected to the county board with thirty-two votes. A bond issue went down with only five votes in favor.[392]

By early summer 1944, nonofficial use of company equipment had become a problem. Frank W. Gilchrist wrote a memorandum to the Gilchrist Timber Company's foremen in which he discussed the excessive use of the company's red Dodge pickup and Chevrolet stake truck for nonofficial purposes. Rationing remained in effect, so it had become ever more difficult to obtain spare parts, tires, and fuel for the vehicles. All too often such items were only available if one used informal suppliers.[393]

The federal government's scheme to bar employers from raising wages, then binding men to their current positions so as to assure firms engaged in defense work a labor force wasn't successful. The men, especially those who had only been hired because of the labor shortage created by the war, resented it, particularly since the Kaiser Shipyards located near Portland, Oregon, were allowed to pay higher wages than was the Gilchrist Timber Company. On June 30, 1944, the Gilchrist

*Mary G. Gilchrist Ernst, 1944.
Collection of Mrs. Mary G. Ernst.*

Timber Company was short ten men for laborer positions. The jobs paid $0.90 per hour for a forty-eight hour week with time-and-a-half for all hours in excess of forty hours per week. A vacant planer feeder position paid $0.93 per hour. The vacant tail sawyer position paid $0.95 per hour for a sixty-hour week with time-and-a-half for all hours per week in excess of forty.[394]

Frank W. Gilchrist wrote a letter dated July 5, 1944, to Harry Fletcher which discussed the ongoing labor shortage, the federal government's ever more oppressive regulations and, of particular significance for the future of the Gilchrist Timber Company, select cutting:

> We are having the devil out here. There are no men coming in for employment and we are losing one or two all along. This has hurt us some and I am afraid, unless we get some new men, our production is going to be curtailed somewhat. We lost two days in the planing mill last week and we were down the first two days this week in the planing mill, starting up again this morning. We have about a million and a half feet in our dry shed and we can take care of twice that much if are forced to do it, but during these times I hate to build up an inventory and I am just hoping something will happen so we will be able to ship our product out.
>
> The new government regulations which go into effect with reference to shipment of lumber after August 1st, are not entirely clear to me but it looks as if we will have to ship about twice as much as we have been in the past direct to the government.
>
> We are getting ready to mark our trees for selective cutting in the woods. I have given considerable study and we may be starting off on the wrong foot, but it looks now as if we will not take over one-third of the timber at the first cutting. This may run up our costs but, the way conditions are now, we can afford to try this kind of experiment.[395]

Frank W. Gilchrist reported in the same letter that repainting of the section of Gilchrist located south of the school and mall had commenced. He also wrote that Frank R. Gilchrist would spend another two weeks in Seattle before proceeding to a station near Pasco, Washington.[396]

At the end of July 1944, Frank W. Gilchrist reported to the Gilchrist Timber Company that the operating costs for June were out of line, that he expected the same (if not worse) for July and shuddered to think what August would bring. Shipments were off, too, because of the manpower shortage. He wrote in the matter of the Gilchrist Timber Company's manpower crisis:

> The manpower situation is so acute that we never have a full crew in any department and at times some departments we are forced to shut down one in order to keep the other one going. The net result is that our costs have increased considerably and we are not about to ship our production.
>
> I thought when the newer ruling went into effect July 1st that possibly the United States Employment Service would furnish the lumber industry with some men since lumber is one of the critical war materials at the present time. Up to the present the Employment Service has

*Mary M. Gilchrist.
Collection of Mrs. Mary G. Ernst.*

been able to give very little help and they do not even give us any encouragement about help in the future. We have been going along the best we could but I am sorry to say that prospects of economical operation for the next few months do not look very good.[397]

The letter concluded with a report that the mill would shut down on August 25 to give the employees a vacation week, to allow timber for repairs, and to make the mill ready for the winter months. Operations would resume on September 6.[398]

The labor shortage had not abated with the coming of autumn. Frank W. Gilchrist wrote to James Applewhite that on the preceding Thursday he had shut the mill and green chain down, then shifted the crews to work in the shipping and planing departments. There was some positive news reported, too. The repairs to the steam turbine had been satisfactory. The turbine's efficiency had increased. The paving contractor had finished on September 11 and had performed satisfactorily.[399] Less than a week later, Frank W. Gilchrist wrote to A. T. Blackwell of McNary, Arizona, to offer him a position as millwright with Gilchrist Timber Company. The position paid $1 per hour with time-and-a-half for all hours over forty hours per week. The millwrights, he reported in the letter, were averaging fifty hours per week. Access to a house in Gilchrist was mentioned as an incentive. Rents ranged from $22 per month for the smallest to $31.75 for the largest. Water, electricity, and garbage were included.[400]

*Mary M. Gilchrist.
Collection of Mrs. Mary G. Ernst.*

During the first week of October 1944, Frank W. Gilchrist wrote to James P. Applewhite, then currently serving with the 50th USN Construction Battalion. In the letter he mentioned that Floyd Green and Dee Warner had contracted with Gilchrist Timber Company to load boxcars. They were paid $0.32 per thousand board feet. As of the date of the letter, October 4, 1944, they had loaded in excess of half a million board feet of lumber. Mr. Gilchrist expressed the hope that at last the shipping bottleneck was eliminated. He then noted that it was too soon to tell if the selective cutting which had been carried out had been done correctly. The close of the fire season was reported, too.[401]

During the middle of the month, the Gilchrist Timber Company recognized the thirty-five members of the mill's staff who had served continuously since the mill commenced operation during October 1939. Some men who were there when Gilchrist Timber Company commenced service would return once they were released from military service. Earlier during 1944, Alva Hendry returned to Laurel, Mississippi, where he went into business for himself. He remained in Laurel until his death in 1985 at the age of 83.[402] F. A. Hendry and his grandsons went on to make careers working for the Gilchrist Timber Company, then its successors. During the autumn of 1944, Benjamin V. Wright died. He had represented Gilchrist interests in Central Oregon since 1925 and was significantly involved in the construction of Gilchrist, the mill, and Klamath Northern Railroad. William T. Sherman, after years of service for the Gilchrist-Fordney Company then the Klamath Northern Railroad as Engine Number 204's engineer, returned to Shady Grove, Mississippi, a community located on the northern edge of Laurel. He farmed there until his death in 1960. He was succeeded by Dowell Garner as the Klamath Northern Railroad's engineer.[403] The group of men and their families who came west with Frank W. Gilchrist were succeeded by a generation, led by Frank R. Gilchrist, a significant percentage of whom were the sons of the men who had helped build Gilchrist.

Fuel shortages continued as long as wartime rationing remained in effect. On October 23, 1944, Frank W. Gilchrist wrote a letter to the rationing board which had jurisdiction of Mr. J. P. Adams of Vanport, Oregon. The purpose of the letter was to obtain an authorization for him to drive to Gilchrist to go to work for the Gilchrist Timber Company.[404] In a letter that Frank W. Gilchrist wrote to James P. Applewhite during the final week of October, he described how the mill was operating eight hours a day, six days a week, then noted that the labor shortage continued.[405]

Frank W. Gilchrist also mentioned in the same letter that selective cutting was going well. He cautioned that it still remained too soon to judge whether or not the new forest management practices would prove successful for Gilchrist Timber Company. Gilchrist Timber Company, since it operated its logging trucks entirely on its own, privately owned road system didn't need to pay registration fees for them to the State of Oregon. It could operate the largest available trucks, too, since it wasn't restricted by the weight limits that the State of Oregon imposed on trucks which operated on state and county roads. There was one place where Gilchrist Timber Company trucks occasionally crossed, but did not travel on, a state road (Highway 97). The State of Oregon, Frank W. Gilchrist explained to James P. Applewhite, was attempting to use crossing the highway as a basis to collect registration fees from the Gilchrist Timber Company and to regulate the size of the company's log trucks. The Gilchrist Timber Company responded by building an underpass for its trucks which was located approximately one mile north of Gilchrist. He concluded the letter by reporting that Frank R. Gilchrist was in San Diego where he was waiting to join his ship.[406]

In the next letter Frank W. Gilchrist wrote to James P. Applewhite, there was news that the manpower situation was no worse than had previously been the case. This, after several years of a state of near-constant crisis involving manpower, was very good news. At least, the problem wasn't growing worse. During October 1944, the mill shipped three million board feet. Frank W. Gilchrist remarked that this was the first time in many months that shipping equaled production. The team contracted to load boxcars was making a difference. The departure of Ted McMahan from the service of Gilchrist Timber Company was noted as was the fact that William T. Sherman, Engine Number 204's engineer, would move back to Laurel on December 15, 1944. Frank W. Gilchrist then mentioned that he intended to contact A. L Griffin to see if he was interested in becoming Number 204's engineer. The first snowfall of the season fell on November 2, 1944. It didn't stick and was a mere dusting. Frank R. Gilchrist had reported on board the USS *Belleau Wood* (CVL-24). He was serving as one of her pilots. Frank W. Gilchrist explained that his eldest son had recently returned to San Diego after spending a few days underway on board her.[407]

Motion pictures were one of the tools the Roosevelt administration used to maintain support for the war effort, toleration of rationing, high taxes, and restriction on the freedom of employees to change jobs as well as wage and price controls. On November 10, 1944, Maj. Harry D. Williams, an Industrial Services Officer, showed a film entitled *Timber To Tokyo* at the Gilchrist Theatre. Films of this type were routinely shown at the Gilchrist Theatre throughout the Second World War.[408]

USS Belleau Wood (CVL-24).

War bond purchases by Gilchrist Timber Company employees remained high even after almost three years had elapsed since the attack on Pearl Harbor. One of the results of Roosevelt's centralized control of the nation's economy was that there was little available to buy. Frank W. Gilchrist reported in a letter to the Oregon War Finance Committee, whose subject was the 6th War Loan Drive, that Gilchrist and the Gilchrist Timber Company had raised $10,425 in bond sales, that it had exceeded its quota of $9,960. The bond sales total included Saving Stamps which had been purchased by students attending the Gilchrist School as well as the town's concessionaires and their employees.[409]

At the end of January 1945, Frank W. Gilchrist reported in a letter to Lt. James P. Applewhite that the mill had shipped 34 million board feet during 1944. He also noted that the mill was fully staffed, though the woods crew was not made up of the sort of men who were of the quality he desired.[410]

During the Gilchrist Bowling League, teams were raised by the townsite, planing mill, shipping, sawmill, woods, fallers, and dry sorting. The season consisted of twenty matches. The first match didn't count. Its purpose was to establish each team's handicap. Each team furnished a scorer and a man or two whose purpose was to watch the foul lines and to call fouls. Matches were conducted at 8 p.m. on Mondays, Tuesdays, and Thursdays. At the end of the season, the members of the teams gathered together for a party which was funded by a nickel per match fee each team member was assessed. Bowling on the two-lane alley located in the Gilchrist Mall has remained an enduring feature of life in Gilchrist.[411]

Frank W. Gilchrist proposed the construction of a small log mill to the Gilchrist Timber Company's board of directors in a letter dated February 17, 1945. A small log mill was suited for the milling of lodgepole pine, a species that is common to Central Oregon and which produces smaller logs than those typical of ponderosa pine. The facility was not constructed though a comparable, much more sophisticated mill was constructed thirty-four years later by Frank R. Gilchrist.[412]

USS *Belleau Wood* (CVL 24) departed Pearl Harbor on January 30, 1945, for Ulithi where she joined Task Force 58.[413] Frank R. Gilchrist

The Club membership card of Mr. Applewhite. Collection of Mrs. Mary G. Ernst.

remained assigned to her as a pilot. Over the next six months, he would see action in a succession of several of the bloodiest battles of the Pacific Theater to include Okinawa and Iwo Jima. His squadron was decimated during the first six months of 1945. On the day of his twenty-first birthday, Frank R. Gilchrist was providing air support for the soldiers and marines who were fighting for Okinawa.

On March 13, 1945, Frank W. Gilchrist wrote to Harry Fletcher with news of his son and of the operations of the Gilchrist Timber Company. The snow was almost entirely gone. He expressed the hope that within the next ten days no ice would remain on the millpond. Frank W. Gilchrist wrote of his eldest son, "We hear from Frank every once in a while. He is with the 58th Task Force and has seen some action." Frank W. Gilchrist also reported that Stewart J. Gilchrist had arrived at University of California (Berkeley) where he was serving in the United States Navy's V-12 Program.[414]

During the preceding months, Gilchrist Timber Company's labor situation had stabilized if not become satisfactory. Once again there was action by the federal government which boded ill for the operation of the mill. In this instance, the government had changed the rules for conscription to include all males, even ones working for war industries, between the ages of eighteen and twenty. By 1945 the United States had more or less exhausted its reserves of manpower. Preparations were underway for the invasion of Japan, for Operation Olympic and Operation Coronet. The Japanese had already proved to be a determined adversary who, unlike the Germans, routinely fought to the death rather than surrender. Kamikaze attacks had already commenced and had proven an effective weapon. One had struck USS *Belleau Wood* (CVL 24). The closer Allied forces came to Japan's home islands, the more inevitable seemed its defeat, the more tenaciously the Japanese forces fought. For just Operation Olympic and Operation Coronet, it was projected that the Allied nations would sustain 2 million casualties and that the Japanese would sustain 10 million casualties. Frank W. Gilchrist, in a letter to Harry Fletcher, discussed the effects of the changes to the federal government's conscription policies:

> This new change in drafting procedures has raised the dickens with the lumber industry, and if They do take all the boys between 18 and 29, well will lose twelve men. I am afraid it is going to be a very serious handicap on our operations. I was in Klamath Falls last week for a day and the consensus of opinion down there was that all the boys would not be drafted but that they were sure to take two or three. There is nothing much to do about it, but there have been no people looking for work for some time now.[415]

In 1945 Oregon's state government had not yet degenerated to the level it would sink to, during the 1970s and onward, of implementing laws and regulations which intended to destroy the forest products industries. It did do harm through its sloth. The matter of Gilchrist Timber Company logging trucks crossing, not driving on, Highway 97 is a case in point. Frank W. Gilchrist continued in his March 13, 1945, letter to Harry Fletcher:

> I am going to Portland tomorrow to see if I cannot work out some scheme whereby we can get a permit to cross the Dalles-California Highway with our logging trucks. Last fall, when the matter was taken up, everyone thought that the legislature, which is in session now, would pass an amendment to the Oregon Highway Act which would give logging trucks permission to cross highways without putting a license plate on them. The legislature failed to do it and the highway department will not give us permits to cross the highway unless we license our trucks. Our trucks are oversize in that they have 10' bunks instead of 8', and it is unlawful for the State to license trucks of that size. I do not know what the outcome will be, but it may be that we will have to build an overpass over the Dalles-California Highway.[416]

Winter's hold on Gilchrist Timber Company lands eased enough by March 26, 1945, that the woods crew was able to return to work. It was reported that, after weeks of idleness or performing other work, they were glad to do so. The naval air station at Klamath Falls was short of fuel. It purchased 135 cars of hog fuel from Gilchrist Timber Company. The sale didn't yield much but did clear the hog fuel pile. Frank W. Gilchrist wrote to Lt. James P. Applewhite that he feared the mild winter boded ill for the coming fire season. In the same letter he reported that the Gilchrist Timber Company would build an underpass for its trucks since Oregon's state government was adamant in its determination to bar the Gilchrist Timber Company from crossing Highway 97 with its logging trucks. Stewart J. Gilchrist, it was anticipated, would complete his coursework at Notre Dame by July. Mary Geales Gilchrist was home for Easter vacation. The demand for lumber remained high. A tight labor market, coupled with the chronic challenge of obtaining cars to ship orders out in, made the mill's operation an ongoing succession of close-run crises.[417]

Mrs. Frank W. Gilchrist wrote the American Red Cross on April 4, 1945, to report that the residents of Gilchrist and Crescent had raised $1,243.53 for the organization. This sum included $100 that she had personally donated. The residents of Gilchrist never stinted in their support of the armed forces throughout the whole of the Second World War.[418]

The labor shortage continued into the spring of 1945. On April 16, 1945, C. E. Shotts offered a position as blocksetter and extra sawyer to Glen Fisk. The position paid $1.205 per hour with time-and-a-half for all hours in excess of forty hours per week. The position was on the day shift which was then working fifty hours per week.[419]

The influx into Gilchrist of new hires resulted in some peculiar problems, such as individuals who did not understand the town's customers or unwritten rules. An example was the presence in Gilchrist of residents who did not know the places from which one should not fish. Frank W. Gilchrist wrote and distributed a memorandum dated April 20, 1945, to the residents of Gilchrist. The memo stated, "Our insurance prohibits fishing in the pond from boats, rafts and logs. Fishing is only allowed from the banks."[420] Still other individuals who did fish from the banks of the millpond would walk across Mr. Gilchrist's backyard while fishing. Frank W. Gilchrist, even though his labor force now included many newcomers, still maintained the Gilchrists' custom of taking an active interest in the well-being of their employees. On May 1, 1945, Frank W. Gilchrist wrote to Audrey Kiehn. He began the letter with an expression of sympathy, then told her not to concern herself with the rent due on her house until she was able to return to work.[421]

During the middle of May 1945, the Gilchrist Timber Company furnished Brooks-Scanlon, in response to their request, with five years of log production costs. Brooks-Scanlon was considering shifting from railroad logging to truck logging.[422] Gilchrist Timber Company then had more experience than any other mill in Central Oregon conducting logging using log trucks. Gilchrist Timber Company, Shevlin-Hixon, and Brooks-Scanlon continued to maintain amiable relations after the war ended.

On May 14, 1945, the mill's whistle sounded to announce V-E Day. German's National Socialist government was destroyed as well as defeated. The war continued in the Pacific. Plans were already in place, in motion, to move entire army corps to the Pacific for the invasion of Japan. The prospect of more years of war tempered the jubilation that followed victory in Europe. Mrs. Ernst described her brother Frank's motivation for choosing to serve as a carrier pilot as well as his experiences with his squadron while deployed and while training in the Pacific Northwest:

> He was stationed in Walla Walla, he was a fighter pilot, so the squadron flew down here all the time. Mother and Daddy were "Mom & Pop" to the Squadron. Their first week out, half of them were killed, that included their commanding officer. So they wrote home and said, "Mom, if one more person dies we'll be home within the week." They didn't lose anymore thank goodness. That was a rough week for him I'm sure. He became a fighter pilot because he said, "I only have me to decide. I don't have someone with a wife or kids to think about." I thought that makes sense, its just you. Oh, now they just flew over, they didn't get to land. One time they flew over the mill and that night they called daddy, he said I don't mind you flying over it, but when you fly under it you get out of there. They'd cut between the Jack Pines, and they saw me at the Post Office one time and they kept dive-bombing until I came home. So I came home, stood out there in the yard and watched. They flew down from Pasco, and when they had to put in flight time they'd come here and bother

Members of VF-30 and (right to left) Frank W. Gilchrist, Mary G. Gilchrist Ernst, and Frank R. Gilchrist. Collection of Mrs. Mary G. Ernst.

us and then tell us about it. It was fun and nice having them around too.[423]

During July 1945, the USS *Indianapolis* delivered to Tinian the components for the atomic bomb which was detonated over Hiroshima. No one in Gilchrist knew of this event. The expectation was that the war would continue until 1948 or 1949 and that the country had ahead of it a much larger-scale repetition of the carnage which had occurred when fighting occurred on Iwo Jima, then Okinawa. Frank W. Gilchrist's correspondence reflected an expectation of several more years of war with its attendant problems. In his letter dated July 24, 1945, to Harry Fletcher, he wrote that on July 13 for the first time in two years he had all three of his children home together. Stewart J. Gilchrist had departed for Fort Schuyler on the preceding Thursday. Frank R. Gilchrist was to report to a new squadron on August 10.[424] The expectation was that both his sons as well as those of many of his employees would take part in the invasion of Japan. All stoically endured and prayed that Japan would soon surrender.

Frank W. Gilchrist, in his July 24, 1945, letter to Harry Fletcher, next discussed the mill's operations. The manpower shortage remained the mill's biggest trouble. Meddling by the federal government continued to exacerbate the difficulties the Gilchrist Timber Company faced when filling the federal government's lumber orders:

> The War Labor Board has given the employees with five years' continuous employment another week's vacation so we will be down, I imagine, the week. This will cut our production by six or seven hundred thousand feet, but there is nothing we can do about it.[425]

As always, weather remained a concern. The weather during July of 1945 was such that Gilchrist Timber Company's timberlands, as well as those of its neighbors, were fairly dry. Several lightning-caused fires had occurred but no green timber had been destroyed.

Japan's surrender during mid-August was unexpected. Once again the mill's whistle sounded to announce the news. Now the Gilchrist employees and the sons of Gilchrist employees who had gone off to war could return home.

> A bunch of them were here on VJ Day. They'd all signed up to go back, they'd finished their tour of duty but they told the commanding officer that if they'd take them they'd go back with him.
>
> VJ Day came and they went down and changed that tune. Daddy had the keys to the store so he sent Frank up to get steaks out of the meat market, the next day they said someone's been in here and daddy said it was me, I sent the

Mary G. Gilchrist Ernst, Frank R. Gilchrist and Buss, 1945.
Collection of Mrs. Mary G. Ernst.

kids up to get steaks last night and I cooked them all steaks. They were a happy bunch.⁴²⁶

Frank W. Gilchrist wrote Lt. James Applewhite on September 8, 1945, to report that Frank R. Gilchrist had resigned his commission and was expected home within a matter of days. He also wrote, "Stewart is at home on leave and has to report outside San Francisco on September 15 for duty outside the continental United States so I presume he will take a cruise."⁴²⁷

Next in his letter of September 8 to James P. Applewhite, Frank W. Gilchrist discussed the mill's labor situation. The mill remained shorthanded. The leadership of the union which represented the mill's staff was planning on striking. It was a component of the union's plans for an industrywide strike of Pacific Northwest lumber producers. The strike was something that the rank and file did not support. The majority of the mills in Klamath County had already had their employees go out on strike. Frank W. Gilchrist wrote, "The story today is that all lumber producers in the Northwest will be down on strike by October 1ˢᵗ. It is rather hard for me to believe that due to the fact that so many people are being laid off but one can't ever tell."⁴²⁸

There were men who, at the same time as the International Wood Workers of America's leadership was preparing to take the rank and file out on strike, sought early release from active service with the United States Army to return to work for the Gilchrist Timber Company. Frank W. Gilchrist wrote a letter, dated September 13, 1945, to Lt. McGrew. The purpose of the letter was to request Edward H. McConnell's early release from active duty so that he could return to work for the Gilchrist Timber Company in his former capacity of edgerman.⁴²⁹

Frank R. Gilchrist, Mary G. Gilchrist Ernst and Frank W. Gilchrist.
Collection of Mrs. Mary G. Ernst.

Labor strikes began to occur throughout the timber industry of the Pacific Northwest almost as soon as World War II ended. Within two months of the Japanese surrender, millworkers had struck for higher wage rates and forest products manufacturers were urging that lumber prices be deregulated and the Office of Price Administration be abolished. Mill owners reasonably argued that production was stifled by government-controlled price regulations, because it prevented them from charging the equilibrium market price, reflected only by the price charged by black market lumber dealers.[430] The lumber industry was in turmoil. Controls by the federal government on the sale of lumber were lifted effective September 30, 1945.[431] Price controls remained in place so what the federal government was actually offering was a license to sell lumber at a loss to all comers. While the lumber manufacturers argued with the government in favor of the restoration of a free market or, at the very least, price increases, their employees struck for higher pay rates.[432] At the outset of what would prove to be a protracted work stoppage, Mr. Gilchrist offered his employees an agreement that would have given them whatever settlement the other timber companies eventually agreed to give their employees, providing that they did not strike against Gilchrist Timber Company. The agreement was never accepted by the mill's labor force, but it did continue to operate for one day until pressure from the regional office of the International Wood Workers of America compelled the employees of the Gilchrist Timber Company to strike.[433]

Frank W. Gilchrist, in a letter to the directors of the Gilchrist Timber Company dated September 25, 1945, described the circumstances surrounding the start of the strike, including the lack of support it had among the rank-and-file members of the union:

> Last Sunday night about seven o'clock two of the union representatives called on me at my house and said the plant was going on strike Monday morning. I came to work a little before starting time.
>
> There were two pickets on the East side, or rather the town side, of the highway and, upon arriving at the mill, I found men coming to work. At seven o'clock we had enough men to start the mill as usual and the green chain and stacker. The mill ran until noon and the men went home for lunch and, when they returned, the picket line had been changed from the East side to the highway to the west side of the Highway and there were about seven men standing in the middle of our entrance road to the mill with a sign and, as the men drove by or walked by, the pickets held up the sign and showed it to the men. We had a few more men report after lunch so we were able to start the dry chain.
>
> The organizers of the A. F. of L., in Prineville, called me and wished a meeting last evening at five o'clock. We had the meeting and, after considerable discussion, they said they were going to bring outside pickets to stop our employees who wanted to work from working. The meeting was adjourned upon my statement that we would run if the men at the plant were available. In a little while, I gave it more thought and decided I did not want any of our employees hurt and probably some of the outside pickets which the union would bring in would use violence to stop the men from working or coming to work, so I went and got hold of the union representatives and offered to give them the additional week's vacation, which we were going to give next week, starting this morning and concluding next Tuesday morning, October 2nd. They put the proposition to their membership and they agreed to do that, so this morning the entire operation is down and will be down until next Tuesday morning.
>
> We were the only A. F. of L. plant that operated at all in six States and I would have continued to operate if I could have gotten police protection for our employees who wished to work. It was impossible to do that so, I gave the vacation and I hope that something will be done between now and next Tuesday so that we can start up. We are in a little difficult position, due to the fact that in order to dry out lumber in the kilns, we will have to use up practically all of our fuel and, if the mill does not start up next week, we will have to start our diesels in order to keep water and what few lights are necessary to protect our property.
>
> As things develop, I shall keep you people posted but, from the looks of things now, I would say maybe our plant would be down until Spring.[434]

Gilchrist Timber Company's involvement in the regional timber industry strike, which neither management nor most of the Gilchrist Timber Company's employees had wanted, was unlike that of any of the other firms which had been struck. Gilchrist Timber Company employees who lived in Gilchrist were at liberty to remain in their houses if they wished to do.[435] Many, particularly those employees who had come west with the Gilchrist Timber Company, did so. The ones who left were more often than not war-time hires who had no loyalty to the firm More likely than not wouldn't have been hired had war-related labor shortages not existed. The Gilchrist grocery store continued to extend credit to the residents of Gilchrist even though virtually the heads of its household were striking, albeit unwillingly, against the Gilchrist Timber Company. The mill was, however, very much idle. Frank W. Gilchrist wrote to Harry Fletcher, "We have shut down the plant lock, stock and barrel and have let all the office force go with the exception of Albert . . . By the first of November we will have no pay roll except those men I expect to use when we start up."[436]

Activity that did occur at the mill was subdued. It focused on maintenance and electricity generation for Gilchrist and Crescent. Frank W. Gilchrist, in a letter to Joseph B. Knapp, discussed cutting lodgepole pine poles. He wrote that though the mill was currently shut down by a regionwide strike that he expected to continue until spring, there remained a demand for lodgepole pine poles, that he thought he could assemble a crew to harvest them.[437] The mill's powerhouse generated electricity by burning hog fuel, which was waste produced in the course of milling logs. Electricity generation, without hog fuel, was accomplished by using diesel-powered generators. Gilchrist Timber Company, prior to the strike, had been supplying Crescent with electricity. This practice wasn't feasible during the strike.[438] Mill maintenance and the lodgepole pine pole business was the subject of the letter Frank W. Gilchrist wrote to LT. James P. Applewhite on December 13, 1945. He wrote that rotten timbers had been found near the head rig, that he planned to replace them the following March or April, and that he was currently busy changing the resaw into a head rig. The pole business, pending board approval, was on track. The strike continued and he anticipated that it would take several months to restart the mill. He reported that Jud Willingham was conducting maintenance work on Klamath Northern Railroad's tracks. Frank W. Gilchrist concluded the letter by noting that his daughter only had four days off for Christmas vacation.[439] The board of directors, towards the end of December 1945, approved Frank W. Gilchrist's proposed changes to the mill and instructed him to proceed with the pole business. It was his expectation, Frank W. Gilchrist wrote in a letter to James P. Applewhite, that the strike would continue until the spring. He observed that the men were anxious to return to work.[440] The strike, Albert Carmichael wrote in a letter dated December 31, 1945, to Cal L. Adams, was something that neither the leaders or employees of the Gilchrist Timber Company had desired. They were dragged into it by outsiders.[441]

During January 1946, much of the correspondence consisted of letters in which Albert Carmichael explained that the mill, because of the strike, wasn't currently accepting orders, that they expected to resume operations during March or April. In response to a letter from Mrs. Anderson, owner of Dealers Lumber and Coal Company, Albert Carmichael wrote that Frank W. Gilchrist remembered him from his childhood in Laurel.[442]

This strike was the only occasion in the history of the Gilchrist Timber Company's Central Oregon operations that it had to suspend the production of lumber because of labor turmoil. It is a testimony to the relationship the Gilchrists had with the employees, of the manner in which they treated them, that the Gilchrist-Fordney Company was only struck once. That strike occurred during April of 1918 and was also a consequence of the effects that World War II and attendant government meddling were having on the market's operation.[443] This strike was six months long; it began in September of 1945 and ended on April 9, 1946. Along with the Gilchrist Timber Company, every other sawmill in the Pacific Northwest whose labor force was unionized was unable to produce lumber because their employees had struck.[444]

The employees of Gilchrist Timber Company had been on strike for almost three months when the mills of the Klamath Basin began to reach agreements with their striking employees. The

Hines Lumber Company of Burns, Oregon, agreed upon a settlement with its workers on December 12, 1945.[445] Strikes occurring in the Klamath Basin were settled on December 29, 1945.[446] The next month, on January 12, 1946, Shevlin-Hixon reached an agreement with its workers.[447] While the mill owners were making agreements that would bring their striking employees back to work, the Office of Price Administration (O.P.A.) was near the end of its existence. Lumber prices were raised by the O.P.A. on February 21, 1946.[447] With the end of strikes and price controls, the production of forest products for domestic consumption began to increase throughout the Pacific Northwest. Though the sawmill workers of Central Oregon and the Klamath Basin had ended their strikes and gone back to work, the labor force of the Gilchrist Timber Company continued to strike against its employer. Gilchrist waited for winter to end, so that logging operations could be resumed, before settling the strike.

Gilchrist Timber Company made an agreement with its employees, which ended their strike, on April 9, 1946.[448] The strike the employees had staged as a response to pressure from affiliated union locals lasted six months. It was led by leaders of the Gilchrist Union Local and was the longest of all the sawmill strikes which took place in Central Oregon in 1945 and 1946. During the strike, Gilchrist Timber Company employees continued to live in company-owned houses and were still extended credit by the Gilchrist supermarket. Some of the employees of the Gilchrist Timber Company left its town and service during the strike, but most remained. When the company resumed operations in April of 1946, after a strike which had been prolonged by the winter weather,[449] price controls had been eased and the demand for lumber was increasing. Once the strike was settled, the population of Gilchrist, the Gilchrist Timber Company, and its employees resumed the patterns that had characterized their lives before the outside world had intruded and compelled a strike that neither the management nor the workers of the Gilchrist Timber Company had sought or desired.[450] The effects of federal price and wage controls as, arguably, the decisive factor in precipitating the strike, presaged the much farther reaching and long-term effects that state and federal regulations would have forty years later on the Gilchrist Timber Company, the Pacific Northwest's forest products industry, and the town of Gilchrist. With the strike settled, the Gilchrist Timber Company reassembled its work force. The mill and town now entered the period that was its golden age.

CHAPTER V

1946-1982

Gilchrist in its Heyday

"Some days in late August at home are like this, the air thin and eager like this, with something in it sad and nostalgic and familiar..."

— The Sound and the Fury
by William Faulkner

During the months of the strike, Gilchrist employees and sons of Gilchrist employees who had served during the Second World War began to return home to Gilchrist and to take positions with the Gilchrist Timber Company. These demobilized veterans, for the next forty years, would constitute Gilchrist Timber Company's core as well as setting the tenor for the town. Frank R. Gilchrist returned home during the fall of 1945. He worked for Gilchrist Timber Company for a year, went back to Oregon State University to resume working on his degree, then returned home to Gilchrist and the Gilchrist Timber Company. James Applewhite, after resigning his commission, returned to work for Gilchrist Timber Company. Among the many sons of men who had come west with Gilchrist Timber Company in the late 1930s who returned to Gilchrist and the Gilchrist Timber Company were Alva Hendry, Jr., F. A. Hendry, Robert Sherman, Arthur Sherman, and Charlie Shotts. As of March 14, 1946, the list of veterans who had returned to Gilchrist and the employ of the Gilchrist Timber Company included David Penny, Harry Garner, Lester Snider, Oren Bowman, Woodrow Edgar, J. T. Edgar, Lee Snider, Wyatt Ward, Bill Anderson, Huelan Foreman, Lambert Speed, William T. Sherman, Albert Ford, Ellsworth Caproon, W. C. Foreman, and Kenneth Christianson.[451]

There were new hires following the strike who would make their mark on Gilchrist and the Gilchrist Timber Company. Their number included Clem C. Caldwell, Jr., of Yelgar, Allen Parrish, Louisiana, William Steers, and Wayne Ernst. William Steers, said James Childre, was the discovery of his father, Rufus Childre. William Steers was Rufus Childre's successor and was with him in the woods marking the corners of forties when he suffered a fatal heart attack. Wayne Ernst, before entering the employ of the Gilchrist Timber Company during 1946, served in the Pacific Theater as a technical sergeant. Wayne Ernst assigned to a medical hospital unit. He earned the Bronze Star for his service. Wayne Ernst became Frank R. Gilchrist's second in command and married Mary Geales Gilchrist. Their sons (Gil, Will, and John) were crucial in the continued existence of Gilchrist, Oregon.

During the spring of 1946, the mill came back into full operation. The shipping and planing departments resumed operations on April 8, 1946.[452] By April 3, 1946, the mill had fully resumed operations. The reconstituted crew was proving satisfactory.[453] Orders were satisfactory too. Albert Carmichael reported to Frank W. Gilchrist:

> Have been pretty busy for the last couple of weeks getting orders in shape for shipment, etc. We received a $4.50 advance effective April 4th, and this was taken into account in pricing our orders as it became effective before we started the planing mill on the 8th. We shipped 16 cars last week and mailed our first invoices on Saturday, so we should be getting returns by the end of this week.

The saw mill is cutting 95,000 feet per day now and we still have some ice in the logs.

When the logs are all free of ice, etc., I believe we will get 100,000 feet or better.[454]

Other mills during the spring of 1946 continued to experience labor turmoil. Gilchrist did not. The fir mills of the Pacific Northwest were going out on strike. There were rumors of additional wage demands. These new labor troubles bypassed Gilchrist and the Gilchrist Timber Company. Albert Carmichael wrote, "Union activity is rather quiet. They are letting us alone for the most part."[455]

Businesses in Gilchrist were reopening too. Most had closed during the strike. Albert Carmichael reported to Frank W. Gilchrist that an agreement had been entered into that he'd reopen the barbershop on April 22, 1946. Dutch Stover reopened the theatre on May 1, 1946.[456] The beauty shop reopened April 1946. The concessionaire, Mrs. Spencer, operated the shop on the basis of a 20 percent commission on sales to the Gilchrist Timber Company. Terms were subject to renegotiation if they proved unsatisfactory. Mrs. Spencer purchased the shop's fixtures and equipment. She was, Albert Carmichael reported to Frank W. Gilchrist, an accomplished beautician and businesswoman.[457] The Snack reopened too. Frank W. Gilchrist wrote to Mr. E. F. Ritche, "I have been able to open up The Snack. It is not just exactly what I wanted but I was desperate so made arrangements."[458] Spring cleanup was underway. The Club reopened on Saturday, June 8, 1946, at 1:30 p.m. The hours were 6:30-9 p.m., Tuesday through Friday; 1:30 p.m.-midnight, Saturday; and 1:30-9 p.m., Sunday. Dues were $1 per person per month for everyone over sixteen. Children under sixteen were admitted free. Mr. and Mrs. J. P. Gibson were in charge of The Club's operation.[459] Albert Carmichael wrote, "We have had several days of real spring weather already and it is surprising how dusty it is getting already. The people in the Village are beginning to clean up their yards and burn trash, etc., so I guess spring is here."[460] Gilchrist's streets were paved during the early 1970s.

During the spring of 1946, James P. Applewhite, who had returned to Gilchrist Timber Company to serve in the same capacity as he had prior to the Second World War, answered a letter from A. J. Glassow, Brooks-Scanlon's general manager. In his letter to Brooks-Scanlon's general manager, James P. Applewhite furnished a schedule of wages, by position, which Gilchrist Timber Company was paying its woods crew. Brooks-Scanlon was shifting from using trains to using trucks to move its timber from the woods to its mill. Gilchrist Timber Company was the region's most experienced firm when it came to using trucks for logging operations.[461] The cooperation among the mills that flowered during the Second World War continued afterwards. Employees of the mills routinely exchanged information pertaining to such matters as sharpening saw blades during the winter when the logs came up from the pond frozen.

By the spring of 1946, all the houses in Gilchrist were occupied. It was noted when Carl Wilson was offered a position with the Gilchrist Timber, that no houses in town were currently available.[462] Plans for the town's expansion were under consideration. None of the houses constructed based on those plans was available until 1946.

Frank W. Gilchrist, writing to Gilchrist Timber Company's board of directors on May 16, 1946, was able to report strong demand for the mill's lumber. Lumber was averaging a sale price of $40 per thousand board feet. The employees seemed contented. Turnover was low since the strike ended. The logs the mill was currently cutting had been in the pond throughout the strike. The logs yielded wet, low-quality hog fuel. The wet hog fuel the powerhouse had been receiving was adversely affecting powerhouse operation. The wet fuel made it necessary to operate the mill on Saturdays to produce enough fuel to maintain steam over the weekend. This increased costs.[463] By the middle of May, the mill was back to 75 percent of its usual production.[464] The mill's labor force, as of May 27, 1946, numbered 106 men. An across-the-board pay increase of five cents an hour went into effect on June 10, 1946.[465]

Children using the pond as a play area, as well as a place to fish, was a matter of concern for the residents of Gilchrist and Crescent as well as the Gilchrist Timber Company. Frank W. Gilchrist, in a letter dated May 21, 1946, informed his sawmill foreman, C. E. Shotts, "Will you please

1946-1982 – Gilchrist in its Heyday

*Logging operations, late 1940s.
Collection of Milton Hill.*

instruct your pond men to keep all children off the logs, log booms and out of the pond house at all times."[466]

The bank which had been planned for the Gilchrist Mall wasn't established in it until the 1990s. Prior to the establishment of a bank in La Pine during the late 1970s, the nearest banks were in Bend or Klamath Falls. Bank hours were limited by federal regulations imposed during the Franklin Roosevelt administration. These regulations made it impractical to visit a bank unless the business was very important, since doing so required taking time off from work and also required the better part of a day to travel to Bend or Klamath Falls, transact the business, and return home. The grocery store and drugstore made up for the lack of a bank by cashing checks free of charge. The post office sold money orders. The lack of a bank usually wasn't a hardship. The grocery store and drugstore, because of the role they played in absence of a bank, kept large sums of cash on hand to coincide with paydays. Albert Carmichael informed Frank W. Gilchrist on October 22, 1946, of a robbery which had occurred the preceding Friday night. The nighttime burglary of the Gilchrist Mall was one of the biggest robberies that had occurred, as of the date of the incident, in the history of Central Oregon. The burglars entered the Gilchrist Mall by forcing doors which provided access to a central hallway that led to the back of the grocery store, and by a similar route to the drugstore which was at the opposite end of the Gilchrist Mall. The criminals used nitroglycerine to open the safes located in the drugstore and the grocery store. The total loss was estimated at $14,000.[467] Approximately $7,000 in cash was taken. The burglars also made off with all the liquor store's cased whiskey as well as two guns, a radio, and some jewelry.[468] The burglars were never caught. Some papers from the drugstore's safe were found in a gravel pit near Mowich.[469]

On November 4, 1946, The Club was used as the location for Gilchrist's voting booths. This had been the usual location from which Gilchrist's electorate cast their ballots.[470]

During the autumn of 1946, Gilchrist Timber Company was steadily increasing the number of employees. On September 29, 1946, the mill employed 133 men. The following month, on October 27, 1946, the number had grown to 138. The interest the Gilchrist family took in the well-being of their employees and their families, which they did without engaging in the intrusive and annoying paternalism which was the downfall of the progressive company town operators of the nineteenth century, is one of the reasons why Gilchrist, Oregon, was the model company town. An example of the Gilchrist family's taking time to assist the employees of the Gilchrist Timber Company occurred on November 21, 1946. James E. Griffin wanted to go into debt to place a large order with the Montgomery Ward Company. Frank W. Gilchrist developed a budget for James E. Griffin which made it possible for him, by purchasing one or two items every two weeks rather than ordering all the items at once, to acquire the goods he desired without going into debt.[471] At Christmastime, besides a Christmas card for each employee, the Gilchrist Timber Company also gave each of their employees a turkey. By the 1970s, twenty-two years was the average amount of time an employee of the Gilchrist Timber Company had been with the firm. Mrs. Mary G. Ernst explained that the reason Gilchrist Timber Company's employees were so loyal was more than competitive wages and benefits including access to quality housing at below prevailing market rents. It was that the Gilchrists took a personal interest in their employees and treated them decently and as individuals.[472]

During January 1947, Clem C. Caldwell, Jr., of Yelgar, Allen Parrish, Louisiana, joined the Gilchrist Timber Company. He had served with the United States Navy during the Second World War. He was assigned to Gilchrist Timber Company's machine shop. His duties included making repairs to Engine Number 204 and serving as Walter Rigdon's assistant. He was subsequently assigned to the powerhouse which, in 1947, still furnished power for the town as well as the mill.[473]

Use of the design for Gilchrist's service station for other Texaco stations was the subject of a letter, dated March 10 1947, that Hollis Johnston sent to Frank W. Gilchrist.[474] Texaco, following the Second World War, built a series of service stations which were outright copies of Gilchrist's service station. Others were variations of its design.

During early 1947, preparation and planning continued for the construction of another series of houses. Gilchrist Timber Company acquire two new ten-passenger buses which were used to transport the woods crew.[475] The decision was made during 1947 that the Gilchrist Timber Company would not engage in the production of lodgepole pine products.[476] Mill operations continued satisfactorily during the summer of 1947. Forest fires were not a problem that summer, though there was a boxcar shortage which was expected to grow more acute during the months ahead.[477] Selective cutting had been established since 1944 as the basis for the Gilchrist Timber Company's timber management practices. Frank W. Gilchrist discussed the ongoing process of refining selective cutting timber management in a letter to Gilchrist Timber Company's board of directors which was dated October 23, 1947.[478] During 1947, Frank R. Gilchrist left Oregon State University to resume working for the Gilchrist Timber Company as a lumber salesman who worked out of Memphis, Tennessee. Frank R. Gilchrist, during his time in Memphis, met Helen Gertrude Hill, a native of Memphis. They married during September 1949, then moved back to Gilchrist where Frank R. Gilchrist continued his apprenticeship by working as his father's special assistant.[479] Gilchrist continued to attract favorable attention from individuals who visited the town. Mrs. W. P. Lyon, in a letter dated September 30, 1947, wrote to Frank W. Gilchrist that she had recently stopped by Gilchrist for lunch. She was very favorably impressed by what she saw and she now wanted to move there.[480]

Mr. Wilmer McCallum was offered a position by C. E. Shotts in November 1947. The position paid $2.30 an hour. A similar position prior to 1940 paid $0.98 per hour.[481] The increase in wages was a function of inflation as well as the mill's increasing productivity.

Gilchrist continued expanding during November 1947. Frank W. Gilchrist requested sketches from Hollis Johnston for "our house, Jim's and the guest house."[482] An apartment complex had been constructed for the teachers who were assigned to the Gilchrist Schools.[483] The apartments were located south of the school's shop and science room. Another complex of apartments, located northwest of the school and east of the highway patrol substation, was subsequently constructed after Gilchrist School expanded. Rents for the apartments were collected monthly by the school district from the teachers' salaries and remitted annually to Gilchrist Timber Company[484] A substation for the highway patrol was constructed in Gilchrist during this period. Assignment to this substation, which included game enforcement, became a coveted assignment.[485]

Christmas 1947 was observed with a holiday which ran from the 24th thru the 29th of December. The powerhouse, which supplied both the town and mill with electricity, was excluded. Each employee also received a turkey which was available for pickup at the Gilchrist supermarket commencing on December 24.[486] This was a part of Gilchrist Timber Company's routine which continued more or less without significant alteration for the next forty-two years.

Gilchrist Timber Company was renowned for the quality of its lumber. Other Central Oregon mills such as Brooks-Scanlon and Shevlin-Hixon produced more lumber. What Gilchrist Timber Company did was to produce better-quality lumber. Its ponderosa pine lumber was used for finish work such as paneling. Nelson F. Brown of Dixie Lumber Company wrote, "We have almost completed disposing of a car of ponderosa pine and do want to say it is one of the finest cars of lumber that I have received in this yard."[487]

During January 1948, wages paid by the Gilchrist Timber Company rose by five percent. This was an across-the-board increase.[488] The mill shipped 3,183,188 board feet during January 1948. The sales price for the mill's output averaged $74.79 per thousand board feet. Demand was described as satisfactory as was the collection of accounts receivable.[489] The mill's gross profit for 1947 was $990,000. More of the mill's net profits, with the repeal of Roosevelt's more oppressive tax rates, were available for reinvestment and for disbursal as dividends. The investment Ralph Gilchrist and Frank W. Gilchrist had made in Central Oregon more than ten years before was at last paying off.

Frank R. Gilchrist, by the spring of 1948, had settled into his routine as a lumber salesman. During February 1948, he dispatched his eldest son to New Orleans to verify that lumber shipped to the New Orleans Manufacturing Company conformed to specifications. Frank W. Gilchrist wrote

Mr. Ed Hill.
Collection of Milton Hill.

regarding his son's service to the Gilchrist Timber Company as one of its lumber salesmen:

> We are shipping your orders fairly promptly and I hope some of the lumber will have arrived by time you make your second round. As I told you, I think that if the people would ever buy some of our pattern stock, they would be well pleased with it and it would sell. Nelson Brown, I am sure, has told you that when you called on him in New Orleans, so it would help us if you could sell some Commons run to pattern.[490]

On the morning of April 6, 1948, Engine Number 204, along with one car load of lumber, jumped the tracks just south of Crescent. It tied up the railroad for two days. The incident was uncommon enough that Frank W. Gilchrist mentioned it in a letter to his eldest son.[491] In the same letter, he noted that four inches of snow had fallen since the preceding Thursday and that snow was still falling as of April 6.

Wage rates as of April 1, 1948, had doubled since the Gilchrist Timber Company commenced operations. Blocksetters were paid $1.8075 per hour. Millwrights earned $1.5525 per hour. The hourly wage for a sawyer was $2.3275. The mill's least-skilled employees (clean-up men and laborers) were each paid $1.425 per hour.[492]

The construction of Rainbow Circle, which was then known as the Prenco Subdivision, was well underway by May 8, 1948. The houses located on Rainbow Circle were war surplus. They were of the type which was constructed to provide housing for officers. The houses were moved to Gilchrist. What was not known until after the houses were in place and occupied was that they weren't as represented. They were described as having been designed for regions with hard winters. They weren't. Robert F. Johnson and Associates of Portland, Oregon, was the general contractor. A. H. Barbour & Sons, who had previously done work on the mill, shopping center, and houses of

*Engine 204.
Collection of Louie Jordan.*

Gilchrist, was a subcontractor.[493] The houses were ready for occupancy by July 10, 1948. The cost per house was $14,000. Mrs. Ernst commented that she thought her father had overpaid for them.[494] The houses rented for $45 a month. Tenants were charged 1½ cents per kilowatt hour for electricity. The houses were located at the north end of Gilchrist. The streets they were on were curved, unlike the other streets in Gilchrist, all of which were straight. The houses, until the mid-1970s, were not painted Gilchrist Brown; hence, the name Rainbow Circle. The houses had an almost whimsical quality. They had flat roofs and a style of architecture that suggested something from southern California and contrasted with the Norwegian Modern style which was employed when the rest of Gilchrist was constructed.

Frank W. Gilchrist wrote in a memorandum to the tenants of Rainbow Circle:

> The new houses will be completed before July 10th. As they are completed Mr. Sample will deliver the keys to your house to you and one week after the keys are delivered, rent will be charged.
>
> We think the houses are very complete and hope that you will enjoy living in them. If, for any reason, you wish to change your mind about occupying one of these houses, do not hesitate in telling us as there are several applications on file for same.
>
> It will be appreciated if you and your wife will sign this letter in the spaces provided and return the same to us, if the terms are acceptable.[495]

Louie Jordan, who raised a family in one of the Rainbow Circle houses and who was growing up in Gilchrist when they were delivered, recalled the delivery of the houses and life in them:

> To ease up on the housing situation, they bought the houses in Rainbow Circle. As for those houses, I can remember sitting on my bicycle and watching them being trucked in

there. I would say it was around 1950 or 1951. Each one of those houses was delivered in three pieces. They had been bought out of a military housing complex in California. They were built out of 2x2's, not 2x4's or 2x6's. Inside of the walls, they were not insulated. They had a flat roof, with about six inches of tar on the top. So, they were hard to heat. In later years, they put a gabled roof on them, to help in the winter time, and during the summer, when the sun would just cook that hot tar. Fairly recently, they blew insulation into the walls and put metal siding on them.[496]

The construction of Gilchrist, which had started in 1938, was now completed. The town, other than the addition of the police substation and the construction of two churches, would grow no larger, had no reason to grow larger. The number of houses in Gilchrist, as of 2011, has neither increased nor decreased since the construction of Rainbow Circle was finished. On August 10, 1948, Frank W. Gilchrist wrote to S. I. Ritchey, district manager for the California-Oregon Power Company, that Gilchrist consisted of approximately 160 dwellings, a business district, and a consolidated school for grades one through twelve. He also noted that water was furnished and not charged to the town's tenants.[497]

Beginning on October 1, 1948, Gilchrist Timber Company began billing its tenants two cents per kilowatt hour. What this change entailed was switching from the previous arrangement, which had been established in 1938, of a basic charge for electricity then additional charges for each major appliance such as a washing machine or a refrigerator.[498]

Gilchrist Timber Company received many peculiar requests. Jack R. Blair, in a letter dated January 20, 1949, proposed buying all of Gilchrist Timber Company's pine cones. Frank W. Gilchrist explained that the timber company had no pine cones for sale then suggested he might meet with more success if he contacted the Forest Service.[499]

Rufus W. Childre, early during March 1949, returned from a tour of the Crossett Experimental Forest. He had been dispatched there to gather information that might be of use to Gilchrist Timber Company in managing its timberlands. He was favorably impressed by what he saw. He concluded his letter with, ". . . I did a little wandering around on my own just to see if the stuff really grew like they had been telling me. In another week or so I probably would have been as enthusiastic as they were about it."[500] Rufus W. Childre was a self-trained forester. His son credits him with discovering Bill Steers, who subsequently became Gilchrist Timber Company's woods superintendent. By the late 1980s, Gilchrist Timber Company lands, using individual tree management, were yielding 15 to 20 million board feet of timber each year. The quality of the timber was exceptional and, due to Gilchrist Timber's Company's forest management practices, the land might have indefinitely produced similar annual yields of timber.

During April 1949 Frank W. Gilchrist received a letter from Charles E. Ogle of Associated Forest Industries of Oregon. The letter was a harbinger of things to come. In it he described the first steps of a process which would culminate four decades later with the near destruction of Oregon's forest products industry and the impoverishment of the communities the mills supported, before forest policy was made to suit the aesthetic sensibilities of environmentalists who lived in cities and suburbs hundreds or even thousands of miles away from the individuals whose lives and communities their policies impoverished.[501]

During the spring of 1946, Mary Gilchrist's health began to deteriorate to such an extent that she required hospitalization and was unable to carry out her normal duties involving a membership and fund-raising drive for the Red Cross.[502] Two months later Frank W. Gilchrist reported to Gilchrist Timber Company's board of directors that his wife's health was starting to fail.[503] Mrs. Mary Gilchrist, following a prolonged illness, died during the summer of 1949. She had married Frank W. Gilchrist when she was sixteen and he was nineteen. They had three children, had spent most of their lives as husband and wife, and were always very much in love with each other. Mary Gilchrist was returned to Laurel, Mississippi, and was buried at Lake Park Cemetery. A few years later, Frank W. Gilchrist joined her there, to rest beside her in the soil of Mississippi, where they had met then fallen in love all those years before. Mary Geales Gilchrist, following her mother's death, took charge of running the Gilchrist family household.

While Frank W. Gilchrist was back in Laurel for his wife's funeral, he received a letter dated May 13, 1949, from Frank X. Seaton of the American Red Cross of Klamath Falls, Oregon. Frank Seaton produced a swimming program for the children of Gilchrist and Crescent. Frank W. Gilchrist, upon his return to Gilchrist, in his response dated July 28, 1949, said only that it was probably too late in the season for such a commitment for the current year.[504] Over the years the millpond had been used for boating, swimming, and fishing. During the winter it had been skated on, traversed by snowmobiles, and been driven on by the occasional car and at least once a lawn tractor.

The state patrol substation, located at Gilchrist, went into operation during the first week of August 1949. Gilchrist Timber Company constructed on the north side of the street bordering the north side of school, across the street from Our Lady of the Snows, a Catholic Church, and abutting the east side of Highway 97, a rectangular building which housed an office, garage, and two apartments. It was staffed by two state patrol officers. One was responsible for game enforcement, and the other was assigned traffic enforcement duties.[505]

On October 16, 1949, the tenth anniversary of the day when Gilchrist Timber Company commenced operating the mill, a dinner was held at The Club. It was attended by the men who had been continuously employed by Gilchrist Timber Company since the mill first commenced operations. Twenty-two men, not counting Frank W. Gilchrist (the host) plus wives or family members were present. Most of these men had sons who were soon to begin their own careers with Gilchrist Timber Company and as residents of Gilchrist.

Later during the summer of 1949, Frank W. Gilchrist received a letter from A. R. Entrican, Directory of Forestry, State Forest Service, Wellington, New Zealand. A. R. Entrician had visited Gilchrist and the Gilchrist Timber Company late that spring. He wrote of the mill and town:

> Your shopping and community center at Gilchrist also impressed me as being the best of its size that I have seen anywhere. We also are endeavoring to establish a similar center in one of our forest communities, and again I should be grateful if you could make your plans for these buildings available.
>
> I should be quite happy, of course pay any costs for printing and air mailing.[506]

Ralph Gilchrist and Frank W. Gilchrist intended to build the best possible town for their employees. There is no reason to suspect they ever imagined that their little mill town would have international influence. That, however, is what occurred.

On September 19, 1949, in what is yet another example of the Gilchrists taking a personal interest in the well-being of Gilchrist Timber Company staff, Frank W. Gilchrist sent his wishes for a speedy recovery to Robert W. Anderson and, in an eminently practical gesture, also included a check for $300.[507]

Gilchrist was recognized yet again as a model community in an article published during the first quarter of 1950 by *Unasylva: An International Review of Forestry and Forest Products*. In the article, which was illustrated with photographs, it was noted that Gilchrist was a complete community that included provisions for all employees' routine needs as well as a school, theater, restaurant, lounge, library, and churches.[508]

On July 18, 1950, so as to meet near-term financial requirements, Gilchrist Timber Company amended its charter. Capital stock was increased to $3 million with 30,000 shares issued. On September 5, 1950, all timber company shares were still held entirely by the heirs of Frank W. Gilchrist (1845-1912).[509] Each of the three branches, descended from Frank W. Gilchrist, held 9,306 shares. The branches were Grace Gilchrist Fletcher; the Estate of Frank R. Gilchrist, Frank W. Gilchrist, Successor Trustee; and Hester Hill Gilchrist and Joseph A. Vance, Jr. Trustees under the will of Ralph E. Gilchrist. Each branch had representation on the board of directors though only one branch, that of Frank R. Gilchrist, lived in Gilchrist, Oregon.[510] Over the next forty years the shares, though remaining within the extended family group descended from Frank W. Gilchrist, became more dispersed among relatives who had limited contacted with Gilchrist, Oregon.

During the early 1950s, more of the men

departed who had come out west during the late 1930s with the Gilchrist Timber Company from Laurel, Mississippi. Albert Carmichael moved to Memphis, Tennessee, where he established himself as a lumber salesmen for the Gilchrist Timber Company. His years of service with the Gilchrist-Fordney Company and Gilchrist Timber Company, including service as office and sales manager, made this a potentially very lucrative move for him. It was also a position which required extensive automobile travel. During 1954 Albert Carmichael, while off on a business trip, died following a motor vehicle accident.[511] Dan Denham, who had worked for the Gilchrist-Fordney Company before coming west with the Gilchrist Timber Company, retired during 1950, then moved back to Laurel where he died at the age of 79 on September 29, 1956. Walter W. Smallwood, the master mechanic who had gone to work for the Gilchrist-Fordney Company in 1920, also retired in 1950. He decided to remain in Central Oregon. He died at the age of 82 on October 25, 1964. Ervin Griffin died of a heart attack while on the job, loading logs, on October 22, 1951. His wife and children, following his death, returned to Mississippi. Jud Terrell, yet another employee whose connection with the Gilchrists began with the Gilchrist-Fordney Company, retired in 1952. He was serving as sawmill superintendent at the time of his retirement. He was another of the team who came west in the late 1930s with the Gilchrist Timber Company and who decided to remain in Central Oregon. He died, aged 70 years, at Saint Charles Hospital on June 2, 1957.[512] Many of the Gilchrist Timber Company employees who decided to remain in Central Oregon are buried in Bend at the Pilot Butte Cemetery or else in the adjoining Greenwood Cemetery.

During the early 1950s, television came to Gilchrist. Louie Jordan recalled that the first television sets in Gilchrist were sold at the Gilchrist supermarket: "Around 1950 or 1951, we bought our first black and white TV from that grocery store."[513] In Gilchrist, as in other company towns of the Pacific Northwest, the television tended to undermine the town's social life. Some residents of Gilchrist started staying at home rather than bowling at the Club. The arrival of the VCR and DVD players reduced the Gilchrist Theatre's business. Even more residents of Gilchrist stayed at home with their television sets once reception improved and expanded with the coming of cable and satellite systems.[514]

Also during the early 1950s, improvements to Highway 97 were completed. The road became straighter and wider. It was possible to travel the roads at higher speeds. Moreover, the price of gasoline, in relative terms, was declining. The amount of time to travel from Gilchrist to Klamath Falls or Bend was significantly reduced. The effect of the both the coming of television and the improvements to Highway 97 was to reduce Gilchrist's relative isolation.

In 1951 small parcels of Central Oregon real estate were placed on sale. They were located near La Pine and were sold by Burdette and Pearl Lechner of La Pine. Though these sites, and others sold by similar developers, were offered as summer cabin sites, people, including employees of the Gilchrist Timber Company, established permanent year-round residences. Some chose to live on their own property as a matter of preference. Others did so because they wished to provide themselves with housing after they retired, when they would no longer be able to live in company-owned houses. The woods near Crescent, as well as around La Pine and to the south of it, began to be divided into small parcels of land, whereas previously there had been only empty sections of wood and pasture.[515] People, including some who had taken jobs with the Gilchrist Timber Company, were moving into Central Oregon because they were attracted to the region for reasons in addition to economic ones.

During 1952, Wayne H. Ernst began working for the Selective Service Board as a volunteer. He continued to work as a part of it into the 1970s. On March 1, 1972, it recognized him for having completed twenty years of service.

In 1953, Frank R. Gilchrist, who had returned from Memphis with his wife, was selected to serve as the Gilchrist Timber Company's sales manager. His experience as a lumber salesman prepared him for the position which, since Albert Carmichael's departure, had been vacant.

The marriage of Mary Geales Gilchrist to Wayne H. Ernst on May 9, 1953, is remembered as one of the most memorable events of Gilchrist's

Robin-egg blue tent used for wedding reception of Wayne H. Ernst and Mary Geales Gilchrist. May 9, 1953. Collection of Mrs. Mary G. Ernst.

golden age. The wedding ceremony was conducted on a floating dock, located on the millpond, which served the Gilchrist house. Among attendees at the wedding was Mr. Frank W. Gilchrist's mother as well as virtually the entire population of the town plus most employees of Gilchrist Timber Company and Klamath Northern Railroad. A tent was erected over the tennis court which was located east of the Gilchrist house. The reception was held inside the tent. Louie Jordan, who attended the reception, recalled:

> They got married between the Gilchrist house and the pond, on the dock down there. After that, they had a big reception in a huge circus tent, they erected over the tennis court, between the house and the highway. It was huge.[516]

Mrs. Ernst recalled her reception:

> We put a tent over the tennis courts. Leslie Norlin, who was our gardener, got plants and trees and decorated it. He sold those to people in town. He got things that would grow here and used them for our wedding, and then people bought them. I guess some of them still have them, I don't know. We were married right here on the lake then had the reception on the tennis court. It was a big wedding, but it was fun.[517]

From the marriage of Mary Geales Gilchrist and Wayne H. Ernst came five children, two daughters and three sons. Their sons, Wayne G. "Gil" Ernst, William L. "Will" Ernst, and John S. Ernst would figure prominently in Gilchrist's future. Their first daughter, Mary Geales Ernst, born on January 4, 1957, died tragically the following year on June 18, 1958. She rests at Greenwood Cemetery beside her father and her brother Will. Jan K. Ernst, youngest of the Ernst children, married Clifford Houck and went on to a career with Oregon Parks and Recreation Department.

Frank R. Gilchrist and Helen Gilchrist adopted four children: Frank Rust Gilchrist, Jr., James Applewhite Gilchrist, Benjamin "Benji" Hill Gilchrist, and Susan Gilchrist-Hosack. Benji Gilchrist worked for the Gilchrist Timber Company for many years and was vice president at the time

Mary and Frank Gilchrist.
Collection of Mrs. Mary G. Ernst.

1946-1982 – Gilchrist in its Heyday

*Mary and Wayne Ernst. May 9, 1953.
Collection of Mrs. Mary G. Ernst.*

Flora and Frank Gilchrist.
Collection of Mrs. Mary G. Ernst.

of the sale of Gilchrist Timber Company to Crown Pacific. He still resides in Central Oregon.

With the marriages of Frank R. Gilchrist and his sister, Mary Geales Gilchrist, as well as the marriages of sons and daughters of the contingent who had come west with the Gilchrist Timber Company during the late 1930s, the next generation of Gilchrist, Oregon, was started.

Time continued to scythe down the members of the contingent which came west with Frank W. Gilchrist to build Gilchrist and its mill, then to live in and work there. Engine Number 204, after forty-six years of service with the Gilchrist-Fordney Company then the Gilchrist Timber Company, was sold for scrap in 1955 when the decision was made to change Klamath Northern Railroad's motive power from steam to diesel. This change was yet another part of a national trend. Engine Number 204's successor was a seventy-ton diesel which was purchased new from General Electric.[518] Engine Number 204's tender remains in service on the Klamath Northern Railroad as a snowplow. Louie Jordan, who knew Engine Number 204 from growing up in Gilchrist, then as an adult employed by Klamath Northern Railroad, said of the engine's fate:

> When they brought in 205, the GE diesel electric, 204 was cut up for scrap. We all thought it should have been put on the lawn in front of the mall, but when you do that there is a tremendous liability for climbing on it and getting hurt.[519]

On April 4, 1956, at 5:30 a.m., Frank W. Gilchrist suffered a massive heart attack, and then died. He was 53 years old. His coffin was taken back to Laurel, Mississippi, to Lake Park Cemetery where he was buried beside his wife. During the preceding month, he had begun to experience chest pain and had been admitted to Saint Charles Hospital a few days prior for a checkup. Perhaps the strain of leading the Gilchrist Timber Company through the Second World War, coupled with the loss of his wife, had at last taken their toll. Ironically, his coffin, accompanied by Wayne and Mary Geales Ernst and Frank and Helen Gilchrist, started back to Laurel on the tracks of the Great Northern Railroad, the railroad whose intransigence was the reason that Klamath Northern Railroad connected with Southern Pacific rather than the closer tracks of the Great Northern Railroad.[520] *The Bend Bulletin* wrote of Frank W. Gilchrist:

> Frank Gilchrist during his too-short lifetime had enjoyed many things. He has his share of personal tragedy and loss. He had more than the normal share of friends.
>
> Frank Gilchrist made friends easily. He kept them long. He was a most generous nature. His hospitality epitomized the South in which he spent most of his early years. His graciousness as a host could not be exceeded.
>
> Frank Gilchrist enjoyed many of the things in life to which others only aspire. He had been willing, even eager, to share those experiences and possessions with his many friends.
>
> Frank Gilchrist's generosity had been extended to those who worked for him. A few years before World War II the town of Gilchrist, across Highway 97 from the mill of the Gilchrist Timber Company, founded.
>
> But due to the personal interest in the community of Frank Gilchrist and members family who made their home there Gilchrist is unlike any company town in the logging West.
>
> Gilchrist is a model town.[521]

Mrs. Ernst said of her father and mother as parents and of her father and his accomplishments:

> They were great parents . . . they were young. They were 16 and 19 when they married and all three of us children were born before my mother was 21. So, we had very young parents . . . . They just cared and daddy took a lot of pride in things.[522]

On April 30, 1956, following a special meeting of the directors of Gilchrist Timber Company, Frank R. Gilchrist was elected to the board of directors, filling the vacancy created by his father's death. The following year, on January 22, 1957, the board of directors met for their regular meeting. Officers were elected. Frank R. Gilchrist was selected to serve as president. The son of Harry Fletcher, Thomas G. Fletcher, was elected vice president. Wayne H. Ernst was voted in to serve as secretary. Joseph A. Vance, Jr., was chosen as treasurer. Frank R. Gilchrist and Wayne H. Ernst,

Above: Engine 204 with cars.
Collection of Mrs. Mary G. Ernst.

Left: Engine 204's name plate.
Collection of John S. Ernst.

until his sudden death by heart attack in 1983, led the Gilchrist Timber Company in the decades ahead.[523]

During the final years of the 1950s Our Lady of the Snows, a Catholic Church was built in Gilchrist, across the street from the Highway Patrol Station, on a lot donated by the Gilchrist Timber Company.

Life in Gilchrist from the period following the strike into the late 1980s was idyllic. It was secure too. Gilchrist Timber Company, unlike other Central Oregon mills, did not layoff employees. The employees did not go out on strike. The mill's labor force was largely hired on the basis of referrals by current employees. Louie Jordan recalled:

> They never hired off of an employment board. If I said, "My brother, my uncle, or my friend, needs a job", he got a job. You couldn't just go there and get a job. You had to be recommended. It was that way for years and years.[524]

The mill's employees constituted a sort of fraternity that grew trees, manufactured very high-quality lumber and had access to an exclusive town. In consequence thereof, esprit de corps existed.

> Growing up in Gilchrist was great. You never had to lock your car. You never had to lock the door to your house. They were all good people... It was that way for years and years. It was a nice small town. Everybody knew everybody else. I delivered papers there for many years. We had a nice school. It was small. We had twelve rooms there, the office, gymnasium, and the cafeteria. Every house was full. There was a waiting list to get into company housing. Company housing was great. They paid everything. You would pay big bucks for a three bedroom house.
>
> It was $35 a month. When I graduated from high school, in 1954, we had a huge graduating class.
>
> We had five boys and four girls! Then, I worked on the Railroad that summer and then I worked for the Crescent Oil Company. I worked there for about three years, and then went into the Air Force for about ten years. After that, I came back and worked in the woods for about five months, and then an opening on the Railroad came up, and I got that. I spent 32 years on the Railroad.[525]

Gilchrist's homogeneous population, size, and relative isolation, coupled with Frank R. Gilchrist's leadership, all resulted in a unique community that it once seemed would exist indefinitely.

Gilchrist Timber Company, early during the summer of 1964, was recognized by the state of Alaska for the numerous donations it had made in response to the Good Friday Earthquake which occurred on March 27, 1964.

Charlie Shotts, son of Charles Shotts and grandson of C. E. Shotts who had come west from Laurel with the Gilchrist Timber Company during the later 1930s, was born on December 30, 1949. He recalled coming of age in Gilchrist during the 1950s and the 1960s:

> Well, from my perspective, it was a great place to grow up. You had the outdoors, with a lot of hunting and fishing, and living in the forest. It was a pretty close knit community and you pretty much knew everybody in town. Kids came in from other towns on school buses and you got to know them. It was a fun place to grow up. We didn't have kindergarten. I started first grade, and each grade had one teacher. I went through elementary school. I thought I got a relatively good education there.
>
> You started at one end of the building and moved down to the other end, by the time you were in twelfth grade. Of course, you were out the other end of the school, and went on with your life. It was a good place to grow up. There were, of course, people that worked for the saw mill, but there were also forest service people, and sometimes different kinds of people would come in. But, most of it was related to the timber industry or the forest service. It was a good company. It had a lot of long time employees. It was pretty fair with the employees. The Gilchrists seemed to be a good family that cared about their employees. It was unique, because it was a company owned town. Rent was cheap in the town, and they had pretty much built all of the facilities a family would need. They had a grocery store, a snack shop, and a lot of stuff. They provided them with a place to live. Most of the management was fair with the employees. A lot of people had long careers with the company.
>
> They would move people up in the company, if there was an opportunity and they had the aptitude.

Logging on Odell Butte, circa 1963.
Collection of Mrs. Mary G. Ernst.

There were always new openings, but a lot of the employees had very long careers. There were a lot of promotions from within.[526]

During the 1960s and into the 1970s, more of the original contingent of employees who came west from Laurel, Mississippi, with Gilchrist Timber Company departed from the scene. Edgar Shotts retired in 1963. He had been the sawmill superintendent. His son, Frank R. Gilchrist's high school classmate, had been working for Gilchrist Timber Company for almost fifteen years. He died in Redding, California, on November 30, 1983. Isom Ezell kept books for the Gilchrist-Fordney Company, then the Gilchrist Timber Company. He had also managed the Gilchrist supermarket. He returned to Laurel after retiring in 1965. He was 74 years old when he died on May 13, 1971. Walter Rigdon, who entered the employ of the Gilchrist-Fordney Company in 1917 and was a resident of Gilchrist prior to the town's construction, retired in 1968. He remained near Gilchrist, a widower since 1947, who lived in a cabin with his dog and at last had the leisure to pursue exclusively his interests in hunting and fishing. He died, aged 89 years, on June 16, 1984. Curtis Breazeale, after suffering a stroke, retired in 1980. Three years later he died. F. A. Hendry, Alva Hendry's son, succeeded him as dry kiln, green chain, and dry shed foreman. James Applewhite died at Saint Charles Hospital on May 15, 1967. He was 68 years old. Save for the years he served with the United States Navy during the Second World War, James Applewhite had been mill superintendent for Gilchrist Timber Company since the first board was cut in 1939. Upon James Applewhite's death, Charles Shotts, who was already Gilchrist Timber Company's logging superintendent, was made plant superintendent. He held both positions until 1974. During 1974 Charles Shotts was appointed vice president of the Gilchrist Timber Company. Stewart M. Jones of the Gilchrist-Fordney Company was the only other nonfamily member who became an officer of a Gilchrist company during the twentieth century.[527]

During 1968 another round of modernization commenced at the Gilchrist Mill. A debarker, chipper, and chip-handling facility were installed. In 1969 the small log mill commenced operations. Also during 1969, the edger and trimmer were replaced. The fuel-handling system for the powerhouse was also replaced during 1969.[528] The town of Gilchrist, during the early 1950s, following the establishment of Midstate Electric Cooperative, began to receive electricity from a source other than Gilchrist Timber Company's powerhouse. Gilchrist was now on the grid, though the town still remained entirely self-sufficient with regard to its water and sewage systems. This change, in part, occurred because the town's residents now had significantly more electrical appliances than they had during the late 1930s. The demand the residents of Gilchrist now had for electricity exceeded the capacity of the mill's powerhouse to fully furnish both the mill and the town. In 1968, Gilchrist Timber Company at last found it more cost effective to buy electrical power from Mid-State than to generate its own. The powerhouse was used to generate steam for the dry kilns and as an auxiliary power source.[529] In 1972, Gilchrist Timber Company installed more efficient sorting equipment.[530]

The 1960s and early 1970s were a particularly busy time for Klamath Northern Railroad. Louie Jordan recalled:

> We graduated from lumber into wood chips, also. Most of our wood chips went to Anderson, California. We started out with 40 foot chip cars. We could haul six of those up the hill. We had about a two and a half percent grade up the hill. As the chip market got better and better, we started cutting more and more chips. Other than chips that were generated out of the mill, from making lumber, we bought a couple of chippers and put them in the woods, cutting small Jack Pine timbers.

> We went from five or six 40-foot cars, to twelve or thirteen 60-foot cars. We would have to make two or three trips a day, to make it up the hill. So, we ordered a new 140-ton GE locomotive that they still have now. That guy has two big Cummins engines on it, one on each end. That guy would haul as much as twelve or fourteen cars up that hill, at one time, if the rail was not wet or snowy. That went on that way, until the chip market took a dive. Then, we went back to eight or nine cars. We had a little outfit down the road there, called Ben Glenville. He started out cutting one boxcar of box shook, out of Jack Pine. That graduated to three or four boxcars, and then he started cutting green 2x4s, 8-foot long, which the state of California would accept in their building code. Then, he started cutting chips, so then we were getting a couple cars of shook, a couple cars of studs, and four or five boxcars of chips, so there was at least one trip from him, every day, sometimes two. Then, he started cutting 1x6, 8-foot long, knotty Jack Pine for Sears and Roebuck to make unfinished furniture with, and he just doubled our capacity.[531]

Fred Southwick, whose family owned a motel in Crescent and who moved to Gilchrist during the late 1960s, offered a perspective as someone who did not have multi-generational connections with Gilchrist and the Gilchrist Timber Company:

> As far as school went, the longest thing I ran in Kansas was 440 yard, and here they ran cross country, which was two miles, so that was a lot longer. I liked it. I liked that you could go on any property, because I was used to being able to run around everywhere. Right behind our house was Gilchrist property, which you could go wherever you wanted to there. I always liked it. Everybody knew each other, which was good, as long as you didn't get in trouble. There were about five state policemen there, and I think their wives talked a lot, so if anybody got in trouble, everybody knew it.

> It was very friendly. It was a great place for me, because it was a B school, and immediately, since I lettered, I became well known. School was always easy for me. I excelled academically. It was a little hard to make friends, because a lot of those people had been there a long time, and had known each other since

Winter Logging, early 1970s.
Collection of Darrell Overland.

1946-1982 – Gilchrist in its Heyday

*Winter Logging, early 1970s.
Collection of Darrell Overland.*

135

Winter Logging, early 1970s.
Collection of Darrell Overland.

1946-1982 – Gilchrist in its Heyday

*Winter Logging, early 1970s.
Collection of Darrell Overland.*

Winter Logging, early 1970s.
Collection of Darrell Overland.

1946-1982 – Gilchrist in its Heyday

Gilchrist Mill and Dam, July 1975.
Collection of Tami Jordan.

Gilchrist houses, July 1975.
Collection of Tami Jordan.

Gilchrist Oregon: The Model Company Town

Gilchrist Mall, July 1975.
Collection of Tami Jordan

*Gilchrist Mall during winter, early 1970s.
Collection of Darrell Overland.*

the first grade. But, if you were there long enough, you made friends. All, the houses were all the same color. I had never lived in a place like that. I didn't have a car when I was first there.

There was one theatre, which is where you went on the weekends. It was fairly cheap, so we always went to the movies. It seemed that a lot of people came to the school activities. They'd come to watch basketball. I don't know if a lot came to watch cross country, because they could only see you when you started and ended. So, it wasn't really a spectator sport. I really liked the principal. He was a really great guy. I don't know if he was the principal to start with, but he was the coach, Jerry Bennett. Some of the teachers were very good. One teacher lived where I was, and he always caused me problems, but that's just because I was a smart alec. I did well in a small town and a small school.

I think one of the problems we have now are these large schools. You just get lost and you lose all of your identity. You didn't lose your identity at Gilchrist. If you did something wrong, your parents knew it by the end of the day. I did work for them one summer on the Railroad, and they paid you the wages that the guys got in the mill, which were excellent wages back then. I knew James Gilchrist.

I had been to their house a lot. They were outstanding people.[532]

Kathy Stice, a 1971 graduate of Gilchrist High School, knew Gilchrist in its heyday from the perspective of the member of a family who had been ranching in north Klamath County and south Deschutes County since 1889, when her grandfather's great uncle homesteaded the land that became the family's ranch. She recalled:

I started first grade at Gilchrist, and finished the twelfth grade. I'm one of four or five in my class that started in first grade and actually graduated from Gilchrist High School. Most of the people that lived in Gilchrist, also worked at Gilchrist Lumber Company. Only people that worked for the lumber company could live in Gilchrist. It was a good place. Everybody knew everybody and we all looked out for one another. We were a little different, because we had a ranch and lived outside of Gilchrist. I raised forage cattle, and I had my own herd. That's what took me to college.

It was a very small community, and we all worked together. If somebody needed a ride somewhere, we always took care of it. My dad was at every basketball game that I can remember. He still worked out in the woods, but he always made sure that we kids always got to town. I was on the drill team and he always made sure I had a way home. Of course, after I was old enough to drive my own car, then I could drive back and forth. We lived fourteen miles outside of Gilchrist, so it was kind of a big deal when we went to town. I would say my high school years were more involved in Gilchrist, than my younger years, which was more involved in La Pine. We were in baseball. He was very involved with us as we were growing up. I would say that more of my Gilchrist memories were from my high school years. Once I got to high school, then I got really involved with the activities in the school. We really got involved in sports. It was cross country in the fall, basketball in the winter, and track in the spring.[533]

Milton Hill, who graduated from Gilchrist High School and whose father came west from Laurel with the Gilchrist Timber Company, recalled of his experiences growing up in Gilchrist:

I was actually born in Bend, Oregon on February 15, 1957. Shortly after my birth, I was taken to Gilchrist, Oregon, where my parents lived. They still live in Gilchrist. I lived in Gilchrist until I was 18 years old, in 1975. I lived there off and on for five or six years after that. I live in Tigard, Oregon now. I want to relate a little story to you. The Gilchrist family owned the saw mill, the property, and the town. It was a private company town. Where I lived, the owners of the town, named the town after themselves. Therefore, it was fairly natural for me to think that, the town down the road, named Crescent, had a Mr. Crescent in it. I also assumed there was a Mr. Bend, a Mr. Portland, and so on . . . I lived in a very unique area. I'll tell you a story that I share with folks, when I'm talking about where I lived, that shows how Gilchrist is different than most places. My earliest memories of Gilchrist are from when I was four years old. This would have been in the very early 60's. Gilchrist had dirt streets, little brown houses, everything was very much the same, and everything oriented to the saw mill. The friends I had and the people who were friends and acquaintances of my parents, all were workers at the saw mill, or were friends and family of workers at the saw mill. The saw mill was kind of a central part of life at that time. I was the only son of my parents. The school system was right in the middle of town, and it still is. I don't know what the arrangement was on all of this private land, to have a county owned school there. They might have donated the land or sold it to them. In the middle of this brown town, there was a different architecture and differently built buildings. Before going to school there, I always kind of saw it as being this different and new place. It was connectivity to the outside world. We had very little connection to the outside world. Most people, where they live, their electricity comes from some other entity, other than who they work for. But, at that time, that wasn't the case in Gilchrist. The saw mill provided electricity to the town. The rural electrification project had not reached out that far yet. In the evenings, I remember, as it would get dusk, the street lights would come on. They didn't come on automatically, like they do now, but because someone over at the saw mill would turn a switch and turn on the lights. We were dependent on the timber company for that. Aside from the school system being something different from the outside, I remember when natural gas was brought into the town, and that was an outside entity. There were pipelines and meters put on the houses. I must not have been over five or six years old, but I remember thinking that it was neat, because it was kind of a connection to the outside. I remember going to my first day of first grade. At that time, the hallways in the school seemed very large and immense. It was kind of awe inspiring. That building was probably the largest building I had ever been in in my life, aside from the large grocery store in Bend. In Gilchrist itself, there was a restaurant, a gas station, and a grocery store; however, my family did most of our commercial activity in Bend, which was about an hour north on highway 97. I have memories of us going up there, usually every weekend. My dad's shift was Monday through Friday, like everyone else. At least one weekend day, we'd drive to Bend, and I remember coming back in the evening and being bored in the car. Coming back in the winters, there would sometimes be a snow storm, and we'd leave Bend, which was a lit up town, with sidewalks and paved streets, and go out into the dark and there were no street lights all the way through to La Pine, because there was no electricity out there yet. In La Pine, everyone had generators at that time, so there was very little lighting once you left Bend. It was very dark. That had to have been in the early 60's, probably 1962 or 1963. I don't know when rural electrification came in. I would guess it was probably the mid 60's. In La Pine, there may have been small electric companies that lit up a few blocks or something, but you didn't have street lights or any public utilities. I remember La Pine as always being dark at night. It was the same way in Crescent too. I'll get off track here for a moment. The big Chevron station in Crescent, if you're facing it, on the left is a large building, and that used to be a stage stop, and the people there used to have a diesel generating plant in there that provided a little bit of electric service to a few customers there in Crescent. There is probably a whole history of little electric projects that went on like that. In Gilchrist, it was a by-product of the power plant for the saw mill that provided electricity for the town. The place was kind of isolated. Often, when we were coming back from Bend to Gilchrist, we would stop at a place called The Timbers. At that time, it was like a bar and restaurant combination, and not too far from Gilchrist. It was a just a few miles away. What I remember, and this is as a young child, probably prior to first grade, was my dad and mom would often stop there and take me into the tavern where I could watch this little train that went around some tracks up near the ceiling. It was just a little novelty for the bar. I think my parents probably stopped there just to give me a break, because I was usually whining so much in the car, or maybe it was a restroom break. But, I remember the little bar, and the train going around, and the thick woods surrounding the tavern at the time. It was kind of an esoteric, little hole-in-the-wall place, but I have very fond memories of that. Just south of where The Timbers was, there was a road that pulled in to the local swimming pool, called the canal. It was actually just a diversion of the Little Deschutes for irrigation. The swimming area was just where people had historically parked and jumped in. There was a diving board and two areas for swimming. I remember going there in the summers. I really liked going swimming there. It's probably taken on epic proportions in my mind since then. Driving into that swimming hole, there was a ponderosa pine tree on the left, just as you left the highway, and there was an Indian face carved into the bark of the tree, and if I remember right, it was painted. The folks that my parents socialized with, in the 60's, in Gilchrist, many of them were like my parents, and had moved out with the timber company from Mississippi. They had a common history of time in the south, and now the good times and solid employment of the timber company there. I remember the folks that lived a few doors down from my parents. There was one couple, Bob and Marie Anderson. I don't think they were from Mississippi, but they were my parents' age. Bob was very proud of the work he did at the mill. They were a childless couple, but they seemed to have a very solid marriage. She had a garden and he had his wood shop, and they kept their house up immaculately. All of the houses in Gilchrist were rentals at that time, in the early 60's. As well as I can remember, all of the houses were very immaculately maintained. There was a sense of pride, accomplishment, and ownership . . . even though people weren't buying their houses. It seemed like everything was stable.[534]

Tom Steers, son of Bill Steers, Gilchrist Timber Company's woods superintendent, and Karen Steers, his wife, first started attending Gilchrist High School after her parents moved to Chemult following her father's transfer there by the Forest Service. They shared recollections:

Driscoll: I guess I'll start at the beginning. Where were you born?

Tom: I was born in Bend. At the time, my parents lived in Silver Lake. About six months after I was born, my parents moved to Gilchrist.

Driscoll: Why did your parents move to Gilchrist?

Tom: He took a job at the Gilchrist Timber Company, as a faller for Rufus Childre.

Driscoll: What about you, Karen?

Karen: I was born in Springfield, Oregon. I moved to Chemult in 1973. I went four years to Gilchrist High School. My dad worked for the Forest Service.

Driscoll: How did your dad end up managing the forest?

Tom: He went to college at the University of Kentucky and then to Michigan State. After that he went into the service. In the summer, during college, he would come out to Oregon and work for the forest service. He stayed on lookouts and things like that. When he got out of college and the service, he joined the forest service, and that brought him to Lake View and Silver Lake. At Silver Lake, he got to know Rufus Childre, who was the woods boss at that time. He needed an assistant, and he asked my dad to come over there. At the same time, Charlie Schotts came in, but he was from the area. He just started working and kind of worked his way up to where he was running the woods operations.

Driscoll: I'd like you both to tell me about your recollections of Gilchrist. Tom, you did all 12 grades there.

Tom: I loved it. A good example of why I liked it, was about 10 years ago, we came back to the Gilchrist Days that they have, and I have a nephew, CJ, and he came whirling in through there on a bicycle, and every person in the entire place knew him. Your kids can go out and be kids without having to worry about what's going to happen to them. They might kill each other, but they don't have to worry about anything else that's going on. It was a great place to grow up. Back in the days, before there were all of these electronic ways to entertain yourself, you were forced to entertain yourself in other ways, and I think it was really good for us.

Karen: I moved to Gilchrist when I was entering high school, and it could have been a really tough time. But, I remember that I was really well accepted. They were like, "Wow, a new person!" The whole time I was there, I never felt like I wasn't involved or that I didn't fit in. It always felt like a big family walking down the halls of the school. I can remember the whole hallway singing, "Oh Black Water."

Tom: That's right!

Karen: Everybody was involved in it. I can remember being very content, and thinking, "This is not so bad!"

Tom: Basically, if you lived in the town, your parents either worked for the timber company, or the police, or the school. That was it. If you lost your job, you were going to be moving. I do remember one time, Frank Gilchrist going up to some people, whose kids were getting in trouble, and telling them, "If you don't get control of your kids, you're going to be gone." It was the idea that we don't tolerate those kinds of behaviors, such as robberies and stuff like that, it just didn't happen. You weren't allowed to. I also remember Wayne Ernst driving through town, and you were expected to keep your property up. He'd go through, and he'd go up to a house and tell them they needed to mow their lawn, or get their junker out of the front yard. It was well taken care of. It was kind of a neat place, and the company took care of its employees. It didn't take advantage of them, it took care of them.

Karen: The theatre was there, and it was priced so kids could afford to go. It would give them something to do. It would keep them out of trouble.

Tom: The timber company just offset the cost of whatever they needed to keep that running.

Driscoll: Describe your dad's practices managing the woods.

Tom: Sustainable forestry. He believed that, at the time, when Crown Pacific bought the land, they could have continued to log the land exclusively, indefinitely. They'd only run one shift at the mill, but they could do it. The idea was they would go into a forest and take out mature trees only. They'd leave everything else in mixed growth, and plant behind them as they came. They would even leave some mature trees, because they would go back, ten years later. They would mark all the timber they wanted to cut, and then leave everything else. It was beautiful, until Crown Pacific cut everything down.

Driscoll: I remember how park-like it was.

Tom: It was. It was cleaned up enough, that you could get through the forest, but even the stand behind town, if you remember that, there was beautiful ponderosa pine in there, and it had been logged about three times. They just kept going and figured they could go back to an area every ten years, and go again.

Karen: My dad worked for the forest service, and he was also in timber sales. He worked with private industry for the forest service, and he always felt like Gilchrist was always easy to work with, even if they weren't always in total agreement, but they always had the best interest of the forest.

Tom: They would buy up timber sales, just to keep other companies out. They would say, "They don't take care of the land, so they're not going to be here." It was good.

Driscoll: The timber company moved up from Laurel, Mississippi.

Tom: I think it really affected the town. It was a small southern town, located in the middle of Oregon. When I started growing up there, two-thirds of the people had southern accents. I think that's probably why my parents were accepted. My mom is from North Carolina, and my dad is from Kentucky. They are southerners. It was just a genteel atmosphere. I'm sure there are still people here, whose grandparents came from Mississippi. There were little things, like they had cocktail hour still. They are nice to people and always polite.

Karen: They had manners. The kids always said, "Yes, ma'am."

Tom: You learned to respect everyone around you, because that's what they do in the south. It was kind of fun.

Driscoll: What other recollections do you have of growing up in the town, such as, the mall?

Tom: The mall? Well, when I was a little kid, the sidewalk around it was the only pavement in town. That's where we learned to skateboard. We'd go around the circle and ride our bikes, and when you could finally pop off the dirt road and onto that smooth concrete, it was great. I'm surprised somebody didn't just wipe out, coming around one of those corners. I remember playing little league baseball, with Ernest Poncil as the coach, and Roger Moore was the coach before that. I just had great times up there. I remember when my dad and Charlie Shotts built a track up there. The school needed a track, and they wanted something. They talked about raising money, and they came and just built it, and Gilchrist Timber Company paid for it. Later, they turned it into a football field. I remember swimming at the pond. Every summer day, all day long, you were at the pond. Then, you'd go play basketball at the Ernst's basketball court, and then you'd go back to the pond. I remember getting water out of the laundry room that they had there.

Karen: When you were in college, the company provided you with a job.

Tom: That's right. If your parents worked for the company, and you were going to college, you were provided with a job in the summer, at union wages, which in those days was like, five or seven bucks an hour. People were raising families on that, and I remember I would go work in the summer for the Railroad, and I'd do the same thing during Christmas break, and I'd make enough money during Christmas break for all of my expenses until spring break. Then, you'd save up during the summer. They took care of you. I sure do miss that old train.

Driscoll: Kind of a de facto Gilchrist scholarship program.

Tom: Yes, it really was, but you earned your scholarship. Some people worked in the woods, and some people worked in the mill.

Tom: I did a speech in college about the history of Gilchrist and growing up in a private logging town. I got to know quite a bit. I actually sat down with Frank Gilchrist and had him explain to me the stuff I had always heard about, but I had him explain how certain things came about. He would have set it up, so that the company kept going. I think Benji would have probably run the company, Will would have been in charge of sales, and the two of them would have kept it going. They are two people that could have, and would have, been very successful.

Karen: John would have probably been a part of that too.

Tom: Yes, John probably would have run the mill, just like he did. When I was in college, I had a friend from Valsetz and another from Beatty. The

*Gilchrist Timber Company Christmas card.
Collection of F.A. Hendry.*

three of us were all from privately owned logging towns. As we talked about what went on, I came to see the difference between Gilchrist and some of these other ones. Gilchrist was there and their philosophy was, "We have a business, we want our employees to be good, and we're going to take care of them and make it a good place. You could trust Mr. Gilchrist. That's the difference between businesses now and businesses then. When they negotiated a contract, they would sit down with Frank and tell him what they needed, and he would say, "Here's what I can do." He would be very open. He would say, "Here's our profit margin, here's what we have to work with." Things worked out for a lot of years that way. There were years that the timber market was down, and Gilchrist Timber Company stayed open, and Frank Gilchrist absorbed the losses to keep people working. Gilchrist Timber Company, in Mississippi, had been logging just like everybody else did, where you just cut it all down. I think Laurel was the third place they moved, and when they moved to Oregon, they decided they were going to do things differently when they got there. Rufus Childre started the sustainable forestry, and when my dad took over, he kind of expanded on it.

Driscoll: I remember little things, like if you stayed on the logging roads, you could stay out of trouble.

Tom: And, they all lead to the same area, if you just keep going. It's downhill to the highway, wherever you go. If you head toward the mountains, you will find the highway, sooner or later, and then you just have to figure out if you're going north or south. I just remember hours, and hours, and hours of playing in those woods. I went to college with people, and they would talk about playing in the woods. Then, we'd go to their house and there would be this little patch of trees, and we'd think, "You guys have no clue!" We're talking about playing in the WOODS! There were no parents, and there was nothing there, except for what we would come up with.

Karen: Well, your mom had four boys, so you would be gone all day, and you'd come back for lunch, and then you'd come back in time to be washed up by five o'clock for dinner.

Tom: Yes, that's right.[535]

In 1970 the Gilchrist Timber Company employed 185 men and was producing 40 million to 50 million board feet of lumber per year. The Gilchrists and Gilchrist were still well and fondly remembered in and near Laurel, Mississippi. According to an article published in 1970 in the *Jackson Daily News,* ". . . With selective cutting practices . . . Gilchrist seems assured of being a, Mississippi, colony in Oregon for many years to come."[536]

In 1972, Bud Keown's situation was typical of that of the rank-and-file employees of Gilchrist

1946-1982 – Gilchrist in its Heyday

*New mill under construction, circa 1979.
Collection of F.A. Hendry.*

Timber Company. The rents charged by Gilchrist Timber Company ranged from $29 per month for a one-bedroom house to $85 for the largest of the four-bedroom houses. The rent had last been increased in 1953. Bud Keown earned $9,600 a year, plus overtime, which was a typical annual income for a Gilchrist Timber Company employee. With his wages, coupled with other benefits such below-market rents on a company house (in 1972, he paid $45 for one of the smaller four-bedroom houses), he was able to afford a boat with trailer, two motorcycles, a new car, and all the household appliances then typical. Said Bud Keown, "You know, I got everything I want here."[537]

"Crime hardly exists here," said Cpl. John Hall who was in charge of the highway patrol station located in Gilchrist.[538] There was no municipal government. None was needed. Gilchrist Timber Company provided municipal services for its employees when most local governments to this day provide ever-decreasing quality at ever-higher costs. Said Bill Steers, Gilchrist Timber Company woods boss and holder of a forestry degree from Michigan State University, regarding the absence of a municipal government, "We don't need it . . I wouldn't live anywhere else. We go to Portland four or five times a year. We hit all the good restaurants and nightclubs. We do plenty of shopping. We love it. But after three days we can't wait to get back here."[539]

Said Frank R. Gilchrist of the town his father had created and the benefits it had for Gilchrist Timber Company, ". . It's paid off. We've been able to attract and hold a much higher caliber of worker. Fifty percent of our employees have been with us more than twenty years."[540] Frank R. Gilchrist continued his father's custom of taking a personal interest in the well-being of the town's inhabitants. He was, however, devoid of ostentation. His usual attire consisted of sports shirts, slacks, boots, and a white hard hat he wore when inside the mill. When asked if he thought of himself

New mill and old mill, circa 1979.
Collection of F. A. Hendry.

as the town's patriarch, he said, "Yeah, whenever somebody grabs my arm and tells me his toilet isn't working."[541]

In 1978 a new lumber-packaging machine had been installed as had been a new trimmer.[542] More significantly, construction began during August 1978 on a new mill. The new mill, in one eight-hour shift, was capable of producing 200,000 board feet a day, which was equal to what the original mill produced in two eight-hour shifts. The new mill had two sides: one for large logs and the other for small logs. The mill was designed by Warren & Brewster Company of Albany, Oregon. Both head rigs combined Klamath Iron Works multi-band mills with Warren & Brewster Maxi-Mill overhead, end-dogging carriages. The large-log side contained twin eight-foot band mills and a carriage which was capable of rotating a log ninety degrees. A hydraulic cylinder moved an arm which pivoted a chuck that was within the end clamp assembly that held the log. The small-log side contained a quadruple six-foot band mill which was nonrotating. An Ausco scanner coupled with a computer system controlled the head rigs. Approximately 95 percent of the logs went through automatically, though the sawyer could override the computer. Another feature of the new mill that was different from the old was that its logs were dry-decked, not floated in the millpond. The log yard, which was created for the new mill, initially had a capacity of three to four million board feet.[543]

Both the large side and small side of the new mill were in operation by October 1979. The old mill, during the period of transition, was run at night. The new mill was operated during the day. The old mill was placed into mothballs on January 11, 1980.[544] It remained in operational condition and was brought back into service from time to time.

Gilchrist was the subject of an article published during 1981 by *The Wall Street Journal*. Gilchrist, without trying, had gained national recognition as the model company town. During the summer of 1985, *Willamette Week* published an article which, as did every other article published about Gilchrist and the Gilchrist Timber Company, reported the wisdom of the Gilchrist family's leadership and management practices, the loyalty these policies engendered in employees, that the Gilchrist Timber Company was operating Oregon's last company town, that it had no plans to discard it, and that Frank R. Gilchrist routinely rebuffed offers from real estate speculators who coveted his town. Gilchrist Timber Company, unlike every other mill, had avoided layoffs during the period of the Carter Recession. Also reported in the *Willamette Week* article was that Rob and Jeanne Hendry were the third generation of the Hendry family to live in Gilchrist and work for Gilchrist Timber Company.[545]

During the spring of 1981, Frank R. Gilchrist recommended to the Gilchrist Timber Company that the firm increase its timber acreage, while continuing to conserve timber and aggressively purchasing federal timber. The purpose of this policy was to assure that Gilchrist Timber Company continued to operate in perpetuity. The board of directors endorsed the plan. Frank R. Gilchrist began its implementation.[546]

What was not noted in articles published during the 1980s, which recognized Gilchrist, Oregon, as the model company town it had been since Frank W. Gilchrist built it then became its first leader, was that the forces which would undo it had already been set in motion. Some were a matter of misadventure; others involved the ongoing meddling by state and federal governments as well as their tax policies. Gilchrist, the company town, and the Gilchrist Timber Company, institutions which seemed features of north Klamath County as permanent as Odell Butte or the Little Deschutes River, would abruptly prove ephemeral. The town, which still endures, would change utterly, though perhaps, not irreparably.

Lumber stacks at Gilchrist.
Stewart J. Gilchrist's photo album, Gilchrist Timber Company papers, Klamath County Museum.

Lumber production mill interior, circa 1939.
Stewart J. Gilchrist's photo album, Gilchrist Timber Company papers, Klamath County Museum.

CHAPTER VI

1982-2012

The Wake of the Flood

*"...only the peak feels so sound and stable that the beginning
of the falling is hidden for a little while..."*

— *Absalom, Absalom* by William Faulkner

"In the wake of the Flood the earth brought forth the serpent Python."

— *Metamorphoses*, Ovid

The starting point for the unraveling of Gilchrist as a company town occurred in a snow storm on January 27, 1982. Frank R. Gilchrist was returning to Gilchrist. A semi had stopped. It was parked partially the road. He did not see the vehicle until a moment, or perhaps two, before he struck it. He was taken by ambulance to Saint Charles Hospital where eventually he was released, though he never entirely recovered from the accident. The Ernst brothers (Gil, Will, and John) as well as Benji Gilchrist stepped into the breach. The mill and town continued outwardly the same as always. In fact, all had utterly changed, had began changing for ill, years before.

The publication of Rachel Carlson's *Silent Spring* marked the separation of the contemporary environmental movement from the conservation movement. Environmental radicalism and extremism grew out of the social protest movements of the 1960s and 1970s in Western Europe and North America. Today, this phenomenon has spread all over the world. The objectives of the conservation movement of the early twentieth century included managing natural resources for long-term utilization for productive purposes. The Gilchrist Timber Company's management of its timberlands was an exemplary example of the management of natural resources in a manner consistent with the principles of the conservation movement.

Sense was the hallmark of the conservation movement. Sensibility is at the heart of the environmental movement which came into its own during the 1960s. The environmental movement originated in cities and suburbs. Its devotees more often than not were individuals who did not earn their livelihoods by utilization of natural resources. They were not connected with the land in the manner that ranchers, farmers or loggers are. The members of the 1960s' environmental movement were a species of tourist who treated nature with religious fervor. Their ranks included numerous politicians, academics, and members of the legal profession. They have been singularly successful in employing the judicial system to advance their agenda.

The National Wilderness Act, passed in 1964, set up a national wilderness preservation system on federal lands and engendered a myriad of successive studies on additional acreage of federal forests. These studies continue to plague the forest industry by keeping ever more federal acreage from being available for the production of timber.

Year after year, legislation and litigation involving the management and utilization of natural resources made it increasingly difficult for the timber industry to obtain supplies of raw material. The Clean Air Act was amended in 1963, 1967, and 1970. The Endangered Species Act was passed in 1966. Two years later the Wild and Scenic Rivers Act was passed. The National Environmental Policy Act was passed in 1969. Oregon passed legislation which duplicated the federal legislation and was even more onerous. The Oregon Forest Practices Act of 1972 was the most significant of acts passed by the state of Oregon. It increased the regulation of productive activities by the timber industry on state and private forests.

By the end of the 1970s, this succession of increasing regulation and anti-productive management practices impeded the productive use of timber, dramatically reducing the availability of federal timber from lands managed by the Forest Service and Bureau of Land Management. These regulations and management practices made it more costly to harvest private timberlands. Litigation by environmental groups, coupled with every expanding regulation and attendant compliance costs, all served to make it ever more difficult for timber companies to manage forest lands to provide a reliable, long-term supply of timber. Forests planted, then managed for years, were barred from harvesting by suits brought by environmental groups.

Hindering timber harvesting suited the sensibilities which motivated the groups bringing the lawsuits and brought into law ever more restrictive regulations. The effect was to idle even more acres of land which had hitherto been producing sustained yields of timber for Oregon's lumber mills.

Besides being less dependent on the Gilchrist Timber Company for housing, the employees and their families began to shop regularly in places other than the Gilchrist Shopping Center. Employees of Gilchrist Timber Company were now traveling more often to Bend (50 miles north of Gilchrist) to shop, because new roads and automobiles made the larger community more accessible and a greater variety of goods could be purchased there. By the first years of the 1970s, the services of the Gilchrist Timber Company became less vital to the well-being of its employees and their families.[547] The option of living in Gilchrist, of renting houses from the Gilchrist Timber Company, remained a very popular benefit among employees of the Gilchrist Timber Company.

Following World War II, the timber companies of the Pacific Northwest began to eliminate company towns by closing and destroying them or by selling the buildings. Economic development, improved transportation systems, and the growth of neighboring communities altered the circumstances in the Pacific Northwest which had once compelled companies to own and operate towns.[548] When Shevlin-Hixon closed its company town in 1951, Gilchrist became the only company town that remained in Central Oregon.[42] Gilchrist, however, not only endured, but expanded.

The first members of the generation born following World War II started to enter the labor force of the Gilchrist Timber Company in the 1970s. This generation was unique in that it had known only prosperity, full employment, and rising expectations. Even members of this generation who might spend all of their years employed by the Gilchrist Timber Company, renting one of the company's houses, expressed less attachment to the company than did their fathers and grandfathers. The post-war generation had not experienced depression, massive unemployment, or deprivation. Some members of the post-war generation were the product of families who had been employed and housed by the Gilchrist Timber Company for as many as four successive generations. Some, almost as soon as they finished attending Gilchrist High School, went to work for the Gilchrist Timber Company, married, and then moved into a company-owned house. Others who came from families that had been employed by the Gilchrist Timber Company for several generations would vary from this pattern by purchasing a house, rather than renting a company-owned one. Both variations of this group took employment with a company they had been acquainted with all their lives. They had emotional ties to it and its town. This group was supplemented by employees who had no prior connection with the Gilchrist Timber Company, but who chose to work for it because it provided them with an alternative to city life, an opportunity to live in Central Oregon and enjoy a wide variety of benefits including inexpensive company housing.[549] The post-war generations supplied the Gilchrist Timber Company with people, who like their fathers, sought a stable, quiet existence in Central Oregon.

Wayne H. Ernst died on August 26, 1983. With his death, Frank R. Gilchrist, still suffering

Old Mill, 1986

Old Mill, 1986

Mill and dam, 1986

the effects of his accident, lost a confidant, right-hand man, and a companion he had known since 1946.

Charles Shotts, following Frank R. Gilchrist's accident, continued as vice president of the Gilchrist Timber Company but was authorized by the board of directors to perform Frank R. Gilchrist's duties while he recovered from his injuries. He never fully did. Frank R. Gilchrist continued to serve as president of the Gilchrist Timber Company until 1988 and as a member of the board of directors until the following year when, at the age of 65, he retired. Charlie Shotts was named president of the Gilchrist Timber Company by its board of directors during the spring of 1988. He was the first nonfamily member to hold that position. During August 1988 the Gilchrist Timber Company, in honor of its 50th Anniversary, published a history, entitled *Gilchrist: The First Fifty Years*. What occurred over the next twenty-four months was unanticipated.[550]

During 1990 Charles Shotts took over Frank R. Gilchrist's place as a member of the Gilchrist Timber Company's board of directors. He oversaw the company's dissolution rather than presiding over, then handing off the Gilchrist of Wayne and Mary Ernst and Frank and Helen Gilchrist as a company with an unlimited future.[551]

The directors of the Gilchrist Timber Company assembled for a special meeting which began on February 2, 1990. The entire board, including Charles Shotts, Allen M. Fletcher, and Jeanne C. Vance, were present. She had been named to the board in 1978, following the death of her father, Joseph A. Vance, Jr. She represented her branch of the family.

Charles Shotts, after Allen M. Fletcher convened the meeting, reported that the expectations for income during the preceding year had been met, that the company's financial condition was favorable. He then proposed to the board, which approved his request, the expenditure of $1 million to build a remanufacturing facility, the purpose of which was to increase the mill's efficiency by utilizing lower grades of lumber.

What next occurred was that Jeanne Vance proposed to the board that it investigate selling the Gilchrist Timber Company. The arguments she presented in favor of her proposal emphasized the desire some of the stockholders had for liquidity for estate-planning purposes, noted that timber prices were currently at record levels, and pointed out that the current favorable tax climate might eventually disappear. The board of directors agreed to her proposal, then said it would notify all Gilchrist Timber Company stockholders of the plan to solicit their recommendations and suggestions. Among other topics discussed that day was a compensation plan for terminated employees. The rough treatment dealt the lumber producers by politicians who pandered to the environmental movement had, by all but denying them access to federal timber, coupled with regulations which restricted (or sometimes denied) property owners their right to harvest their own timber, drove up the cost of timber holdings, such as that which belonged to the Gilchrist Timber Company, creating a nearly irresistible incentive for some of the shareholders to sell the company and its timberlands.

The pay envelopes the employees of the Gilchrist Timber Company received on March 20, 1990, included a notice informing them that the directors of the Gilchrist Timber Company had decided to place the company on the market. After six generations – 123 years – the Gilchrist family was leaving the timber business. Rumors, fear, and uncertainty quickly became the norm for the residents of Gilchrist and employees of Gilchrist Timber Company. Frank R. Gilchrist had adopted the policy of allowing retired Gilchrist Timber Company employees to continue occupying their houses. Valsetz, one of Oregon's last company towns, had been razed in 1984 by Boise-Cascade. Kinzua, following the mill's closure, was demolished in 1978. It was feared Gilchrist might meet a similar fate.[552]

Frank R. Gilchrist died at St. Charles Medical Hospital on February 26, 1991. He was 66 years old. Omitted from his obituary which was published in the *Bend Bulletin* was reference to his service during World War II as a pilot who served aboard the USS *Belleau Wood* (CVL 24) during some of the bloodiest campaigns of the Pacific Theater. What was mentioned was the Gilchrist Timber Company's timber management practices, his service under four consecutive governors as a member of the Oregon Board of Forestry, his service as a member of the Oregon State Parks and Recreation Advisory Committee, that he was a member of the advisory committee to Oregon State University's Forest Products Research Laboratory, director and president of the Western Wood Products Association, and director of the National Forest Products Association. He was buried in Pilot Butte Cemetery beside his wife who had predeceased him in 1978. His grave is not far from that of Wayne Ernst as well as numerous employees of Gilchrist Timber Company and their family members.[553] Frank R. Gilchrist's death was reported in Laurel, Mississippi, where there still remained people who remembered him as a child, the son of Frank W. Gilchrist. His death more or less coincided with that of the Gilchrist Timber Company.

For portions of two years, from late 1990 until early 1991, numerous rumors circulated with regard to the fate of the Gilchrist Timber Company. Leaders of Gilchrist Timber Company's IWA (International Wood Workers of America) unsuccessfully petitioned Barbara Roberts, then serving as Oregon's governor, to take action to save the jobs of the employees of the Gilchrist Timber Company. Their appeal to her was ironic, given that one of the special interest groups which had elected her was the environmentalist movement whose efforts had engendered the circumstances which culminated in the sale. The IWA, because of what was done to the timber industry by environmental legislation, eventually declined from 144,000 members to extinction.

Tom Steers recounted his recollection of the sales and what his father had said regarding the transaction:

> Now, this is from my father, but Charlie Shotts and those people put together a proposal to sell it, and sold it to the stock holders. My dad said he didn't know why. But, generations were changing, and people said, "We want our money now." They wanted that, rather than keep-

Gilchrist houses south of the school, summer 1990.

Gilchrist Supermarket, summer 1990.

Gilchrist house, Nob Hill, summer 1990.

Gilchrist Theatre, summer 1990.

Gilchrist house, Nob Hill, summer 1990.

ing their investment. I think if Frank hadn't had the accident, which kind of changed him, and had other people running things, if Crown Pacific hadn't taken over that mill, he would have worked until they forced him out. It was just a nice place to be and a good place to live. My mother, however, might have been happy to move somewhere else.[554]

Rent in Gilchrist, at the beginning of 1991, ranged from $67 a month for the town's smallest houses to $125 a month for the largest ones.[555]

Early during the spring of 1991, on March 25, news was announced that there was a buyer for the Gilchrist Timber Company's land. The buyer's name was unknown. The offer did not include the mill or the town. It was feared that Cavenham Forest Industries was the unnamed prospective buyer and that the firm would harvest the timber for processing elsewhere.

Later that spring on May 7, 1991, the directors of Gilchrist Timber Company assembled at the L'Enfant Plaza Hotel in Washington, D.C. Charles Shotts reported that Cavenham Industries was the unnamed buyer, the firm's offer was for the entire Gilchrist Timber Company, and the firm's offer had been reduced from $130 million to $100 million. Cavenham Industries was informed that their offer was unacceptable. Other offers, Charlie Shotts reported, had been received. It was one of these other offers, the one from Crown Pacific, which was accepted.

Crown Pacific proposed to purchase for $136,500,000 the Gilchrist Timber Company timber, its 103,000 acres of timberland, the mill, Klamath Northern Railroad, and the town. The mill was to close as soon as Crown Pacific's offer was accepted. The deal, which was very heavily leveraged, was scheduled to close on July 1, 1991. Employees of Gilchrist Timber Company were terminated on July 31, 1991. On October 4, 1991, the mill resumed operations as part of the Crown Pacific organization. During October 1991, Ernst

*Demolition of the original Gilchrist Mill.
Collection of Milton Hill.*

Brothers Corporation (Gil, Will, John, and Jan) purchased the town lock, stock, and barrel in a separate transaction. Their purchase of Gilchrist may very well have saved it from the fate which befell Kinzua and Valsetz. The certificate of dissolution, which dissolved the Gilchrist Timber Company, was filed on December 28, 1993.

The mill which Frank W. Gilchrist constructed in 1938 was sold by Crown Pacific to a Russian firm which dismantled it, then transported it to Siberia where it was reassembled. B. E. Hill, who had participated in the mill's construction, was a member of the crew that dismantled it.

Many changes quickly followed the sales of the town and the mill, railroad, and timberlands. Tom Steers said regarding Crown-Pacific's management practices:

> I remember a lot about it. My brother, Rick, went to work for the new company to sell the lumber. In fact, he still sells the lumber from Gilchrist Mills. My dad, at the time, was ready to retire, and he was hired on as a consultant for a couple of years. My dad tried to convince Peter Stout to continue the practices, but they were in so much debt, that they had to log it off to try to maintain their corporate standing, and they weren't able to do it. I do remember one story that was kind of funny. The first winter they went through here, it was a pretty mild winter, and Peter went through the mill and said, "Take down those walls. We don't need those. They're in the way and they slow things down." My dad said, "You know, it does snow here." So, that year, they took down all those things, and the next year it was just a miserable winter and they had to shut the mill down, and rebuild the walls. My dad said, "They pay me to consult. If they don't ask, I don't tell 'em!"[556]

Crown Pacific accelerated cutting on its Gilchrist timber holdings in an ultimately futile effort to generate enough income to service its debts. Within a few years the forest, which the Gilchrist

Demolition of the original Gilchrist Mill.
Collection of Milton Hill.

family had begun acquiring and transforming into timberlands which were without equal, was cut over. By then, Crown Pacific had filed for protection under Chapter 11 of the Bankruptcy Code.

Ernst Brothers began the transition of Gilchrist from a company town by making improvements to the town's houses. These improvements included new roofs and siding. The town's houses were now painted different colors, which was, after more than fifty years, the realization of Benjamin V. Wright's initial plan for the painting of the town. Gilchrist was platted as a townsite with individual lots. Gil Ernst, during September 2001, described conditions which then existed in Gilchrist as well changes which Ernst Brothers had made during the preceding ten years:

> Crown Pacific and the school are still big. We were big, and we've downscaled quite a lot. But, what has occurred on the town site is that the town was platted in 1996. It used to be just one big plot. We resided, and put new siding, new windows, and roofs for all of the houses. And, the houses have basically been sold. In September of 1997, we relinquished our control of the town site to the owner's association, because we had sold over 80% of the houses. So, the owner's association controls the town site. They are in charge of it. They have an architectural committee that watches over it. If you change things, you have to first go to them. That's the biggest change in the town itself. They have officers and if you have complaints about the town site, you call them. People still call here, but we refer those calls to them. They've tried different things. They just had the town site paved. They started last year and got it completed this summer. There's still a place for people to call, if there are problems. It's not, and probably won't ever be, like it was when Gilchrist was there. Since Gilchrist has sold, there's quite a bit of turnover in the town site. Even the buyers of the houses, there are a few investors who have more than one that rent.
>
> There's quite a bit of turnover. Longevity is not a big thing, like it used to be. I really couldn't tell you the tenants of more than half the houses I've got anymore. That's probably the biggest change in the town site; the turnover. You've constantly got people moving in and moving out. The main thing that is the same is the police department. We've got a new store, Carrie's Corner. We remodeled it when they went in there. That's a good thing. We've got a new video store that went in, and the Oregon State Visitor's Center. The Mill Town Espresso opened up this year and is on its second owner, because its originator moved. We've got some new things happening, and that's good.[557]

Ernst Brothers were responsible for Gilchrist's successful transition from company town to small town with a mill. It is because of them that the town did not pass into oblivion as was the lot of so many other company towns.

The Gilchrist Mill, following Crown Pacific's bankruptcy, was purchased by Interfor of Canada. The Gilchrist Mill, as of 2012, was the only mill other than the one at Warm Springs, which is still operating in Central Oregon. Klamath Northern Railroad is a factor in the mill's survival. It brings logs into the mill and takes lumber out. During 2011, the Gilchrist Mill's annual production was 120 million board feet. Rob Hendry, son of F. A. Hendry and grandson of Alva Hendry, is employed by Interfor's Gilchrist Mill. He is the third generation of the family to work there. During the spring of 2011, he described Interfor's operations:

> We put a lot of hours in over there. We're busy. They run more lumber in a day there than we'd run in a week at the old Gilchrist mill, or maybe even two weeks. I can't believe the amount of wood they are putting through there these days. We ship all over. They are having a little trouble finding logs because they don't own any timber, so wherever they can get them: Oregon, Washington, California. Crown cut everything. That was the worst thing they could have ever done. They just took it and a lot of it didn't even go to this mill. They were selling to logs to pay out their debt and then they went bankrupt. I live in La Pine and hardly go in to Gilchrist much, I just kind of go through there.[558]

Gilchrist, Oregon, remains. It endures as a mill town though no longer a company town. It was fortunate to largely have missed the real estate bubble which afflicted Bend, Oregon, and its environs. Year after year, the town changes into something ever more unlike the model town which

Klamath Northern Railroad and snow plow converted from Engine 204's tender, circa 2002
Collection of Louie Jordan.

Gilchrist Dam, May 2011.

Mr. Frank W. Gilchrist created. Ever more people now reside in Gilchrist who have no connection with the Gilchrist Timber Company or know the Gilchrist family just as has already happened in Laurel, Mississippi. Yet even after the first-person memories of the Gilchrist family, Gilchrist Timber Company, and the knowledge of why Gilchrist, Oregon, exists and what it was have passed away, the knowledge of all that was and had been accomplished will endure in the archives and in what was and what was done. Something wonderful and grand was created, and then lost. Gilchrist endures now as a mill town currently occupied by retirees and vacation homeowners, no longer a company town. There remain a few who knew the generation who established Gilchrist, who are their children. One can walk the streets of Gilchrist and see the town still much as Frank W. Gilchrist planned it. One can still hear the mill if the wind is blowing out of the west. The millpond, the dam and Klamath Northern Railroad all still remain. Outside of town, one can walk the acres that Frank Dushau cruised all those years ago when he was first dispatched to Klamath County to cruise timber for the Gilchrist family. Gilchrist Mall, the first of its kind east of the Cascades and probably the first of its kind in all of the United States, still remains. Listen, see, and perhaps understand how amazing was what the Gilchrists brought into being, which still survives after a fashion, and the tragedy of the circumstances which led to its unraveling.

". . . not might have been, nor even could have been, but was: so vast, so limitless in capacity is man's imagination to disperse and burn away the rubble-dross of fact and probability, leaving only truth and dream . . . across the vast instantaneous intervention, from the long long time ago: listen, stranger; this way myself; this was I."

— William Faulkner, *The Jail*

Log deck, circa 1940.
Stewart J. Gilchrist's photo album, Gilchrist Timber Company papers, Klamath County Museum.

ENDNOTES

Chapter I: Company owned towns in the Pacific Northwest and Central Oregon

1. Green, Hardy. The Company Town: The Industrial Edens And Satanic Mills That Shaped The American Economy, p 3.
2. Ibid
3. Allen, James. The Company Town In The American West, pp 79-82 and see list 167-183.
4. Ibid, pp 122-127
5. Ibid, Interview with Jim Childre, August 12, 2011; Interview with Mary G. Ernst, April 30, 2011; Interview with F. A. Hendry, April 10, 2011; Interviews with B. E. Hill, May 4, 1981, December 30, 1996 and February 2001; Interview with Milton E. Hill, March 15, 1998; Interview with "Louie" Calvin Louis Jordan, March 27, 2011; Interview with Dan Maynard, May 4, 1981; Interview with Charles Shotts, Sr., May 14, 1981; Interview with Charles Shotts, Jr., July 25, 2010; Interview with Fred Southwick, July 25, 2010; Interview with Tom and Karen Steers, July 25, 2010; Stice, Kathy. Personal Interview July 25, 2010
6. Green, p. 123.
7. Ibid, p. 201
8. Ibid, p. 55
9. Crawford, Margaret. Building The Workingman's Paradise: The Design Of American Company Towns, p. 30.
10. Ibid, p. 113.
11. Green, p. 55.
12. Ibid, pp. 55-56.
13. Crawford, p. 178.
14. Green, pp. 70-71.
15. Ibid, 47.
16. Ibid, pp. 204-205
17. Crawford, p. 3
18. Ibid, p. 13
19. Ibid, p. 19
20. Ibid
21. Green, pp. 10-11
22. Ibid, p. 17
23. Ibid, pp. 84-86
24. Crawford, p. 20
25. Green, p. 22
26. Crawford, p. 30
27. Green, p. 69
28. Crawford, p. 32
29. Green, pp. 29-31
30. Almont, Lindsay. The Pullman Strike: The Story Of A Unique Experiment And Of A Great Labor Upheaval, pp. 38-85.
31. Crawford, p. 3
32. Green, pp. 43-47
33. Ibid, p. 5.
34. Ibid, pp. 38-39.
35. Ibid, pp. 92-94.
36. Crawford, p. 51
37. Ibid, p. 177
38. Ibid, p. 45
39. Green, pp. 116-117
40. Crawford, p. 83
41. Ibid, p. 93.
42. Ibid, p. 67
43. Ibid, p. 178
44. Ibid
45. Ibid, p. 179
46. Green, p. 99
47. Crawford, p. 205
48. Green, pp. 192-194
49. Crawford, p. 2
50. Green, p. 105
51. Ibid, pp. 141-142
52. Ibid, pp. 168-169
53. Ibid, pp. 164-165
54. Ibid, pp. 175-181
55. Ibid, p. 170
56. Ibid, pp. 160-161
57. Ibid, p. 191
58. Allen, p. 7
59. Ibid
60. Ibid, pp. 108-115
61. Carlson, Linda. Company Towns Of The Pacific Northwest, p. 49.
62. Ibid, p. 11.
63. Ibid, p. 23
64. Ibid, p. 80
65. Ibid, p. 178; Green, p. 42.
66. Ibid, p. 175
67. Ibid, p. 211.
68. Ibid, p. 11

69. Ibid, p. 19
70. Ibid, p. 35
71. Ibid, pp. 24-25.
72. Ibid, p. 25.
73. Ibid, p. 198.
74. Ibid, p. 29.
75. Ibid, p. 102.
76. Ibid, pp. 102-103.
77. Ibid, p. 102.
78. Ibid, pp. 101-102
79. Ibid, pp. 113
80. Ibid, p. 105
81. Ibid, pp. 70-71
82. Ibid, p. 188
83. Ibid, pp. 79-86
84. Ibid.
85. Ibid, p. 100.
86. Ibid, p. 207.
87. Ibid, p. 168.
88. Ibid.

Chapter II. The Gilchrist Timber Company: Laurel, Mississippi and Before

89. Fisher, Jim. Six Generations In The Forest Industry, p. 6; Hoffman, Gilbert and Howe, Tony. Yellow Pine Capital: The Laurel, Mississippi Story, p. 171.
90. Fisher, p. 6.
91. Ibid, p. 7.
92. Hoffman and Howe, pp. 176-177.
93. Ibid, pp. 172-173.
94. Clark, Norman H. Mill Town: A Social History Of Everett, Washington From Its Earliest Beginnings On The Shores Of Puget Sound To The Tragic And Infamous Event Known As The Everett Massacre. p. 2.
95. Interview with Jim Childre, August 20, 2011.
96. Gilchrist-Fordney Company insurance announcement from the Lauren Rogers Museum's Gilchrist Collect.
97. The Lumber Trade Journal, p. 1. He Provided Employment For Many. New Orleans, LA January 1, 1913, V. 63 No. 1
98. Hoffman and Howe, p. 190.
99. Ibid.
100. Laurel Daily Leader, Laurel MS. p. 1, February 19, 1917
101. Graham, Elise. Dushau Days, pp. 1-2.
102. Hoffman and Howe, pp. 209-210.
103. Graham, p. 22
104. Interview with Mrs. Mary G. Ernst, April 30, 2011. Hoffman and Howe, p. 216.
105. Hoffman and Howe, p. 210
106. Ibid, p. 222
107. Ibid, pp. 221-222
108. Interview with F. A. Hendry, April 10, 2011; Interview with Mrs. Mary G. Ernst, April 30, 2011; Interview with Jim Childre, August 12, 2011. Gilchrist Timber Company Papers, letter dated November 20, 1943. Hoffman and Howe, p. 222.
109. Interview with Jim Childre, August 12, 2011. Hoffman and Howe, p. 222
110. Fickle, James. Mississippi Forests and Forestry, p. 77.
111. Interview with Jim Childre, August 12, 2011.
112. Gilchrist Timber Company papers: Letter from J.P. Applewhite to A. J. Glassow dated April 4, 1946 GTC papers.
113. Gilchrist Timber Company papers: Letter from S.M. Jones to B. V. Wright, dated September 14, 1926
114. Gilchrist Timber Company papers: Letter from S. M. Jones to B. V. Wright, dated September 16, 1927
115. Key, David S. Laurel, Mississippi: A Historical Perspective, p. 63
116. Fickle, p. 101.
117. Howard, James L., Kramp, Andrew and Quevedo, Enrique. Use of Indexing To Udate U.S. Annual Timber Harvest by State, p 23. and p. 25
118. Hoffman and Howe, p. 221
119. Ibid, p. 224, "Lumber Giant Remembered For Contributions To Laurel", Action
120. Interview with Mrs. Mary G. Ernst, April 30, 2011.
121. Hoffman and Howe, p. 225
122. Ibid
123. Ibid, p. 226
124. Ibid.
125. Hoffman and Howe, p. 226; "Lumber Giant Remembered For Contributions To Laurel", Action; Jones County June 15, 1937, p. 125.
126. Hoffman and Howe, p. 232; "Club Women Of Bay Springs Given Virgin Timber Track By Gilchrist-Fordney Co." Laurel Call Leader.
127. Hoffman and Howe, p. 232.
128. Hoffman and Howe, pp. 232-233; Jones County June 15, 1937, p. 125.
129. Hoffman and Howe, p. 233. Letter To B. V. Wright, dated 1935. Gilchrist Timber Company Papers.
130. Hoffman and Howe, p. 233. Letter To B. V. Wright, dated 1936.
131. Hoffman and Howe, pp. 233-235; Jones County June 15, 1937, p. 125. Gilchrist Timber Company Papers; Gilchrist-Fordney History Is Related" The Laurel Call Leader
132. Interview with Jim Childre, August 20, 2011
133. "Gilchrist Joins Deavours & Hilbun" Laurel Call Leader.

Chapter III. 1938-1941 - The Move West and Building the Town

134. Hoffman and Howe, p. 233.
135. Ibid, 236; Schwantes, Carlos A. Railroad Signatures Across The Pacific Northwest, pp. 159-161.
136. Ibid.
137. Hoffman and Howe, p. 238.
138. Letter from Ralph E. Gilchrist to B. V. Wright, dated October 2, 1926, Gilchrist Timber Company papers.
139. Letters from Gilchrist Timber Company dated 1926 and 1927.
140. Hoffman and Howe, pp. 236-237; Schwantes, pp. 159-161.
141. Hoffman and Howe, p. 238; numerous letters from B. V. Wright to Ralph E. Gilchrist, S. M. Jones and Frank W. Gilchrist, dated 1924-1936, Gilchrist Timber Company papers.
142. Letter from B. V. Wright to C.W. Willette, dated October 4, 1927, Gilchrist Timber Company papers.
143. Numerous letters from B. V. Wright to Ralph E. Gilchrist and Frank W. Gilchrist, dated 1933-1936, Gilchrist Timber Company papers.
144. Letter from B. V. Wright to Ralph E. Gilchrist dated August 7, 1936, Gilchrist Timber Company papers.
145. Letter from B. V. Wright to Frank E. Gilchrist dated April 19, 1935, Gilchrist Timber Company papers.
146. Letter from B. V. Wright to Frank E. Gilchrist, dated July 24, 1936, Gilchrist Timber Company papers.
147. Gilchrist Timber Company papers.
148. Ibid.
149. Ibid.
150. Hoffman and Howe, p. 233.
151. Ibid, pp. 238-239.
152. Gilchrist Timber Company papers.
153. Ibid.
154. Ibid.
155. Ibid.
156. Letter from Frank W. Gilchrist to B. V. Wright, dated January 6, 1937, Gilchrist Timber Company papers.
157. Gilchrist Timber Company papers.
158. Ibid.
159. Letter from B. V. Wright to Mr. Loyde Blakley, dated January 28, 1937, Gilchrist Timber Company papers.
160. Letter from B. V. Wright to F. L. Newton, dated January 30, 1937, Gilchrist Timber Company papers.
161. Letter from B. V. Wright to Frank W. Gilchrist, dated January 29, 1937 Gilchrist Timber Company papers.
162. Letter from B. V. Wright to Frank W. Gilchrist, dated January 1937, Gilchrist Timber Company papers.
163. Letter from B. V. Wright to O. U. Addison, dated February 14, 1937, Gilchrist Timber Company papers.
164. Telegram from B. V. Wright to H.W. Klein, dated February 27, 1937, Gilchrist Timber Company papers.
165. Hoffman and Howe, p. 239
166. Ibid and Gilchrist Timber Company papers.
167. Letter from B.W. Wright to Fred Peterson, dated April 8, 1937, Gilchrist Timber Company papers.
168. Letter from B. V. Wright to Frank W. Gilchrist, dated May 24, 1937, Gilchrist Timber Company papers.
169. Letter from Frank W. Gilchrist to B. V. Wright, dated May 24, 1937, Gilchrist Timber Company papers.
170. Letter from B. V. Wright to Frank W. Gilchrist, dated June 7, 1937, Gilchrist Timber Company papers.
171. Letter from B. V. Wright to Frank W. Gilchrist, dated June 28, 1937, Gilchrist Timber Company papers.
172. Letter from B. V. Wright to Frank W. Gilchrist, dated June 14, 1937, Gilchrist Timber Company papers.
173. Letter from B. V. Wright to Frank W. Gilchrist, dated August 4, 1937, Gilchrist Timber Company papers
174. Letter from B. V. Wright to Frank W. Gilchrist, dated August 11, 1937, Gilchrist Timber Company papers
175. Letter from Frank W. Gilchrist to Benjamin V. Wright, dated August 9, 1937 Gilchrist Timber Company papers.
176. Ibid.
177. Letter from B. V. Wright to Frank W. Gilchrist, dated August 21, 1937, Gilchrist Timber Company papers.
178. Letter from B. V. Wright to H. A. Utley of Favell Utley Realty Company, dated September 13, 1937, Gilchrist Timber Company papers.
179. Letter from B. V. Wright to Frank W. Gilchrist, dated September 11, 1937, Gilchrist Timber Company papers.
180. Gilchrist Timber Company papers.
181. Letter from President, Bend Chamber of Commerce to N. G. Wallace, Public Utilities Commissioner, dated September 1, 1937, Gilchrist Timber Company papers.
182. Letter from Francis Foley to J. P. Applewhite, Gilchrist Timber Company papers.
183. Letter from Frank W. Gilchrist to Benjamin V. Wright, dated October 21, 1937 Gilchrist Timber Company papers.

184. Letter from B. V. Wright to Birmingham Rail & Locomotive Company, dated September 2, 1937, Gilchrist Timber Company papers.
185. Hoffman and Howe, p. 239.
186. Letter from B. V. Wright to Harry J. Veldwyk Machinery Company Seattle, WA, dated September 2, 1937, Gilchrist Timber Company papers.
187. Gilchrist Timber Company papers.
188. Letter from B. V. Wright to M. K. Frank Iron and Steel Products, New York, NY, dated September 11, 1937, Gilchrist Timber Company papers.
189. Letter from B. V. Wright to Stulman-Enrick Lumber Company, dated October 13, 1937, Gilchrist Timber Company papers.
190. Letter from B. V. Wright to Frank W. Gilchrist, dated October 25, 1937, Gilchrist Timber Company papers.
191. Letter from R. G. Watts, Deschutes Lumber Company, Mowich, Oregon to B. V. Wright, dated October 26, 1937, Gilchrist Timber Company papers.
192. Letter from F.J. Foley to J. P. Applewhite, dated October 12, 1937, Gilchrist Timber Company papers.
193. Letter from B. V. Wright to F. W. Gilchrist, dated October 26, 1937, Gilchrist Timber Company papers.
194. Letter from B. V. Wright to C. S. Starrett, dated October 26, 1937, Gilchrist Timber Company papers.
195. Letter from Frank W. Gilchrist to B. V. Wright, dated November 4, 1937, Gilchrist Timber Company papers.
196. Letter from B. V. Wright to Frank W. Gilchrist, dated November 13, 1937, Gilchrist Timber Company papers.
197. Letter from Frank W. Gilchrist to B. V. Wright, dated November 16, 1937, Gilchrist Timber Company papers.
198. Letter from Frank W. Gilchrist to Peter Swann, dated November 5, 1937, Gilchrist Timber Company papers.
199. Letter from H.W. Kline to B. V. Wright, dated November 24, 1937, Gilchrist Timber Company papers. Letter from B. V. Wright to Frank W. Gilchrist, dated November 29, 1937, Gilchrist Timber Company papers.
200. The Forgotten Man p. 352, p. 334 and p. xv.
201. Letter from B. V. Wright to Charles H. Mack, Klamath Falls, dated November 12, 1937, Gilchrist Timber Company papers.
202. Letter from B. V. Wright to I. I. Rosen, Camp Pori, Michigan, dated November 16, 1937 Gilchrist Timber Company papers.
203. Letter from B. V. Wright to George O. Updegraff of Modoc Point, Oregon, dated December 6, 1937, Gilchrist Timber Company papers.
204. Letter from Frank W. Gilchrist to B. V. Wright, dated November 6, 1937, Gilchrist Timber Company papers.
205. Letter from Frank W. Gilchrist to B. V. Wright, dated December 16, 1937, Gilchrist Timber Company papers.
206. Letter from B. V. Wright to Frank W. Gilchrist, dated December 10, 1937, Gilchrist Timber Company papers.
207. Glenn Stanton Papers, Oregon Historical Society, Portland, Oregon.
208. Inspection Report prepared by R. K. Byhre, technical representative, LaBow, Haynes, dated June 20, 1975. *From the collection of Tami Jordan*
209. Letter from Hollis Johnston to J. C. Hazen, Associate Editor, The Architectural Forum, dated June 10, 1941 Gilchrist Timber Company papers.
210. Crawford, p. 201.
211. Allen, Carlson, Crawford.
212. Letter from B. V. Wright to Frank W. Gilchrist, dated January 3, 1938, Gilchrist Timber Company papers.
213. Letter from Frank W. Gilchrist to B. V. Wright, dated February 21, 1938, Gilchrist Timber Company papers.
214. Ibid.
215. Ibid.
216. Letter from B. V. Wright to Frank W. Gilchrist, dated March 1, 1938, Gilchrist Timber Company papers.
217. Letter from Frank W. Gilchrist to B. V. Wright, dated March 9, 1938, Gilchrist Timber Company papers.
218. Hoffman and Howe, p. 239.
219. Letter from B. V. Wright to Frank W. Gilchrist, dated March 15, 1938, Gilchrist Timber Company papers.
220. Hoffman and Howe, pp. 239-240.
221. Letter from B. V. Wright to Frank W. Gilchrist, dated April 12, 1938, Gilchrist Timber Company papers.
222. Hoffman and Howe, p. 240.
223. Ibid, pp. 240-241.
224. Ibid, p. 241. Interview with F. A. Hendry, April 10, 2011.
225. Hoffman and Howe, p. 241.
226. Interview with Jim Childre, August 12, 2011.
227. Ibid, Hoffman and Howe, p. 241.
228. Interview with Jim Childre, August 12, 2011.
229. Interview with Mrs. Mary G. Ernst, April 30, 2011.
230. Letter from B. V. Wright to Frank W. Gilchrist, dated April 25, 1938, Gilchrist Timber Company papers.
231. Letter from J. P. Applewhite to B. V. Wright, dated March 31, 1938, Gilchrist Timber Company papers.

232. Interview with Jim Childre, August 12, 2011.
233. Letter from B. V. Wright to J. J. Polin, Polin's Corner Store, Chiloquin, Oregon, dated May 9, 1938, Gilchrist Timber Company papers.
234. Letter from B. V. Wright to Frank W. Gilchrist, dated June 1, 1938, Gilchrist Timber Company papers.
235. Letter from B. V. Wright to Frank W. Gilchrist, dated June 2, 1938, Gilchrist Timber Company papers.
236. Interviews with B. E. Hill, February 21, 2001.
237. Hoffman and Howe, p. 244
238. Ibid.
239. Letter from Thomas H. Burgess, U. S. Forest Service to B. V. Wright, dated July 20, 1938, Gilchrist Timber Company papers.
240. Interview with F. A. Hendry, April 10, 2011.
241. Hoffman and Howe, p. 244.
242. Ibid.
243. Interview with F. A. Hendry, April 10, 2011.
244. Letter from B. V. Wright to M. L. Jenning, Southern Pacific Rail Road, dated October 31, 1938, Gilchrist Timber Company papers.
245. Letter from Frank W. Gilchrist to B. V. Wright, dated November 10, 1938, Gilchrist Timber Company papers.
246. Ibid.
247. Interview with Mrs. Mary G. Ernst, April 30, 2011.
248. Klamath Falls Herald and News "Crescent" p. 2, December 17, 1938.
249. Letter from M. L. Jennings Southern Pacific Rail Road to B. V. Wright, dated 22 December, 1938, Gilchrist Timber Company papers.
250. Klamath Falls Herald and News, December 23, 1938, p. 9 "Christmas Tree Up At Gilchrist"
251. Klamath Falls Herald and News, January 8, 1939 p. 5 "Gilchrist gets a new fire truck"
252. "Gilchrist Telephone Exchange is Opened" Undated newspaper article from scrap book created Stewart J. Gilchrist.
253. Shlaes, Amity. The Forgotten Man: A New History Of The Great Depression, 354.
254. Klamath Falls Herald and News, April 21, 1939 "Activity Seen at Gilchrist"
255. Interview with Jim Childre, August 12, 2011.
256. Carlson, p. 102.
257. Undated newspaper articles from scrap book created Stewart J. Gilchrist.
258. The Club Organization, dated July 1, 1939, Gilchrist Timber Company papers.
259. Interview with Jim Childre, August 12, 2011.
260. Undated newspaper articles from scrap book created Stewart J. Gilchrist. Hoffman and Howe, p. 245.
261. Undated newspaper articles from scrap book created Stewart J. Gilchrist.
262. Ibid.
263. Artifact, a document, from scrap book created by Stewart J. Gilchrist.
264. Shlaes, p. 366.
265. Hoffman and Howe, p. 245.
266. Ibid.
267. Article from Klamath Falls Herald and News included in scrap book created by Stewart J. Gilchrist.
268. Interview with B. E. Hill, February 2001.
269. Hoffman and Howe, p. 245.
270. Ibid.
271. Ibid, p. 246.
272. Hoffman and Howe, 246. Carlson, pp. 43-44.
273. Hoffman and Howe, p. 246. Articles from a scrap book created by Stewart J. Gilchrist.
274. Hoffman and Howe, p. 246.
275. Ibid.
276. Artifact, a Christmas program, from scrap book created by Stewart J. Gilchrist.
277. Letter from Frank W. Gilchrist to Jack N. Bryant Seattle Washington, dated January 11, 1940, Gilchrist Timber Company papers.
278. Ibid.
279. Artifact, Gilchrist Theatre program, from scrap book created by Stewart J. Gilchrist.
280. Artifact, Gilchrist High School Class of 1940 Graduation Announcement, from scrap book created by Stewart J. Gilchrist.
281. Hoffman and Howe, pp. 247-248. Interview with "Louie" Calvin Louis Jordan, March 27, 2011.
282. Hoffman and Howe, p. 248.

Chapter IV: 1941-1946: World War II and the Strike

283. Shlaes, p. 366.
284. Folsom, Burton W. Jr. and Folsom, Anita: FDR Goes To War: How Expanded Executive Power, Spiraling National Debt And Restricted Civil Liberties Shaped Wartime America, pp 1-5.
285. Letter from William Albert Carmichael to J. P. Applewhite, dated December 31, 1940, Gilchrist Timber Company papers.
286. Letter from Frank W. Gilchrist to J.A. Denton of Portland Oregon, dated January 15, 1941, Gilchrist Timber Company papers.
287. Letter from William Albert Carmichael to editor, Bend Bulletin, Bend Oregon, dated, January 19, 1941, Gilchrist Timber Company papers.
288. Letter from William Albert Carmichael to John Heriza, dated January 15, 1941, Gilchrist Timber Company papers.
289. Letter from William Albert Carmichael to Frank W. Gilchrist, dated February 22, 1941, Gilchrist Timber Company papers.

290. Letter from William Albert Carmichael to Frank W. Gilchrist, dated March 6, 1941, Gilchrist Timber Company papers.
291. Letter from Frank W. Gilchrist to Jack W. Bryant, dated, March 15, 1941, Gilchrist Timber Company papers.
292. Letter from Frank W. Gilchrist to Mrs. Catherine Bauer, Secretary, California Housing Association, dated March 17, 1941, Gilchrist Timber Company papers.
293. Letter from James Applewhite to Horner Temple, dated April 3, 1941, Gilchrist Timber Company papers.
294. Letter from Frank W. Gilchrist to L. Orth Sisemore, Klamath County District Attorney, dated May 12, 1941, Gilchrist Timber Company papers.
295. Letter from Frank W. Gilchrist to Hollis Johnston, dated May 22, 1941, Gilchrist Timber Company papers.
296. Letter from William Albert Carmichael to Frank W. Gilchrist, dated June 14, 1941, Gilchrist Timber Company papers.
297. Ibid.
298. Letter from William Albert Carmichael to Frank W. Gilchrist, dated June 21, 1941, Gilchrist Timber Company papers.
299. Letter from James P. Applewhite to Vernon Applewhite, dated June 23, 1941, Gilchrist Timber Company papers.
300. Letter from Fred H. Heilbronner to William Albert Carmichael, dated June 23, 1941 Gilchrist Timber Company papers.
301. Letter from Frank W. Gilchrist to Reverend J. M. B. Gill, Lakeview Oregon, dated June 27, 1941, Gilchrist Timber Company papers.
302. Agreement dated July 30, 1941, Gilchrist Timber Company papers.
303. Letter from Hollis Johnston to Frank W. Gilchrist, dated July 12, 1941, Gilchrist Timber Company papers.
304. Letter from Frank W. Gilchrist to Hollis Johnston, dated July 16, 1941, Gilchrist Timber Company papers.
305. Letter from Frank W. Gilchrist to Hollis Johnston, dated August 7, 1941, Gilchrist Timber Company papers.
306. Letter from Frank W. Gilchrist to Hollis Johnston, dated August 22, 1941, Gilchrist Timber Company papers.
307. Letter from Frank W. Gilchrist to Davis Lumber Company, Hutchinson Kansas, dated August 2, 1941, Gilchrist Timber Company papers.
308. Letter from Bruce Blahnik to Albert Carmichael, dated October 1941, Gilchrist Timber Company papers.
309. Letter from Hollis Johnston to Frank W. Gilchrist, dated November 12, 1941, Gilchrist Timber Company papers.
310. Letter from Hollis Johnston to Frank W. Gilchrist, dated November 12, 1941, Gilchrist Timber Company papers.
311. Newspaper announcement from scrap book created by Stewart Gilchrist..
312. Letters from William Albert Carmichael to various vendors, dated December 3, 1941, Gilchrist Timber Company papers.
313. Letter from Frank W. Gilchrist to James Applewhite, dated December 20, 1941, Gilchrist Timber Company papers.
314. Letter from Frank W. Gilchrist to James Applewhite, dated December 31, 1941, Gilchrist Timber Company papers.
315. Letter from Frank W. Gilchrist to James Applewhite, dated December 31, 1941, Gilchrist Timber Company papers.
316. Letter from William Albert Carmichael to James Applewhite, dated January 7, 1942, Gilchrist Timber Company papers.
317. Letter from William Albert Carmichael to James Applewhite, dated January 7, 1942, Gilchrist Timber Company papers.
318. Letter from Frank W. Gilchrist to Savings Staff, Treasury Department, dated January 19, 1942, Gilchrist Timber Company papers.
319. Letter from Gilchrist Timber Company to H. H. McCall of Portland Oregon, dated February 20, 1942, Gilchrist Timber Company papers.
320. Letter from Jack N. Bryant to Frank W. Gilchrist, dated April 6, 1942, Gilchrist Timber Company papers.
321. Interview with F. A. Hendry, April 10, 2011.
322. List of Gilchrist Timber Company employees currently serving on active duty, dated 1944, Gilchrist Timber Company papers.
323. Fisher, *Six Generations In The Forest Industry*, p. 29. Interview with Mrs. Mary G. Ernst, April 30, 2011.
324. Hoffman and Howe, p. 248. Gilchrist Timber Company papers. Interview with Mrs. Mary G. Ernst, April 30, 2011. Interview with F. A. Hendry, April 10, 2011.
325. Letter from R. D. Bedinger, Commerce Department, Civil Aeronautics Administration, Seattle Washington to Gilchrist Timber Company, dated April 9, 1942.
326. Interview with Mrs. Mary G. Ernst, April 30, 2011.
327. Letter from the Gilchrist Timber Company to Joe Webb, dated April 10, 1942, Gilchrist Timber Company papers.

328. Letter from the Gilchrist Timber Company to Glen I Talley, LaPine Oregon, dated March 19, 1942, Gilchrist Timber Company papers.
329. Letter from Frank W. Gilchrist to W. R. Cabaniss, of Klamath Falls Oregon, dated April 23, 1942, Gilchrist Timber Company papers.
330. 1942 correspondence, Gilchrist Timber Company papers.
331. Letter from Frank W. Gilchrist to Herbert Penny, Eugene Oregon, dated May 18, 1942, Gilchrist Timber Company papers.
332. Letter from Frank W. Gilchrist to Jack N. Bryant, dated April 8, 1942 in response to a letter from Jack N. Bryant to Frank W. Gilchrist, dated April 8, 1942, Gilchrist Timber Company papers.
333. Letter from Frank W. Gilchrist, dated May 1, 1942, Gilchrist Timber Company papers.
334. Letter from Frank W. Gilchrist to the Board of Directors of the Gilchrist Timber Company, dated May 29, 1942, Gilchrist Timber Company papers.
335. Memorandum from Frank W. Gilchrist to the employees of the Gilchrist Timber Company, dated June 12, 1942, Gilchrist Timber Company papers.
336. Folsom and Folsom, p. 178.
337. Letter from Frank W. Gilchrist to the Board of Directors of the Gilchrist Timber Company, dated June 30, 1942, Gilchrist Timber Company papers.
338. Letter from Frank W. Gilchrist, dated August 1, 1942, Oregon Historical Society Research Library.
339. Letter from Frank W. Gilchrist to Don B. Drury, dated August 7, 1942 Gilchrist Timber Company papers.
340. Letter from Frank W. Gilchrist to M. E. Kenfield, dated August 7, 1942, Gilchrist Timber Company papers.
341. Letter from M. E. Kenfield, Kenfield Lumber Company to Frank W. Gilchrist, dated August 11, 1942, Gilchrist Timber Company papers.
342. Letter from Frank W. Gilchrist to Charles M. Cooper, W. E. Cooper Lumber Company, dated August 17, 1942, Gilchrist Timber Company papers.
343. Bill of Lading from Valley Tractor and Equipment Company, Los Angeles California, dated September 25, 1942, Gilchrist Timber Company papers.
344. Letter from Albert Carmichael to Frank W. Gilchrist, dated August 29, 1942 Gilchrist Timber Company papers.
345. Letter from William Albert Carmichael to Art Burnside & Company, dated September 16, 1942.

346. William Albert Carmichael to Gilchrist Timber Company customers. Dated 1942. Gilchrist Timber Company papers.
347. Letter from Earl Reynolds, Klamath County Chamber of Commerce to Frank W. Gilchrist, dated September 22, 1942, Gilchrist Timber Company papers.
348. Letter from Frank W. Gilchrist to Albert S. Rayner of Hattisburg Mississippi, dated September 26, 1942, Gilchrist Timber Company papers.
349. Letter from William Albert Carmichael to Frank W. Gilchrist, dated October 24, 1942, Gilchrist Timber Company papers.
350. Memorandum from Frank W. Gilchrist to All Residents, Gilchrist, Oregon, dated October 10, 1942, Gilchrist Timber Company papers.
351. Klamath Falls Herald and News p. 1 "War Savings Flags Fly Over Wonder Town", October 19, 1942.
352. Memorandum from Frank W. Gilchrist to all employees, dated November 30, 1942, Gilchrist Timber Company papers.
353. Insurance Announcement for Gilchrist-Fordney Company dtd 1912 collection of Lauren Rogers Museum, Laurel Mississippi.
354. Letter from Frank W. Gilchrist to Russell Dieterich, dated December 30, 1942 Gilchrist Timber Company papers.
355. Gilchrist Timber Company papers.
356. Letter from William Albert Carmichael to F. A. Hoagland of LaGrande, Oregon, dated January 6, 1943, Gilchrist Timber Company papers.
357. Letter from B. V. Wright to Robert E. Graham, dated January 7, 1943 Gilchrist Timber Company papers.
358. Letter from Frank W. Gilchrist to HQ, Northern Security District, dated January 25, 1943, Gilchrist Timber Company papers.
359. Letter from Frank W. Gilchrist to James P. Applewhite, dated February 10, 1943, Gilchrist Timber Company papers.
360. Letter from Frank W. Gilchrist to James P. Applewhite, dated February 10, 1943, Gilchrist Timber Company papers.
361. Letter from Frank W. Gilchrist to A. B. Lytton, dated March 11, 1943, Gilchrist Timber Company papers.
362. Frank W. Gilchrist to D. F. Denham, Laurel Mississippi, dated March 19, 1943, Gilchrist Timber Company papers.
363. Telegram from Frank W. Gilchrist to C. U. Addison, Laurel Mississippi, dated March 27, 1943, Gilchrist Timber Company papers.
364. Letter from Frank W. Gilchrist to W. C. Anderson, Planing Mill Foreman, dated April 2, 1943, Gilchrist Timber Company papers.

365. Letter from Frank W. Gilchrist to Maurice H. Ashton, dated April 6, 1943, Gilchrist Timber Company papers.
366. Letter from Frank W. Gilchrist to K. W. Rolison, dated May 5, 1943, Gilchrist Timber Company papers.
367. Letter from W. A. Carmichael to Virgil Sickels, dated May 12, 1943, Gilchrist Timber Company papers.
368. Letter from Frank W. Gilchrist to Henry Kieper, dated June 22, 1943, Gilchrist Timber Company papers.
369. Letter from Frank W. Gilchrist to Fletcher, Vance and Foley (Gilchrist Timber Company directors), dated July 13, 1943, Gilchrist Timber Company papers.
370. Ibid.
371. Interview with Mrs. Mary G. Ernst, April 30, 2011.
372. Klamath Falls Herald and News p. 1, August 11, 1943 #9878 "Bend Klamath Falls Road Promoters Pool Efforts for Dalles-California Route.
373. Letter from Frank W. Gilchrist LTJG James P. Applewhite, dated August 12, 1943, Gilchrist Timber Company papers.
374. Letter from Frank W. Gilchrist to Fletcher, Vance and Foley (Gilchrist Timber Company directors), dated September 4, 1943, Gilchrist Timber Company papers.
375. Letter from Frank W. Gilchrist to L. L. Tannehill, Valsetz Oregon, dated September 15, 1943.
376. Letter from L. Parker Martinez Modoc Council, Boy Scouts of America, Klamath Falls Oregon to William Albert Carmichael, dated October 5, 1943 papers.
377. Letter from Frank W. Gilchrist to LTJG James Applewhite, dated November 11, 1943, Gilchrist Timber Company papers.
378. Letter from Frank W. Gilchrist to J. W. Kerns Klamath Falls Oregon, dated December 30, 1943. Gilchrist Timber Company papers.
379. Letters dated December 31, 1943, June 14, 1944, December 30, 1943 and November 29, 1943. Gilchrist Timber Company papers.
380. Letter from Frank W. Gilchrist to Joseph P. Knapp & Co, Portland Oregon. Gilchrist Timber Company papers.
381. Letter from Frank W. Gilchrist to Fletcher, Vance and Foley (Gilchrist Timber Company directors), dated February 4, 1944. Gilchrist Timber Company papers.
382. Memorandum from Frank W. Gilchrist to all Gilchrist Timber Company employees, dated February 17, 1944, Gilchrist Timber Company papers.
383. Letter from Frank W. Gilchrist to W. G. Simpson, American Lumberman, Chicago Illinios, dated April12, 1944, Gilchrist Timber Company papers.
384. Letter from Jay M. Allen to Frank W. Gilchrist, dated April 15, 1944, Gilchrist Timber Company papers.
385. Fisher, p.26.
386. Hoffman and Howe, p. 249.
387. Ibid.
388. Telegram from George N. Comfort Lumber Company Cleveland Ohio to Gilchrist Timber Company, dated June 16, 1944, Gilchrist Timber Company papers.
389. Memorandum from Frank W. Gilchrist to all Foreman, dated June 13, 1944, Gilchrist Timber Company papers.
390. Memorandum from Frank W. Gilchrist to all Gilchrist Timber Company Employees, date June 26, 1944, Gilchrist Timber Company papers.
391. Letter from Frank W. Gilchrist to the Oregon War Finance Committee, dated December 14, 1944, Gilchrist Timber Company papers.
392. Letter from B. V. Wright to Fred Peterson, County Superintendant, Klamath Falls Oregon, dated June 20, 1944, Gilchrist Timber Company papers.
393. Memorandum from Frank W. Gilchrist to all Foremen, dated June 26, 1944, Gilchrist Timber Company papers.
394. Letter from Frank W. Gilchrist to Ross Handbury, dated June 30, 1944 Gilchrist Timber Company papers.
395. Letter from Frank W. Gilchrist to Harry Fletcher, dated July 5, 1944 Gilchrist Timber Company papers.
396. Ibid.
397. Letter from Frank W. Gilchrist to Fletcher, Vance and Foley (Gilchrist Timber Company directors), dated July 27, 1944 Gilchrist Timber Company papers.
398. Letter from Frank W. Gilchrist to Harry Fletcher, dated July 5, 1944, Gilchrist Timber Company papers.
399. Letter from Frank W. Gilchrist to LTJG James P. Applewhite, dated September 15, 1944, Gilchrist Timber Company papers.
400. Letter from Frank W. Gilchrist to A. T. Blackwell, McNary Arizona, dated September 22, 1944, Gilchrist Timber Company papers.
401. Letter from Frank W. Gilchrist to LT James P. Applewhite, 50th U.S.N. Construction Battalion, dated October 6, 1944, Gilchrist Timber Company papers.
402. Hoffman and Howe, p. 248. Interview with F. A. Hendry, April 10, 2011.

403. Hoffman and Howe, pp. 248-249.
404. Letter from Frank W. Gilchrist to Mr. J. P. Adams, Vanport Oregon, dated October 23, 1944, Gilchrist Timber Company papers.
405. Letter from Frank W. Gilchrist to LT James P. Applewhite, dated October 25, 1944, Gilchrist Timber Company papers.
406. Ibid.
407. Letter from Frank W. Gilchrist to LT James P. Applewhite, dated November 2, 1944, Gilchrist Timber Company papers.
408. Letter from MAJ Harry D. Williams to the Gilchrist Timber Company, dated November 10, 1944, Gilchrist Timber Company papers.
409. Letter from Frank W. Gilchrist to the Oregon War Finance Committee, dated December 14, 1944, Gilchrist Timber Company papers.
410. Letter from Frank W. Gilchrist to LT James P. Applewhite, dated January 26, 1945, Gilchrist Timber Company papers.
411. Gilchrist Bowling League 1945 Season, Gilchrist Timber Company papers.
412. Letter from Frank W. Gilchrist to Fletcher, Vance and Foley (Gilchrist Timber Company directors), dated February 17, 1945, Gilchrist Timber Company papers.
413. Letter from Frank W. Gilchrist to Harry Fletcher, dated February 21, 1945, Gilchrist Timber Company papers.
414. Letter from Frank W. Gilchrist to Harry Fletcher, dated March 13, 1945, Gilchrist Timber Company papers.
415. Ibid.
416. Ibid.
417. Letter from Frank W. Gilchrist to LT James P. Applewhite, dated April 5, 1945, Gilchrist Timber Company papers.
418. Letter from Mrs Frank W. Gilchrist to American Red Cross, dated April 4, 1945, Gilchrist Timber Company papers.
419. Letter from C. E. Shotts to Glen Fisk, dated April 16 1945, Gilchrist Timber Company papers.
420. Memorandum from Frank W. Gilchrist to Gilchrist, Crescent and surrounding territory, dated April 20, 1945, Gilchrist Timber Company papers.
421. Letter from Frank W. Gilchrist to Audrey Kiehn, John Day Oregon, dated May1, 1945, Gilchrist Timber Company papers.
422. Letter from Gilchrist Timber Company to Brooks Scanlon, dated May 15, 1945 in response to a letter Brooks Scanlon, dated May 15, 1945, Gilchrist Timber Company papers.
423. Interview with Mrs. Mary G. Ernst, April 30, 2011.
424. Letter from Frank W. Gilchrist to Harry Fletcher, dated July 24, 1945, Gilchrist Timber Company papers.
425. Ibid.
426. Interview with Mrs. Mary G. Ernst, April 30, 2011.
427. Letter from Frank W. Gilchrist to LT James P. Applewhite, dated September 8, 1945, Gilchrist Timber Company papers.
428. Ibid.
429. Letter from Frank W. Gilchrist to LT McGraw, Fort Lewis Washington, dated September 13, 1945, Gilchrist Timber Company papers.
430. Hindy, Hill and Nivens, *The Weyerhauser Story*, pp 466-467. The price of lumber was not modified by the O.P.A. until March 1946. Lumber price controls were not ended until November 1946. Lumber prices, once controls were removed, rose until they reached the equilibrium price, which during the period of federal price controls was only reflected by the black market price. *Herald and News*, January 24, 1946.
431. Letter from Frank W. Gilchrist to Harry Fletcher, dated September 21, 1945, Gilchrist Timber Company papers.
432. Hindy, Hill and Nivens, p. 466. *Herald and News*, December 29, 1945, p. 1.
433. Interview with B. E. Hill, May 4, 1981.
434. Letter from Frank W. Gilchrist to Fletcher, Vance and Foley (Gilchrist Timber Company directors), dated September 25, 1945 Gilchrist Timber Company papers.
435. Memorandum from Frank W. Gilchrist to all residents, dated October 8, 1945 Gilchrist Timber Company papers.
436. Letter from Frank W. Gilchrist to Harry Fletcher, dated October 1, 1945, Gilchrist Timber Company papers.
437. Letter from Frank W. Gilchrist to Joseph P. Knapp, dated October 5. 1945, Gilchrist Timber Company papers.
438. Letter to Crescent Light & Power/Crescent Garage, dated October 17, 1945, Gilchrist Timber Company papers.
439. Letter from Frank W. Gilchrist to LT James P. Applewhite, dated December 13, 1945, Gilchrist Timber Company papers.
440. Letter from Frank W. Gilchrist to LT James P. Applewhite, dated December 20, 1945, Gilchrist Timber Company papers.
441. Letter from William Albert Carmichael to Cal L. Adams, dated December 31, 1945 in response to Cal L. Adams' letter dated December 18, 1945 Gilchrist Timber Company papers.

442. Letter from William Albert Carmichael to Fred D. Allen, dated January 16, 1946 in response to Fred D. Allen's letter dated January 13, 1946 Gilchrist Timber Company papers. Letter from William Albert Carmichael to Mrs. Anderson, Dealers Lumber & Coal Company, Columbus Ohio, dated, January 16, 1946.
443. Hoffman and Howe, p. 248.
444. Interview with B. E. Hill, 4 May 1981.
445. Klamath Falls Herald and News, "15 Cent Raise OK'd At Burns" December 19, 1945, p. 1.
446. Klamath Falls Herald and News, December 29, 1945, p. 1.
447. Klamath Falls Herald and News, "OPA Hikes Mill Price Ceiling" February 21, 1946, p. 1.
448. Klamath Falls Herald and News, "Gilchrist Lumber Resumes Operations", April 9, 1946, p. 3.
449. Ibid.
450. Interview with B. E. Hill, May 4, 1981. Interview with Charles Shotts, May 14, 1981. Klamath Falls Herald and News, "Gilchrist Lumber Resumes Operations", April 9, 1946, p 1.

Chapter V. 1946-1982: Gilchrist in its Heyday

451. Memorandum to Gilchrist Timber Company employees, dated March 14, 1946, Gilchrist Timber Company papers.
452. Letter from shipping foreman to Floyd Greene, Milton-Freewater Oregon, dated March 26, 1946, Gilchrist Timber Company papers.
453. Letter from William Albert Carmichael to Frank W. Gilchrist, dated April 3, 1946, Gilchrist Timber Company papers.
454. Letter from William Albert Carmichael to Frank W. Gilchrist, dated April 15, 1946, Gilchrist Timber Company papers.
455. Ibid.
456. Letter from William Albert Carmichael to Frank W. Gilchrist, dated April 3, 1946, Gilchrist Timber Company papers.
457. Letter from William Albert Carmichael to Frank W. Gilchrist, dated April 18, 1946, Gilchrist Timber Company papers.
458. Letter from Frank W. Gilchrist to Mr. E. F. Ritchie, Dorman Hotel Supply, Portland Oregon, dated June 19, 1946, Gilchrist Timber Company papers.
459. Notice, dated June 7, 1946 Gilchrist Timber Company papers.
460. Letter from William Albert Carmichael to Frank W. Gilchrist, dated April 15, 1946, Gilchrist Timber Company papers.
461. Letter from James P. Applewhite to A. J. Glassow, General Manager, Brooks-Scanlon, dated April 10, 1946 in response to a letter from A. J. Glassow, dated April 6, 1946, Gilchrist Timber Company papers.
462. Letter from R. B. Ward to Carl Wilson, dated May 3, 1946, Gilchrist Timber Company papers.
463. Letter from Frank W. Gilchrist to Fletcher, Vance and Foley (Gilchrist Timber Company directors), dated May 16, 1946, Gilchrist Timber Company papers.
464. Letter from Frank W. Gilchrist to D. W. Winn, Green Lumber Company, Laurel MS, dated May 16, 1946, Gilchrist Timber Company papers.
465. Memorandum from Frank W. Gilchrist to all foreman, dated June 10, 1946, Gilchrist Timber Company papers.
466. Memorandum from Frank W. Gilchrist to C. E. Shotts, Saw Mill Foreman, dated May 21, 1946, Gilchrist Timber Company papers.
467. Klamath Falls Herald and News "Two Gilchrist Firms Robbed In Night By Burglars, With Loss Estimated at $14,000.00" p. 1., October 19, 1946.
468. Letter from William Albert Carmichael to Frank W. Gilchrist, dated October 22, 1946, Gilchrist Timber Company papers.
469. Letter from William Albert Carmichael to Frank W. Gilchrist, dated November 4, 1946, Gilchrist Timber Company papers.
470. Ibid.
471. Letter from Frank W. Gilchrist to James E. Griffin, dated November 21, 1946 Gilchrist Timber Company papers.
472. Interview with Mrs. Mary G. Ernst, April 30, 2011.
473. Hoffman and Howe, p. 249.
474. Letter from Hollis Johnston to Frank W. Gilchrist, dated March 10, 1947, Gilchrist Timber Company papers
475. Letter from Frank W. Gilchrist to Harry Fletcher, dated February 20, 1947, Gilchrist Timber Company papers.
476. Letter from Frank W. Gilchrist to Mildred Benson, Dalles Oregon, dated April 1, 1947.
477. Letter from Frank W. Gilchrist to James P. Applewhite, dated August 14, 1947, Gilchrist Timber Company papers.
478. Letter from Frank W. Gilchrist to Fletcher, Vance and Foley (Gilchrist Timber Company directors), dated October 23, 1946, Gilchrist Timber Company papers.
479. Hoffman and Howe, p. 249.
480. Letter from Mrs. W. P. Lyon to Frank W. Gilchrist, dated September 30, 1947, Gilchrist Timber Company papers.
481. Letter from C.E. Shotts, Sawmill Foreman to Mr. Wilmer McCallum, dated November 11, 1947, Gilchrist Timber Company papers.

482. Letter from Frank W. Gilchrist to Hollis Johnston, dated November 19, 1947 Gilchrist Timber Company papers.
483. Letter from Klamath County School District to Frank W. Gilchrist, dated November 20, 1947, Gilchrist Timber Company papers.
484. Letter from Klamath County School District to Frank W. Gilchrist, dated June 30, 1948 with Warrant #25997 for $925.00, Gilchrist Timber Company papers.
485. Undated newspapers paper article from scrap book created by Stewart J. Gilchrist.
486. Memorandum from Frank W. Gilchrist to all employees, dated December 18, 1947, Gilchrist Timber Company papers.
487. Letter from Nelson F. Brown, Dixie Lumber Company, New Orleans Louisiana to Frank W. Gilchrist, dated January 16, 1948, Gilchrist Timber Company papers.
488. Letter from William Albert Carmichael to Frank W. Gilchrist, dated February 12, 1948, Gilchrist Timber Company papers.
489. Letter from William Albert Carmichael to Frank W. Gilchrist, dated February 18, 1948, Gilchrist Timber Company papers.
490. Letter from Frank W. Gilchrist to Frank R. Gilchrist, dated March 19, 1948, Gilchrist Timber Company papers.
491. Letter from Frank W. Gilchrist to Frank R. Gilchrist, dated April 6, 1948, Gilchrist Timber Company papers.
492. Memorandum to all Gilchrist Timber Company employees, dated April 1, 1948, Gilchrist Timber Company papers.
493. Letter from Frank W. Gilchrist to A. H. Barbour and Sons, dated May 8, 1948, Gilchrist Timber Company papers.
494. Interview with Mrs. Mary G. Ernst, April 30, 2011.
495. Memorandum to lessees of Houses in Prenco Subdivision, dated June 25, 1948, Gilchrist Timber Company papers.
496. Interview with "Louie" Calvin Louis Jordan, March 27, 2011.
497. Frank W. Gilchrist to S. I. Ritchey, District Manager, California-Oregon Power Company, dated August 10, 1948, Gilchrist Timber Company papers.
498. Memorandum from Frank W. Gilchrist to all tenants dated September 30, 1948, Gilchrist Timber Company papers.
499. Letter from Jack R. Blair to Frank W. Gilchrist dated June 29, 1949, Gilchrist Timber Company papers.
500. Letter from Rufus W. Childre to Frank W. Gilchrist and James Applewhite dated March 19, 1949, Gilchrist Timber Company papers.
501. Letter from Charles E. Ogle, Secretary-Manager Associated Forest Products Industries of Oregon to Frank W. Gilchrist dated April 26, 1949, Gilchrist Timber Company papers.
502. Letter from Frank W. Gilchrist to Fred Peterson, American Red Cross, dated March 26, 1946, Gilchrist Timber Company papers.
503. Letter from Frank W. Gilchrist to Gilchrist Timber Company Directors dated May 16, 1946, Gilchrist Timber Company papers.
504. Letter from Frank W. Gilchrist to Frank X. Seaton, American Red Cross, Klamath Falls Oregon dated July 28, 1949, Gilchrist Timber Company papers.
505. "State Police Open Gilchrist Substation" Bend Bulletin, Bend Oregon date August 6, 1949, Article contained in a scrap book created by Stewart J. Gilchrist.
506. A. H. Etrican, Director of Forestry, State Forest Service, Wellington, New Zealand, Gilchrist Timber Company papers.
507. Letter from Frank W. Gilchrist to Robert W. Anderson dated September 19, 1949, Gilchrist Timber Company papers.
508. Homes For Forest Workers Unasylva V. IV, #1 JAN-MAR 50, Unasylva: An International Review of Forestry and Forest Products, Washington, D.C. pp 10-11.
509. Hoffman and Howe, p. 249.
510. Fisher, p. 31.
511. Hoffman and Howe, p. 249.
512. Ibid, pp. 249-250.
513. Interview with "Louie" Calvin Louis Jordan, March 27, 2011.
514. Carlson, p. 207.
515. U.S. Department of Commerce, Sixth Census of The United States: 1940 (Washington D. C., 1943), 1016-1020; U.S. Department of Commerce, Sixth Census of The United States: 1950 (Washington D. C., 1952), 1048-1052; Rand McNally Commercial Atlas (New York City, New York, 1970) 432.
516. Interview with "Louie" Calvin Louis Jordan, March 27, 2011.
517. Interview with Mrs. Mary G. Ernst, April 30, 2011.
518. Hoffman and Howe, p. 250. Koch, Michael. Steam And Thunder In The Timber: Saga Of The Forest Railroads. pp 303-304.
519. Interview with "Louie" Calvin Louis Jordan, March 27, 2011.
520. Hoffman and Howe, p. 250. Interview with Mrs. Mary G. Ernst, April 30, 2011. Frank Gilchrist, 1903-1956 The Bend Bulletin, April 5, 1956, p. 4; Frank W. Gilchrist Succumbs After Sudden Heart Attach, Bend Bulletin April 4, 1956, p1.

521. Frank Gilchrist, 1903-1956 The Bend Bulletin, April 5, 1956, p. 4; Frank W. Gilchrist Succumbs After Sudden Heart Attach, Bend Bulletin April 4, 1956, p1.
522. Interview with Mrs. Mary G. Ernst, April 30, 2011.
523. Hoffman and Howe, p. 250-251.
524. Interview with "Louie" Calvin Louis Jordan, March 27, 2011.
525. Ibid.
526. Interview with Charles Shotts, Jr., July 25, 2010.
527. Hoffman and Howe, p. 252.
528. Ibid.
529. Ibid.
530. Ibid.
531. Interview with "Louie" Calvin Louis Jordan, March 27, 2011.
532. Interview with Fred Southwick, July 25, 2010
533. Interview with Kathy Stice, July 25, 2010
534. Interview with Milton E. Hill, March 15, 1998.
535. Interview with Tom and Karen Steers, July 25, 2010.
536. Mississippi Pilgrims built town a Gilchrist in Oregon, Jackson Daily News, Jackson Mississippi, p. B-1 June 26, 1970.
537. Idyllic Timber Town Pays Bonus Of Contentment, The Commercial Appeal, Memphis Tennessee May 21, 1972.
538. Ibid.
539. Ibid.
540. Ibid.
541. "Company Town Has Aspects of Utopia" Press Register. Mobile Alabama p. 5-A May 21, 1972.
542. Hoffman and Howe, p. 252.
543. "Sawmill emphasized recovery from wide range of logs" David A. Pease, Forest Industries November 1980, p. 34.
544. Hoffman and Howe, p. 253.
545. "The Last Company Town In Order" Willamette Week, Vol 11, No. 42, August 22-28 1985. P. 1.
546. Hoffman and Howe, p. 254.

Chapter VI. 1982 to Present: The Wake of the Flood

547. Interview with Milton E. Hill, April 29, 1981; Interview with B. E. Hill, April 29, 1981, Interview with Charles Shotts, May 14, 1981.
548. Allen, p. 145
549. Interview with Milton E. Hill, April 29, 1981; Interview with B. E. Hill, April 29, 1981, Interview with Charles Shotts, May 14, 1981.
550. Hoffman and Howe, p. 254. Fisher, pp 42-46.
551. Hoffman and Howe, p. 254.
552. Carlson, p. 204.
553. Timber titan Gilchrist, 66, died in Bend, Bend Bulletin February 1991.
554. Interview with Tom and Karen Steers, July 25, 2010.
555. Carlson, p. 25.
556. Interview with Tom and Karen Steers, July 25, 2010.
557. Interview with Gil Ernst, September 10, 2001.
558. Interview with F. A. Hendry, April 10, 2011.

BIBLIOGRAPHY

ARTICLES

"15 Cent Raise OK'd At Burns" *Klamath Falls Herald And News*. 19 December 1945: p. 1.

"350 Employees At Gilchrist-Fordney Mills" *Laurel Leader-Call*. December 1928: p. 1.

"After Sitting Idle, Gilchrist Sawmill Set To Run Again" *The Bulletin*. July 1, 2009: p. B-1.

"Champions Of The Free Word" *The Bulletin*. October 31, 2009: p. C-1.

"CIO Pine Men Get Wage Boost: Increase To Equal AFL Level" *Klamath Falls Herald And News*. 24 January 1946: p. 1.

"Christmas Tree Up At Gilchrist" *Klamath Falls Herald And News*. December 23, 1938: p. 9.

"Clearing For Townsite Near Crescent Starts" *Klamath Falls Herald and News*. April 30, 1938: p. 1.

"Club Women Of Bay Springs Given Virgin Timber Track By Gilchrist-Fordney Co." *Laurel Call Leader* Undated

"Company Town Has Aspects Of Utopia – No Government In Gilchrist, Ore." *Press Register, Mobile*. May 31, 1972: p. 5A

"Crescent Resort Gets Tentative Approval: *The Bulletin*. December 5, 2008: p. C-1

"Crescent School Gets Vacation To View New Engine" *Klamath Falls Herald And News*. April 27, 1938, p. 5.

"Deal Appears Close For New State Forest Near Gilchrist" *The Bulletin*. December 10, 2009: p. C-1.

"Deal For New Forest Around Gilchrist Close – If State Can Pay For It" *The Bulletin*. May 28, 2009: p. 1.

"Death Suddenly Takes Frank Rust Gilchrist" *American Lumberman*. February 24, 1917: p. 60.

"Forest Service Auctions Timberland" *The Bulletin*. September 26, 2007: p C-1.

"Frank W. Gilchrist Succumbs After Sudden Heart Attack" *The Bend Bulletin*. April 4, 1956: p. 1.

"Frank Gilchrist, 1903 – 1956" *The Bend Bulletin*. April 5, 1956: p. 4.

"From Tree-Cutting In Laurel, He Found Happiness Westward" *Sun Herald, Biloxi-Gulfport*. May 21, 1972:

"Giant Resort On Drawing Board Near Tiny Gilchrist: *The Bulletin*. November 22, 2007: p1.

"Gilchrist Church Is Dedicated" *The Bend Bulletin*. October 29, 1957: p. 1.

"Gilchrist Firm Plans Sawmill At Crescent" *The Bend Bulletin*. January 16, 1937: p. 1.

"Gilchrist Gets New Fire Truck" *Klamath Falls Herald And News*. January 8, 1939: p. 5.

"Gilchrist Joins Deavours & Hilbun" *Laurel Call Leader*. Date and page unknow From Gilchrist-Fordney Collection, Lauren Rogers Museum, Laurel, Mississippian.

"Gilchrist: Life Is Slow And Basic In Oregon Company Town" *The Atlanta Journal And Constitution*. May 21, 1972: p. 20-C.

"Gilchrist Lumber Resumes Operations" *Klamath Falls Herald And News*, 9 April 1946: p. 3.

"Gilchrist, Oregon, A Company town" John C. Driscoll. *Oregon Historical Quarterly*, Vol 85, No 2 (Summer, 1984), pp. 135-153

"Gilchrist-Fordney History Is Related" The Laurel Call Leader. Date unknown, page 16. From Gilchrist-Fordney Collection, Lauren Rogers Museum, Laurel, Mississippi.

"He Provided Employment For Many" *The Lumber Trade Journal*. V. 63, #1. January 1, 1913: p. 1.

"Homes For Forest Workers" *Unasylva: An International Review Of Forestry And Forest Products*. V. IV, #1, January – March 1950: pp. 10-11.

"Idyllic Timber Town Pays Bonus Of Contentment" *The Commercial Appeal.* Memphis. May 21, 1972.

"Logging Stalls Forest Proposal Near Gilchrist" *The Bulletin.* February 13, 2009: p. 1.

"Lumber Giant Remembered For Contributions To Laurel" *Action.* Laurel, Mississippi. V. 2, #28, July 15, 1987.

"Lumber Strike Truce Reached: 15 Cent Increase In Wages Agreed At Session Here" *Klamath Falls Herald And News.* 12 January 1946: p. 1.

"Mill Stoppage Carries Ripple Effect" *The Bulletin.* March 3, 2009: p. C-1.

"News Of The Midland Empire – Crescent" *Klamath Falls Herald And News.* December 17, 1938: p. 2.

"News Of The Midland Empire – Crescent: Gilchrist News" *Klamath Falls Herald And News.* February 4, 1938: p. 4.

"OPA Hikes Mill Price Ceiling". *Klamath Falls Herald And News.* 21 February 1946: p. 1.

"Picturesque Village Of Gilchrist Is Model Community" *The Bend Bulletin.* July 9, 1949: p. 6

"Planned Resort Near Crescent To Get Hearing" *The Bulletin.* September 8, 2008: p. C-1

"Sawmill Emphasizes Recovery From Wide Range Of Log Sizes." *Forest Industries.* November 1980: pp. 34-36.

"Show Down Brewing On Price Issue" *Klamath Falls Herald And News.* 24 January 1946: p. 1.

"Spring Slumber Is Over For Gilchrist Lumber Mill" *The Bulletin.* July 1, 2009: B-1.

"The Economic Impact Of Privately-Owned Forests" F2M Forest To Market. Prepared for the National Alliance Of Forest Owners, September 8, 2009.

"Town Of Gilchrist Now Has Post Office" *The Bend Bulletin.* November 19, 1938: p. 3.

"Two Gilchrist Firms Robbed In Night By Burglars, With Loss Estimated at $14,000.00" *Klamath Falls Herald and News.* October 19, 1946: p. 1. 19OCT46.

"Work Moves A Pace On Crescent Mill" *Klamath Falls Herald And News.* June 15, 1938: p. 7.

"Yellow Pine For Shipbuilding" *The Lumber Trade Journal.* January 1, 1913.

BOOKS, PAPERS AND THESES

Allen, James. The Company Town In The American West. Norman, Oklahoma: The University of Oklahoma Press, 1966.

Almont, Lindsay. The Pullman Strike: The Story Of A Unique Experiment And Of A Great Labor Upheaval. Chicago, Illinois: University Of Chicago Press, 1942

Anonymous. Jones County June 15, 1937. Monograph from Gilchrist-Fordney Papers. Lauren Rogers Muesum, Laurel, Mississippi.

Bowden, Jack. Railroad Logging In The Klamath Country. Hamilton, Montana: Oso Publishing. 2003.

Braden, Rose. "Gilchrist Lumber Mill". Lumber Pioneers - Western Wood Products Association. September 2006, Number 2.

Carlson, Linda. Company Towns Of The Pacific Northwest. Seattle: University Of Washington Press, 2003.

Clark, Malcolm Jr: Eden Seekers: The Settlement Of Oregon, 1818 - 1862. Boston, Massachusetts: Houghton, Mifflin Company, 1981.

Clark, Norman H. Mill Town: A Social History Of Everett, Washington From Its Earliest Beginnings On The Shores Of Puget Sound To The Tragic And Infamous Event Known As The Everett Massacre. Seattle, Washington: University Of Washington Press, 1970.

Crawford, Margaret. Building The Workingman's Paradise: The Design Of American Company Towns. New York, New York: Verso, 1995.

Edwards, Thomas G. and Schwantes, Carlos A., Editors. Experiences In A Promised Land: Essays In Pacific Northwest History. Seattle, Washington: University of Washington Press, 1986.

Fickle, James. Mississippi Forests and Forestry. Jackson, Mississippi: Forestry Foundation, Inc., University of Mississippi Press, 2001.

Fisher, Jim. Gilchrist - The First Fifty Years. Bend, Oregon: Oregon Color Press. 1988.

Fisher, Jim. Six Generations In The Forest Industry. Sisters, Oregon. 1995.

Folsom, Burton W. Jr: The Myth Of The Robber Barons: A New Look At The Rise Of Big Business

In America. Herndon, Virginia: Young America's Foundation, 1996

Folsom, Burton W. Jr. and Folsom, Anita: FDR Goes To War: How Expanded Executive Power, Spiraling National Debt And Restricted Civil Liberties Shaped Wartime America. New York, New York: Thresh Hold Editions, a division of Simon and Schuster, 2011

Garner, John. The Company Town: Architecture And Society In The Early Industrial Age. New York, New York and Oxford: Oxford University Press: 1992

Gilchrist Timber Company Papers. Klamath County Museum, Klamath Falls, Oregon

Gilchrist Fordney Company and Gilchrist Timber Company Papers. Lauren Rogers Museum, Laurel, Mississippi.

Graham, Elise. Dushau Days. Laurel, Mississippi, 1989

Gray, Edward. An Illustrated History Of Early North Klamath County. Bend, Oregon: Maverick. 1986

Gray, Edward. Historical Sites Along The Paved Roads Of Northern Klamath County, Oregon. Bend, Oregon: Maverick. 1991.

Gray, Edward. Roughing It On The Little Deschutes River, 1934-1944: A History Of A Sawmill Camp And Its People. Eugene, Oregon: K & M Printing & Lithography, 1986

Green, Hardy. The Company Town: The Industrial Edens And Satanic Mills That Shaped The American Economy. New York, New York: Basic Books, 2010.

Gregory, Ronald L. "Life In Railroad Logging Camps Of Shevlin-Hixon Company, 1916-1950 – Anthropology Northwest Number 12". Corvalis, Oregon: Oregon State University Department Of Anthropology, 2001.

Hickman, Nollie. Mississippi Harvest: Lumbering In The Long Leaf Pine Belt, 1840 – 1915 Montgomery, Alabama: University of Mississippi, 1962.

Hidy, Ralph W., Hill Frank E. and Nivens, Allan. Timber And Men, The Weyerhauser Story. New York, 1963.

Hodge, Jo Dent. "Lumbering In Laurel At The Turn Of The Century." MA thesis, University of Mississippi, 1965.

Hoffman, Gilbert and Howe, Tony. Yellow Pine Capital: The Laurel, Mississippi Story. Lamar County, Mississippi: Toot Toot Publishing, 2010.

Hoover, Herbert. Freedom Betray: Herbert Hoover's Secret History Of The Second World War And Its Aftermath. Stanford, California: Hoover Institute Press, 2011.

Howard, James L., Kramp, Andrew and Quevedo, Enrique. Use of Indexing To Udate U.S. Annual Timber Harvest by State. United States Department Of Agriculture: Forest Service, Forest Service Products Laboratory. Research Paper FPL-RP-853, February 2009.

Key, David S. "Laurel, Mississippi: A Historical Perspective" MA thesis, East Tennessee State University, 2001

Koch, Michael. Steam And Thunder In The Timber: Saga Of The Forest Railroads. Denver, Colorado: World Press, 1970.

Martin, Albro. James J. Hill And The Opening Of The Northwest. Saint Paul, Minnesota: Minnesota Historical Society Press, 1991

McCarthy, Karen F. The Other Irish: The Scots-Irish Rascals Who Made America. New York, New York: Sterling Publishing, 2011

Osgood, Judy, editor. Desert Sage Memories. Bend, Oregon: RSVP, 2002

Petersen, Keith C. Company Town: Potlach, Idaho And The Potlach Lumber Company. Pullman, Washington: Washington State University Press, 1987

Robbins, William G. Landscapes Of Conflict: The Oregon Story, 1940-2000. Seattle: University of Washington Press, 2004.

Schwantes, Carlos A. The Pacific Northwest: An Interpretive History. Lincoln and London: University of Nebraska Press, 1989.

Schwantes, Carlos A. Railroad Signatures Across The Pacific Northwest. Seattle, Washington: University Of Washington Press, 1993

Shlaes, Amity. The Forgotten Man: A New History Of The Great Depression. New York, New York: Harper & Collins, 2007.

INTERVIEWS

Addison, O. U. Personal Interview by Nell Davis. Undated. From the collection of the Lauren Rogers Museum, Laurel, Mississippi.

Childre, Jim. Personal Interview August 12, 2011

Ernst, Mary G. Personal Interview. April 30, 2011

Ernst, Gil. Personal Interview October 14, 1996 and September 10, 2001

Gilchrist, Frank R. Personal Interview November 28, 1981

Hendry, F. A. Personal Interview April 10, 2011

Hill, B. E. Personal Interview. May 4, 1981, December 30, 1996 and February 2001.

Hill, Milton E. Personal Interview. April 29, 1981; Personal Interview. March 15, 1998

Jordan, "Louie" Calvin Louis, Personal Interview March 27, 2011

Maynard, Dan. Personal Interview May 4, 1981

Shotts, Charles Sr. Personal Interview. May 14, 1981.

Shotts, Charles Jr. Personal Interview. July 25, 2010

Southwick, Fred. Personal Interview July 25, 2010

Steers, Tom and Karen. Personal Interview. July 25, 2010

Stice, Kathy. Personal Interview July 25, 2010

INDEX

A
Addison, Oliver (O.U.): 24, 82
Allenton (Camp Allen), Mississippi: 18, 22-25, 44
Anderson, Happy: 92
Applewhite, James: 19, 32, 34, 36-38, 42, 48-50, 64, 69, 86-91, 97, 99-100, 105-107, 109, 111, 113, 115-116, 132

B
Barrell, C. H.: 53
Bay Springs, Mississippi: 23
Bend, Oregon: 31, 34-36, 39, 43, 48-49, 51-53, 67, 87, 95, 99, 101, 118, 124, 142-143, 152, 161
Bend Bulletin: 35-36, 86, 129, 155
Bend Chamber of Commerce: 39, 99
Black Diamond, Washington: 9
Boar & Cunningham Civil Engineers: 40
Boarding House: 45-46, 49
Boise Cascade: 155
Bowling: 10, 45, 53, 75, 107, 124
Bryant, Jack N.: 67, 86, 90, 92
Breazeale, Curtis: 20, 47, 64, 132
Brooks-Scanlon: 11, 20, 36-37, 67, 101, 109, 116, 119
Bunk House: 45, 48-49
Bureau of Land Management: 152

C
Caldwell, Clem C.: 115, 118
Caldwell, George: 88
Cameron, W. J.: 53
Camp Abbot: 92
Carbonado, Washington - 9
Carmichael, William Albert: 19, 49-50, 61, 64, 69, 86-89, 94-95, 97, 99-100, 103, 113, 115-116, 118, 124
Chemult, Oregon: 32, 38, 49, 53, 61, 143-144
Childre, Jim: 20, 115
Childre, Rufus: 20, 25, 47-49, 53, 63. 98, 101, 115, 122, 144, 146

Clean Air Act: 151
Corey, Alabama: 3
Cottington, Keith: 51
Coxen, W. F.: 53
Crescent, Oregon: 33, 37, 48-49, 51, 53, 61, 68, 109, 113, 116, 120, 123-124, 133, 142-142
Crescent School: 37, 48, 50-51
Crown-Pacific: 129, 144, 158, 159, 161
Curry, Will: 47

D
Dahl, A. J.: 49
Denham, Dan F.: 47, 63-64, 124
Deschutes County, Oregon: 10, 141
Deschutes Lumber Company: 41
Dupont, Washington: 10
Dushau, Frank S.: 14, 18, 31, 101
Dushau, Mississippi: 18-19, 22-23, 44, 52, 64, 67

E
Endangered Species Act - 152
Engine Number 204: 15, 24, 40-41, 47-48, 64, 68, 106, 118, 120-121, 129-130, 162
Ernst Brothers, Ltd.: 53, 159-161
Ernst, John S.: 115, 125, 131, 145, 159
Ernst, Mary G.: 125
Ernst (Gilchrist), Mary G.: 19, 49-51, 60, 72, 98, 100, 104, 109-111, 115, 118, 122, 124-127, 129, 154
Ernst, Wayne G. (Gil): 151, 159, 161
Ernst, Wayne H.: 91, 115, 124-125, 127-129, 144, 152, 155
Ernst, William L. (Will): 125, 145, 151, 159
Estes, Annie: 92, 96

F
Fletcher, Allen M.: 154
Fletcher (Gilchrist), Grace: 32, 123
Fletcher, Harry E.: 18, 24, 32, 34-36, 103-104, 108, 110, 113, 123, 129

Fletcher, Thomas: 129
Forest Management: 5, 20-21, 101, 103, 106, 122
Forest Service: 36-37, 122-123, 131, 143-145, 152

G
Garner, Dowell E.: 67, 106
Garner, Harry F.: 90, 115
Gary, Indiana: 1-2, 11
Gilchrist (Corliss), Abigail): 13
Gilchrist, Albert: 13
Gilchrist, Alexander: 13
Gilchrist, Benjamin (Benji): 125, 145, 151
Gilchrist, David: 13
Gilchrist (Smith), Flora: 17, 19, 32, 128
Gilchrist, Frank R. (1871-1917): 17-18
Gilchrist, Frank R. (1924-1991): 19, 68, 91, 93-94, 100, 104, 106-108, 110-111, 115, 119, 123-125, 129, 131-132, 147-149, 151-152, 154-155, 158-159
Gilchrist, Frank R. (Rust): 125
Gilchrist, Frank W. (1845-1912): 13-15, 17
Gilchrist, Frank W. (1903-1956): 18-20, 22, 24-25, 31-32, 34-37, 40-44, 46-52, 61, 63-64, 67, 69, 86-116, 118-125, 128-129, 149
Gilchrist (Hill), Helen G.: 119, 125, 129, 154
Gilchrist, James A.: 125, 141
Gilchrist (Kennedy), Hannah: 13
Gilchrist (Shirley), Martha: 13
Gilchrist (Moorman), Mary: 19, 49-50, 63, 105, 122
Gilchrist, Ralph: 17-19. 21, 24, 32-34, 43, 47, 69, 119, 123
Gilchrist, Robert: 13
Gilchrist, Stewart J.: 49, 63, 91, 98-100, 108-111
Gilchrist, William: 13
Gilchrist-Hosack, Susan A.: 125

181

Gilchrist Barber Shop: 43, 45, 53, 116
Gilchrist Beauty Shop: 45, 53, 116
Gilchrist Brown: 40, 45, 51-52, 121
Gilchrist Club (The Club): 45-46, 53, 75, 87, 107, 116, 118, 123-124
Gilchrist Community Church: 61, 67, 89
Gilchrist Dam: 34, 37-42, 48, 53, 62, 139, 154, 162-163
Gilchrist Electricity and Electrification: 9, 45, 51, 97, 105, 113, 119, 121-122, 133, 142-143
Gilchrist Highway Patrol Substation: 119, 122-123, 131, 147
Gilchrist Mall: 18, 44-45, 53, 55, 57, 88,104, 107, 118, 129, 140-141, 145, 163
Gilchrist Mill: 61, 101, 103, 133, 139, 159-161
Gilchrist Mill Pond: 34, 37-39, 41-42, 45-48, 50, 52, 64, 86-87, 101, 109, 116, 118, 123, 145, 148, 163
Gilchrist Post Office: 44-45, 47-48, 52, 97, 109, 118
Gilchrist Rents: 9, 45-46, 51, 95, 97, 99-100, 105, 118-119, 121, 131, 147, 158
Gilchrist Restaurant: 53, 98, 123, 142-143
Gilchrist Sale: 125, 155, 159
Gilchrist School: 10, 50-52, 56-61, 63, 67-68, 70-71, 86, 89-91, 103, 107, 119, 131, 133, 141-142, 144-145, 152, 161
Gilchrist Service Station: 54, 118, 142
Gilchrist Telephone System: 45, 54
Gilchrist Transportation Company: 13-14
Gilchrist Theatre: 44-46, 67, 78, 87-89, 106, 116, 124, 141, 144, 157
Gilchrist-Fordney: 9, 11, 14-15, 17-25, 27, 31-32, 37, 40, 44-45, 47-48, 64, 67-68, 86, 88, 106, 113, 124, 132-133
Graham, Elise: 18-19
Great Northern Railroad: 31-32, 34-35, 37, 129
Griffin, Ervin: 64, 67, 87, 106, 124
Griffin, Jasmes: 118
Grisdale, Washington: 9

H
Hall, John: 147
Hendry, Alva: 47, 49-50, 63, 65, 67-68, 90-92, 106, 115, 132
Hendry, Forrest (F. A.): 20, 47, 49-51, 68, 90-92, 115, 132, 147, 161
Hendry, Jeannie: 149
Hendry, Phil: 47
Hendry, Rob: 47, 149, 161
Highway 58: 38, 40, 42
Highway 97: 38, 44-45, 99, 106, 108-109, 123-124, 129, 142
Hill, B. E. (Ed): 49, 63, 120, 159
Hill, James J.(Great Northern Railroad): 31-32
Hill, Milton: 142-143
Hines Lumber Company: 22, 114
Holden, Washington: 9
Holmes, Alf: 49
Holmes, Nellie: 49
Houck (Ernst), Jan K.: 125, 159
Humphreysville, Connecticut

I
Indian Hill, Massachusetts: 2-3
Interfor: 161
Ezell, Isom A.: 19, 49-50, 64, 132

J
Jasper County, Mississippi: 14, 20, 22, 24-25, 27
Jennings, M. L. 52
Johnston, Hollis: 43-46, 87-89, 93, 103, 118-119
Jones County, Mississippi: 25
Jones, Stewart M: 18-19, 21-25, 32, 133
Jordan, Louie: 121, 124-125, 129, 131, 133

K
Kannapolis, North Carolina: 1, 5
Keihn, Audrey: 53
Keown, Bud: 146-147
Kern & Kibbe: 37, 40-41, 48
Kinzua, Oregon: 155, 159
Klamath County, Oregon: 7-8, 10, 17, 31, 48, 61, 87, 93, 95-97, 102, 111, 141, 149, 163
Klamath County Chamber of Commerce: 95, 99
Klamath County School District: 36
Klamath Falls, Oregon: 32, 38, 47, 51, 86, 92, 94-95, 100, 108, 118, 123-124
Klamath Falls Herald and News: 52, 63
Klamath Northern Rail Road: 32-34, 36-38, 40-43, 46-47, 50, 52, 67-68, 90, 97, 106, 113, 125, 129, 133, 158, 161, 163
Kline, H. W.: 34-35

L
Lake County, Oregon: 17, 31
LaPine, Oregon: 53, 92, 118, 124, 142-143, 161
Laurel, Mississippi: 13-15, 17, 20, 22-25, 28, 31, 40, 44, 47-49, 52, 86, 88, 92, 98, 106, 113, 122-124, 129, 131-132, 142, 145-146, 155, 163
Lowell, Massachusetts – 1-4, 7
Little Deschutes River: 34, 48, 50
Logging: 7-8, 10-11, 15, 18-22, 31, 33, 45, 68, 76, 87, 103, 106, 109, 114, 116-117, 129, 132-138, 145-146
Logging Camps: 8, 11, 18, 22, 36, 44
Logging Trucks: 20-21,, 68, 106, 108-109, 116
Logging Trainings: 15, 20-21, 27, 68, 116

M
Morris, Chuck: 91
Morris Run, Pennsylvania: 1
Mowich, Oregon: 41-42, 61, 92, 118

N
National Environmental Policy Act: 152
National Wilderness Act: 151

O
Office of Price Administration (OPA): 112, 114
Oregon Forest Practices Act of 1972: 153
Oregon Trunk Line (railroad): 31
Our Lady of The Snows (Catholic Church): 123, 131
Owens, A. R.: 32

P
Pine Ridge, Oregon: 11
Port Gamble, Washington: 1, 9
Potlatch, Idaho: 3, 9-10

Index

Potlatch Mercantile: 53
Pryor, John N.: 47
Pullman, George: 4-5
Pullman, Illinois: 1-3, 5, 11

R

Rigdon, Walter: 47, 49, 63-64, 118, 132
Rainbow Circle: 45, 51, 120-122
Rintala, Alice: 49
Rust-Owen Lumber Company: 13

S

Scotia, California: 1, 3, 5
Script: 3-4, 10, 23
Selleck, Washington - 9
Sherman, Arthur: 92, 94. 115
Sherman, Robert: 92. 94, 115
Sherman, William T.: 64, 92, 106, 115
Shevlin, Oregon: 8, 10
Shevlin-Hixon: 8, 11, 33, 36-38, 67, 101, 109, 114, 199, 152
Shinn (Hendry), Char: 68

Shotts, Charles E. Sr (Charlie): 61, 91-92, 103, 109, 115-116, 119, 132-133. 145, 154-155, 158
Shotts, Charles Jr.: 131-132
Shotts, Edgar: 20, 47-48, 64, 98, 132
Simpson Lumber Company: 8
Smith County, Mississippi: 14, 24-25
Smith, Cherry: 49
Southern Pacific Railroad: 32-37, 40-43, 47, 49, 51-52, 129
Southwick, Fred: 133, 141
Steers, Karen: 144-146
Steers, Tom: 143-146, 155, 158-159
Steers, William (Bill): 48, 101, 115, 143-144, 147, 155
Stice, (Miltenburger) Kathy: 141-142
Strike and Strikes: 4-5, 10, 111-116, 131

T

Tax and Taxation: 15, 21-22, 25, 31, 36, 43, 52, 85-86, 88, 97, 106, 119, 155
Terrell, Bill: 51, 91-92

Terrell, Robert Jud: 20, 47-48, 51, 64, 92, 124
Thompkins, Will: 49

U

Union Pacific Rail Road: 31
Unions and Unionization: 46, 92-93, 99, 111-112, 114, 116, 145
USO: 93
USS Belleau Wood (CVL 24): 68, 91, 106-108, 155

V

Valsetz, Oregon: 100, 145, 155
Vanport, Oregon: 7, 106

W

War Bonds: 90, 96, 102-103, 107
Walker Range: 32-33, 67
Wild And Scenic Rivers: 152
Williams, Alice: 49
World War One: 8
Wright, B. V.: 19-21, 31-38, 41-43, 46-52, 57, 61, 64, 69, 89-90, 95, 101, 103, 106, 161

183